FUNDING PUBLIC COLLEGES AND UNIVERSITIES FOR PERFORMANCE

POPULARITY, PROBLEMS, AND PROSPECTS

Joseph C. Burke and Associates

The
Rockefeller
Institute
Press

Albany, New York

Cover photo courtesy of The State University of New York at Geneseo, Office of Communications and Publications

Rockefeller Institute Press, Albany, New York 12203-1003
© 2002 by the Rockefeller Institute Press
All rights reserved.
Printed in the United States of America

The Rockefeller Institute Press
The Nelson A. Rockefeller Institute of Government
411 State Street
Albany, New York 12203-1003

Library of Congress Cataloging-in-Publication Data

Burke, Joseph C.
    Funding public colleges and universities for performance : popularity, problems, and
prospects / Joseph C. Burke and associates.
        p. cm.
    Includes bibliographical references and index.
    ISBN 0-914341-95-2 -- ISBN 0-914341-96-0 (pbk.)
    1. Public universities and colleges--United States--Finance. 2. Higher education and
state--United States. 3. Program budgeting--United States. I. Title.

    LB2342 .B794 2002
    379.1'18'0973--dc21

                                                        2002031770

ISBN: 0-914341-96-0

CONTENTS

FIGURES AND TABLES

PREFACE

Joseph C. Burke

Every book is a personal product of past and present. This volume is no exception. When leaving the position of Provost of the State University of New York System in 1995, I wanted to confront a question that had challenged me as a system officer and a campus president for over two decades: How to forge policies that preserve the internal autonomy required for campus creativity and diversity, yet ensure the external accountability demanded for campus performance and results? I launched the Higher Education Program at The Rockefeller Institute of Government to pursue as a researcher a question that had plagued me as a practitioner.

At the very moment I started the Higher Education Program, performance funding for public colleges and universities was becoming a hot topic in state capitals. This policy initiative forced new demands for external accountability and fueled heated debates on public campuses that feared for their autonomy. Performance funding obviously raised the critical issue of how to reconcile accountability and autonomy, public needs and professional concerns. Its sudden popularity in the 1990s also posed an intriguing question. Why did a practice, which once seemed uninteresting — even unthinkable — in most states, become popular in the early nineties?

Prior to that decade, only three states had directly tied state funding to campus performance. Tennessee launched its comprehensive program in the 1970s; Connecticut started funding a single indicator of minority enrollments in the 1980s; and Hawaii had an aborted experiment in the 1980s. Other states budgeted their colleges and universities based largely on current costs, student enrollments, inflation considerations, and special initiatives.

Tennessee's program certainly offered an attractive and available model. Its architects carefully designed and gradually developed a comprehensive program that other states could have copied. "Legislation by fax," where states borrowed each other's statutes, constituted a common practice in policy making during the 1980s and early 1990s. State mandates on outcomes assessment and performance reporting for public colleges and universities represented classic examples of this practice, in the continuing effort to ensure external accountability. (As a system provost, I had championed initiatives of outcomes assessment and performance reporting to avoid a state mandate.)

The Tennessee program in performance funding seemed ready-made for borrowing. It offered the attractive goals of external accountability and institutional improvement, a restricted but broad list of performance indicators, phased implementation and periodic reviews, success standards stressing institutional improvement and peer comparisons, limited but substantial funding, and stable priorities and program requirements. Its authors also explained and advocated the program in publications read by campus and state policy makers across the country.

John Kingdon's (1995) theory of separate streams of problems, politics, and policies helps to explain why performance funding did not rise to the top of the policy agenda in states until the mid-1990s. Kingdon claims that these three streams exist without connection until problems and politics converge to make a particular policy appear popular. The 1990s produced such a convergence for performance funding. The recession of the early nineties reduced state revenues; and the competition for funding from health care, welfare, corrections, and public schools meant less money available for higher education, one of the few large discretionary items in state budgets. The recession, with its restricted revenues, brought a new accent on efficiency for all levels of government and public services. As the Little Hoover Committee in California commented: "In an era of recession-reduced revenues and increasing demands for services, national, state and local governments are seeking ways to improve delivery of effective services at the lowest possible cost" (1995, 9).

At the same time, state officials increasingly criticized the effectiveness, as well as the efficiency, of public higher education. They complained about the quantity and quality of faculty teaching and student learning, the emphasis on graduate studies and research and the neglect of undergraduate education, and the rising costs of student tuition and administrative positions. These complaints coincided with the emerging recognition that higher education had become a source of state success in a competitive, national economy driven by knowledge and information.

The intersection of problems and politics caused a search for a new budgeting policy. Higher education had become too important and too costly to fund only inputs and ignore results. The movements to reengineer business and reinvent government, started in the early 1990s, supplied a policy perspective that shifted the notion of accountability from accounting for revenues to accounting for results.

The perceived problems and the conservative politics of the 1990s made performance funding an appealing policy. It sought both state accountability and campus improvement as policy goals and both efficiency and quality as policy values. The program directed campus efforts to statewide priorities, and satisfied the new accountability by focusing on campus results rather than bureaucratic rules. Performance funding also appeared to promise a new notion of academic excellence that centered on the quantity and quality of service to states and students rather than on the traditional model of resources and reputation. Budgeting for results could, it seemed, transform public colleges and universities into customer rather than provider-driven enterprises.

These lofty possibilities explain the increasing popularity of performance funding by the mid-1990s. But performance funding proved volatile as well as popular. As more states adopted or considered the program, others abandoned their initiatives. The difficulty of implementing performance funding in practice matched its attractiveness in theory to state but not campus policy makers. Such initiatives proved easier to start than to sustain. These programs required a level of collaboration and cooperation, patience and persistence, seldom found in state policy making for public higher education. They also demanded a commitment to institutional goals, performance standards, and coordinated activities rarely apparent in campus governance. Term limits and changing administrations made policy persistence problematic in state capitals. The difficulty of identifying and evaluating the results of higher education made performance funding controversial on college campuses.

Like most reform movements, performance funding aroused both fervent champions and fevered critics. Champions, mostly from state capitals and the business community, focused on its attractive possibilities. Critics, mostly from campuses, fixated on what they considered its intractable problems. The former tended to ignore the complexity of these programs and viewed campus complaints as a refusal to accept accountability for performance. The latter often dismissed the possibility of tying resources to results and considered any effort as a plot to run campuses like businesses.

This book seeks to separate the reality from the rhetoric of performance funding. It examines the provisions, possibilities, problems, and prospects of this policy by studying its origin, design, and development across the country. Opinion surveys of state and campus policy makers reveal their attitudes toward the program and case studies in five states explore its impact on institutional decisions and performance.

Chapter One describes the shift from the old accountability for expenditures to the new accountability for performance, and early efforts to achieve this goal through outcomes assessment and performance reporting. Chapter Two defines the two methods of linking resources to results, Performance Funding and Performance Budgeting, and details the growing popularity and as well as the volatility of Performance Funding. Chapter Three examines the performance funding indicators and analyzes the types of measures and the concerns, values, and models of excellence that they imply. Chapter Four compares the results of two opinion surveys of state and campus leaders about performance funding.

Chapters Five through Nine present case studies of the origins, developments, impact, and prospects of performance funding in Tennessee, Missouri, Florida, Ohio, and South Carolina. All of the case study authors played active roles in the initiation, development, or study of performance funding in these states. Chapter Ten offers case studies for Arkansas, Colorado, Kentucky, and Minnesota — which abandoned their programs, and suggests reasons for their demise and for the re-adoption in Colorado. Chapter Eleven identifies the characteristics that seem to distinguish stable from unstable programs. Chapter Twelve analyzes the reality and the rhetoric in the arguments for and against performance funding. The final chapter summarizes the possibilities and problems of performance funding, suggests ways to improve the design and implementation of the program, and speculates about the future of linking state funding to campus performance.

The phenomenon of performance funding deserves the careful attention of everyone interested in higher education, public policy, and state budgeting. State officials, campus leaders, and educational researchers on higher education can learn from the desirability and the difficulty of designing and implementing this funding program. Campus planners, budget officers, institutional researchers, and faculty leaders need to learn the details of performance funding, for its goals, indicators, and standards call for significant changes in traditional practices. Interest in linking budget to performance is not limited to those concerned with public higher education. Officials and researchers studying government policy making in general should also examine performance funding as a leading example of the growing practice of performance-based budgeting for public agencies by the federal, state, and local governments.

Every book benefits from many contributors. This one owes a greater debt to others than most volumes. Andreea Serban, first as a doctoral student and later as a senior researcher, helped shape the entire project on performance funding. Shahpar Modarresi, her successor, brought special statistical skills to the analysis of the survey data. Terri Lessard, the current senior researcher, has contributed her special brand of order, caring, and sensitivity to the project. As a graduate assistant, Jeff Rosen performed the tiresome tasks of data entry and presentation of survey results. Henrik Minassians, as a research associate, helped with the tables and graphs and added his appreciation of political theory and policy making. Henrik took on the tough job of final editing.

The authors of the case studies — Grady Bogue, Juan Copa, Pat Dallet, Gary Moden, Robert Stein, David Wright, and Michael Williford —have supplied the diversity and details of performance funding as practiced in particular states. A Program Associate, Tom Moran, reviewed all of the writings for the project on performance funding and supplied insights that improved the clarity and coherence of the work. Tom McCord, a Visiting Fellow at the Rockefeller Institute, read and offered useful comments on a number of the chapters. This book also benefits from the writings of many researchers on accountability, assessment, and performance of colleges and universities. The willingness of several thousand state officials and campus leaders to respond to our surveys provided invaluable insights into their attitudes about performance funding.

Two grants from The Pew Charitable Trusts made this study of performance funding possible. Special thanks must go to Ellen Wert of the Trusts, who recognized the significance of this project by recommending the initial grant and supporting its continuation, and to Russ Edgerton for supporting the second Pew award. Although many collaborators and experts have contributed to this volume, as always, the authors alone are responsible for its presentation and conclusions, and especially its shortcomings.

Chapter 1

THE NEW ACCOUNTABILITY

Joseph C. Burke

Introduction

T he term "paradigm shift" has become a cliché. But the change from the old to the new accountability in state government and in higher education warrants its use. It altered the notion of accountability from accounting for expenditures to accounting for results and shifted the motive from risk avoidance to entrepreneurial efforts. The transition gained momentum from the movements in the early 1990s to reinvent government and reengineer business. Osborne and Gaebler (1994), in *Reinventing Government,* advocated "A New Accountability System" that focused on the performance results rather than on budgetary regulations (p. 136). Hammer and Champy (1993), in *Reengineering the Corporation,* popularized management theories and techniques that stressed product quality and customer service. As with most seminal books that inspire movements, they voiced an emerging consensus rather than broke theoretical ground.

These management movements preached a novel gospel for business and a new heresy for government and higher education. Their creed proclaimed that organizations not only could — but also must — improve quality while cutting costs and increasing productivity. They championed managing for organizational results rather than controlling by bureaucratic rules, and advocated customer- rather than provider-driven enterprises. By concentrating on performance rather than on compliance, managers could combine the goals of accountability and improvement. Organizations could improve performance while decentralizing authority, by being tight on setting goals and assessing results but loose on the means of achieving them.

Osborne and Gaebler (1994) insisted that high-performing organizations required both direction and decentralization.

> ...Organizations that decentralize authority also find that they have to articulate their mission, create internal cultures around their core values, and measure results. Accountability for inputs gives way to accountability for outcomes, and authoritarian cultures give way to the kind of "loose-tight" cultures described by Peters and Waterman in *In Search of Excellence*, in which shared values and missions take the place of rules and regulations as the glue that keeps employees moving in the same direction (p. 254).

These theories suited the times. Success in the new information era demanded autonomy to encourage the creativity and ingenuity of knowledge workers, but it also required commitment to organizational objectives and results. Managing, measuring, and rewarding results became the new trinity. Like all creeds, it proved easier to proclaim than to practice. Like all crusades, it inspired both fervent champions and fevered critics.

Although academics developed many of these management theories, the academic community considered them all right for business and maybe for government, but anathema for academe (Birnbaum 2000). Outsiders could have predicted that the accent on efficiency would arouse campus opposition, but few would have guessed that the focus on quality would prove a greater obstacle. Colleges had declared "Quality Job One" centuries before Ford. Unfortunately, the academic community never determined nor defined — with any precision — the objectives of undergraduate education nor developed systematic methods for assessing campus achievements. By default, the perception of institutional quality reflected what Astin (1985) labeled the Resource and Reputation Model of institutional excellence, which depended on the quantity of campus resources, the quality of admitted students, and the reputation of faculty research. This Model — based entirely on the resource inputs of funding, students, and faculty — said nothing about the quality or the quantity of the services provided to students, states, and society by colleges and universities. Despite its vaunted devotion to quality, the academic community stuck with this quantitative definition of excellence and shied away from identifying and evaluating the qualitative results of higher education. Academics claimed that those results were too complex, diverse, and subjective to be quantified, but then accepted a quantitative model of excellence, because of their reluctance to specify the qualitative outcomes of higher education.

This reluctance to specify quality goals aroused criticism from a few faculty members but increasing complaints from state legislators. A psychology professor at Harvard complained of the academy's failure to identify results while "sniping from the sidelines" when outsiders tried to define them (Lively 1992). The Chair of an education committee in the Texas Legislature spoke of the difficulty of achieving accountability without an accepted definition of quality:

> I have started referring to this as the great national grope for excellence. We're just groping in the dark. I don't know of any other effort that has used this amount of money and human resources where there isn't a clearly defined objective.... I hope the education community...will begin to develop some criteria by which they can be comfortable to be measured accountable" (Lively 1992).

The gap between legislative hope and campus comfort failed to close. Academics welcomed the decentralization of the new accountability but resisted the direction toward clear goals for performance. The new accountability seemed a concept only half fulfilled. It had acceptance on the means of decentralization without consensus on the ends of the enterprise. The consequence now seems inevitable. Since academics failed to act, the state stepped in, leaving academics "sniping from the sidelines."

Assessing Performance

The problem with identifying and assessing results had surfaced with state policies on outcomes assessment in the mid to late 1980s. The cries for reform of public schools, launched by *A Nation At Risk* (1983) soon echoed in calls for changes on public campuses. Criticism of American higher education and student learning came from all quarters of the political spectrum. Bloom (1987), Cheney (1988), and Bennett (1986) issued jeremiads from the right, and groups of leading educators published more liberal prescriptions in *Involvement in Learning* (Study Group 1984) and *Integrity in the College Curriculum* (Association of American Colleges 1985). Although infused with different ideologies and solutions, all of the books criticized the current state of undergraduate education for its lack of a coherent curriculum, level of student learning, and neglect of quality teaching. All of the authors called for the academic community to clarify the goals of undergraduate higher education, although the former focused on prescribing learning outcomes, while the latter favored improving the learning processes. Astin (1985) attacked the traditional resource and reputation model of institutional excellence and sought to replace it with a value added model that stressed student cognitive and affective development from admission to graduation. Writing as early as 1983, Ewell noticed the changed attitude toward higher education and the new demands for outcomes assessment in colleges and universities.

> Until recently, the higher education community saw little point but no small threat in explicit assessment of student outcomes. The positive impact of college upon the student remained an almost righteously unexamined premise — the "great self-evident" of higher education.... Now, of course, things are different. As institutional resources tighten, colleges and university administrators at all levels are growing more concerned about identifying and improving the impact of their programs on students... The same set of forces has produced a demand for greater accountability on the part of those controlling the use of resources in higher education. More and more, institutions are being asked explicitly — somewhat skeptically — to show that they make a difference (pp. 1-2).

Assessment of undergraduate learning appeared to offer an antidote for perceived ills of higher education. It asked colleges and universities to identify the knowledge and skills that their graduates should possess, to design indicators that reflected those objectives, to evaluate the extent of their achievement, and to use the results to improve institutional performance. Assessment proposed to track the basic skills and general knowledge of students from entry to graduation, and the specialized knowledge acquired during the college years in their academic majors. It appeared the answer that could close the gap between legislative hope and campus comfort.

The Assessment movement swept the country in the late 1980s. Governors, legislators, and coordinating boards liked it so much they mandated assessment policies in two-thirds of the states (Boyer 1987). They even wanted it enough to let campuses decide how to do it. Assessment swiftly acquired the accoutrements of academic success, with its own publication, *Assessment Update*, and an annual Assessment Conference of the American Association of Higher Education that attracted nearly 2,000 faculty, administrators, and educational experts. Every one of the six regional accrediting agencies made assessing student outcomes a requirement for accreditation (Nettles et al. 1997). These agencies sought to shift the stress of accreditation from the inputs of admission scores, library holdings, faculty credentials, and the process of academic governance to the outcomes of student learning. Scholarly journals published articles on what assessment was and how to do it. By 1995, a *Campus Trends* survey reported that fully 94 percent of colleges and universities had some type of assessment activity (El-Khawas 1995).

Although assessment spread widely to colleges and universities, its impact rarely ran deep. Many professors thought the task impossible and others believed it unnecessary. Only a distinct minority approached it as a difficult but fundamental duty. Although all of the state programs proclaimed the dual goals of external accountability and institutional improvement, most campuses focused on institutional improvement and resisted the demands for credible evidence of external accountability for improved results (Burke 1999).

The goals of outcomes assessment sounded simple, but designing and developing a program that required faculty collaboration proved exceedingly difficult. A Policy Statement from the State Higher Education Executive Officers (SHEEO) in 1987 acknowledged the need for some statewide aims for assessment but encouraged campuses to develop programs particular to their institutions (Roaden 1987). Lenth (1993) put his finger squarely on the problem when he wrote of the "dynamic tension within assessment between the internal and external, between improvement and accountability, between formative and summative uses, and between those doing it and those who need to know it" (p. 157).

Although eight in 10 campuses had assessment activities underway in 1991, nearly half of the public four-year campuses said that only 10 percent or less of the faculty participated in these activities (El-Khawas 1995). By 1997, a survey of public baccalaureate campuses in California, Florida, Massachusetts, New York, Texas, and Wisconsin found that only 22 percent of the respondents described their assessment activity as extensive (Burke 1998). Sixty-three percent called it limited, and six percent said they had no activities. The rest skipped the question. Whatever the actual percent of implementation, a gap clearly existed between its national popularity and its limited impact on campuses.

Although nearly all campuses claimed to be doing something called assessment, it remained a marginal activity to most professors. A few campuses — usually small and focused on the liberal arts, such as Alverno, Kings College, and Northeast Missouri State (later Truman State) — made assessment the centerpiece of their curriculum. But on most campuses — especially the larger universities — the majority of the faculty considered assessment as an added activity at best, and a bureaucratic burden at worst. All too often, it seemed a routine ritual that diverted too much of their time and expended too much money. Its focus on students rather than on faculty smacked of students as consumers. It ran counter to the ingrain notion of quality as resources and reputations, especially since the faculty could seldom agree on the outcomes of undergraduate education (Burke 1999).

Unfortunately, assessment — like many reforms — remained a cottage industry on campus. Exciting practices flourished in a hundred places, while the institutions plodded their traditional paths. Decentralization and autonomy smiles on individual innovations but stifles systemic reforms. Assessment, like most innovations on campus, had ardent advocates but little institutional acceptance.

The assessment movement failed to meet the needs of the new accountability. Although all of the mandated state programs had the dual goals of external accountability and institutional improvement, the campus programs tended to emphasize improvement and slight accountability. Governors and legislators found the inability to compare institutional results a shortcoming of the assessment reports. The mandates had provided more decentralization but little direction. Campuses had seized the offer of autonomy, while slighting the responsibility of accountability. All too often, assessment activities did not identify the desired results of undergraduate education, develop an acceptable means of evaluating institutional performance, or demonstrate that public campuses were meeting student needs.

The Financial Crisis of Higher Education

The national recession in the early 1990s brought a new urgency to state demands for campus accountability. After several decades of consistent increases, higher education between FY 1992 and 1993 suffered a historic decline in state support (Hines 1993). For the first time in the history of collecting the data, state appropriations for higher education nationally fell below the previous year. Annual budget cuts for higher education became common, as did mid-year recessions in adopted budgets when state revenues fell below projections. Gold (1995) details the problems of revenues and budgeting in the first half of the 1990s. If the period represented a fiscal crisis for most states, it constituted calamity for most public colleges and universities. Gold calls higher education — the only large discretionary item in state budgets — the "real loser" in the budget battles against healthcare, welfare, corrections, and public schools. Not only did state revenues fall and their budgets decline, but higher education received a diminished share of these limited funds.

Public higher education — once considered untouchable — became an easy target for both budget cutters and external critics in the first half of the 1990s. Criticism of public higher education rises during recessions and recedes with recovery. Commentators predicted that the cuts and criticisms could produce dramatic changes on campuses. "The 1990s promise to be a time of wrenching transition for American colleges and universities," reported the *Christian Science Monitor* in 1992. "...With budgets declining and criticism rising, many universities...find they may have to make sweeping changes to stay in business" (Boot 1992). Former Governor Thomas Keane, president of Drew University, lamented the "lost image" of higher education and declared: "People are questioning our mission.... They claim we cost too much, spend carelessly, teach poorly, plan myopically and ... act defensively" (DePalma 1992).

External critics, mostly from government and business, complained about the quality and quantity of faculty teaching and student learning, the preoccupation with graduate studies and research and neglect of undergraduate education, the encouragement of mission creep and program sprawl, and the bourgeoning of administrative positions and support staffs. Much of the criticism centered on the questionable results of undergraduate education — of admitting too many unqualified students, of graduating too few of those admitted, of permitting them to take too long to degrees, and of allowing too many to graduate without the knowledge and skills required for successful careers in a knowledge and information society (Lively 1992). The complaints continued about the quality and performance of undergraduate education that emerged in the 1980s, but charges of falling productivity and efficiency and rising costs and tuitions became added indictments.

Even the friends of higher education joined the fray. A Wingspread Conference of national leaders in higher education in 1993 issued a withering report. It charged higher education with failing to meet societal needs, despite the series of demographic, economic, and technical changes that increased its importance for most Americans. Instead of responding to these changes, the higher education system weeded out students and trivialized undergraduate education. These reactions aroused a public concern that signaled nothing less than a crisis in higher education. The Report insisted that colleges and universities must educate more people and educate them better. It called for a rigorous undergraduate education that focused more on what students learn and put students at the heart of the educational enterprise. In addition, higher education had to help create a nation of learners by being engaged more thoroughly in education from kindergarten through high school.

The combination of rising criticism and curtailed funding led to renewed demands for accountability from colleges and universities. An article in the *Chronicle of Higher Education* declared:

> Accountability is again a hot topic as state budgets shrink and taxpayers complain about rising costs — particularly in tuition — and what they see as decreases in educational quality.... Under the loose rubric of "accountability," states are enacting new laws and policies that require colleges to demonstrate efficiency, quality, and sound stewardship of public money (Lively 1992).

Aims McGuinness, then with the Education Commission of the States, discerned a difference from earlier accountability initiatives. "What may be new in the world of accountability," he said, "are efforts to assess what results can be shown for all the time and money used to measure how well colleges are performing their jobs" (Lively 1992). Public higher education had become too important and too costly to states to be left to its own devices.

Performance Reporting

The lukewarm response to assessment policies, inability to compare campus results, reduced state revenues, and rising costs led state after state to mandate by legislation performance reporting. The head of the University of Maryland System commented on the changing times:

> Strong winds are blowing through the groves of academe. Many of our nation's universities are under financial stress. All face a flood of rising expectations from a public that, at the same time, views them with growing skepticism and mistrust (Langenberg 1992).

Performance reporting became the favored response in state capitols. The Foreword of a SHEEO study of performance reporting in 1998 stated:

> State-level accountability and the use of performance measures have been touchstones of the 1990s. In state after state, legislators have directed all government entities, including public higher education, to state their goals and activities more explicitly and report results as a form of accountability. Many state higher education agencies have adopted performance measures in response to these accountability demands" (Christal 1998, p. vii).

Before the 1990s, only Tennessee (1984), South Carolina (1988), and Oklahoma (1988) had accountability reports mandated through legislation. By 1996, that number leaped to 23 states, spreading from three southern states to every region in the nation (Christal 1998). The reports sought to make public colleges and universities more responsive to lawmakers, students, parents, employers, and the general public. The new mandates stemmed from the "rising cost for attending college, increasing demands for access, and decreased state resources for higher education" (Christal 1998, p. 1). In response, the reports sought to increase the quality, productivity, and efficiency of public colleges and universities.

The mandates for reporting brought a change from those for assessment. Assessment mandates represented decentralization with little direction, while performance reporting added direction as a price of decentralization. In contrast to the assessment mandates, performance reporting generally required comparability among campuses, although the reports themselves often urged comparisons only among the same types of institutions. Many of the state programs granted increased fiscal autonomy to campuses for accountability for performance results (Blumenstyk 1991). The state legislatures or the state higher education agencies usually insisted on a common list of statewide indicators for all public colleges and universities (Ruppert 1998).

Like assessment, the reports dealt mostly with undergraduate education. In addition to the issues of assessing the quality and quantity of student learning, the new mandates added efficiency concerns about rising costs, swelling bureaucracies, and low graduation rates. They also extended the goals of institutional improvement and external accountability to include meeting state needs, especially in economic and workforce development (Ruppert 1994). The SHEFO Study lists the most common performance indicators along with the number of states that used them (Christal 1998, 5).

Table 1. The Most Common Indicators Used by States	
Indicators	*State*
Graduation Rates	32
Transfer Rates	25
Faculty Workload/Productivity	24
Follow-up Satisfaction Studies	23
External/Sponsored Research Funds	23
Remediation Activities/Effectiveness	21
Pass Rates on Licensure Exams	21
Degrees Awarded	20
Placement Data on Graduates	19
Total Student Credit Hours	18
Admission Standards and Measures	18
Number and Percent of Accredited Programs	13

A study of performance reporting in ten states for the Educational Commission of the States (ECS) lists mostly the same indicators. It adds time-to-degree, which had become a growing efficiency issue in the early 1990s and notes that the indicators on enrollment, retention, and graduation usually specified race, ethnicity, and gender, which were still state priorities in the early 1990s. Unlike the indicators for assessment that often dealt with process, those used in performance reporting accented results. Only one of the 11 indicators listed above — admission standards — measured inputs rather than results. Whereas assessment had stressed the goal of institutional improvement and slighted accountability, performance reporting focused on the latter without neglecting the former.

The performance reports broadened the notion of customers of higher education. Typically state government, particularly the legislature, had been considered the principal consumer of performance information about public colleges and universities. The performance reports of the 1990s expanded the clients to include students and their parents, as well as businesses, schools, the media, and the general public (Ruppert 1998). Their use as consumer reports followed the customer-centered and market-driven focus that reinventing government and reengineering business saw as the true test of quality for all organizations.

Policy makers copied the concept and the format of the performance reports for public campuses from the report cards for public schools, started in the mid-1980s. The absence of standardized test scores from most of the higher education reports represented the main difference from the school report cards. Usually published annually or biannually, the accountability reports circulated widely to state officials, campus leaders, and often to the public media. The contents clearly responded to concerns about the results produced by public colleges and universities. Reports addressed these concerns by including from 10 to 20 indicators that illustrated the performance of public campuses in priority areas. Critics complained, with some justification, that the indicators selected owed more to the availability of data than to the importance of their topics. However, the SHEEO survey indicated that over 80 percent of the reports required new data collection (Christal 1998).

The "report card" flavor of these documents tended to favor quantitative data over qualitative information. Statistics, tables, and graphs crammed the reports. Some of the reports ran several hundred pages, such as those from West Virginia and South Carolina. The size and complexity of most of the documents discouraged all but the most diligent and persistent reader, and few of them included easy-to-read summaries. By including so much information on so many items, the reports obscured the results in priority areas for states and students. The "big picture" of the overall performance of public colleges and universities got lost in the welter of details.

Most of the reports presented trends in institutional performance over time and sometimes showed comparisons with peer institutions of similar missions, both in and out of state. Some of them, such as those in

California and South Carolina, present only data by institutional types, such as research, comprehensive, and two-year campuses, rather than by individual colleges and universities. Most of the reports tried to preserve the diversity of institutional types by resisting comparisons among institutions with differing missions. Some programs set institutional targets for performance on each of the indicators. Several reports also allowed campuses to select a few indicators related to their specific missions. Despite these precautions, campus leaders feared that state officials and the popular media would make unfair comparisons and misuse the results by failing to recognize differences of institutional types and campus missions.

The reports, with their prescribed indicators, provoked opposition from educational leaders. Some academics saw the reporting of institutional results as an invasion of campus autonomy over educational matters. "An Essay on Accountability" from three leading academics offered an alternative response to external complaints. Graham, Lyman, and Trow (1996) acknowledged "that there are persistent pathologies in academic life, violations of its own norms and of society's reasonable expectations of colleges and universities" (p. 12). These scholars proposed candid but confidential self-studies that would help initiate internal reforms on campuses, coupled with process audits by academic experts to provide public evidence of quality control.

These authors conceded that their proposal required public trust: "...Where trust is low, the necessity for persuasion is high, since the internal evidence is not accepted outside as an adequate description of reality" (p. 17). The problem with their proposal was that external trust of the academic community was low and the need for public persuasion was high. For state colleges and universities, with their continuing dependence on taxpayer support, it was impossible to keep external and internal assessments distinct. Skeptical officials and a critical media seemed unlikely to accept assurances from process audits conducted by academics. They wanted credible evidence that institutional performance was worth the state investment and demanded public reports that documented results. These process audits failed the test of the "new accountability" of demonstrating results on priority objectives.

A persistent problem with regional and specialized accreditation of campuses and their programs was that it refused to issue public reports of the results of their reviews, other than the status of accreditation. A second fault was that campus administrators dominated the boards of accrediting agencies and wrote the accreditation reports. Evaluations performed by academic insiders appeared unlikely to convince external audiences. The movement for adopting academic audits of colleges and universities, such as those in Great Britain, had the credibility that came from published reports on results, but academics still wrote the evaluations (Trombley 1999).

An initiative of a group of national associations of higher education showed that some educational leaders sought to respond by improving the performance indicators and their supporting data, rather than resisting the irresistible trend toward accountability reports. The Joint-Committee on Accountability Reporting (1995) of the American Association of State Colleges and Universities, the National Association of State Universities and Land Grant Colleges, and the American Association of Community Colleges recommended a detailed program for performance reporting. The National Governors Association, The National Conference of State Legislatures, the Education Commission of the States, and the Association for Institutional Research encouraged and monitored this effort. A number of governing boards of university systems and individual campuses have endorsed this Joint-Committee Report.

Although these national organizations supported performance reporting, the state mandates stirred the ire of some faculty members. A psychology professor at Winthrop University and director of the South Carolina Higher Education Assessment Network dismissed the reports as costly make work. "We are in a financial crisis unique in our history, and every penny spent to answer this report card is at least a penny not spent working on things to improve us" (Mercer 1993). Others claimed that the reports reveal nothing about institutional quality. One faculty member made a comment that highlighted the narrow notion of quality that reigned on campus, which could hardly have been well received by lawmakers, students, and the general public. He wondered what the number of graduates working in jobs related to their academic majors had to do with educational quality (Mercer, 1993). A frequent criticism centered on the comparative nature of the reports. Campus leaders called it unfair to compare institutions with different missions, enrollments, and programs.

Although the spread of performance reports across the states is clear, their use by state and campus policy makers remains cloudy. Unfortunately, no study of their use has occurred. A 1993 analysis from the Southern Regional Education Board in twelve states concluded that no one has examined the impact of performance reporting in state capitols and on public campuses (Bogue et al. 1993). Grady Bogue, one of the authors, asked the pertinent question: "Are political and educational leaders using the extensive accountability reporting?" (p. 126). Although a project of the Higher Education Program at the Rockefeller Institute is now conducting such a study, none has yet been completed.

Anecdotal evidence suggests that state and campus policy makers all too often ignored the reports in their planning and policy-making. "We … put together a report which we thought would provide more useful information," said an officer of the New Mexico Commission on Higher Education. "So far, we've had the same reaction to the latest report that we had to the first two reports, which was silence…. The lack of response makes some people wonder what's the point of it all" (Mercer 1993). The hope for results from the performance reports rested on the logical, but apparently mistaken, assumption that merely reporting the results of higher education would improve performance. Undoubtedly, the lack of fiscal consequences helps to explain this neglect. Projects without budget impact get little attention in state capitols or on public campuses.

Some policy experts think that performance reporting may make a comeback. The National Center for Public Policy and Higher Education issued in November 2000 its first state-by-state Report Card on the performance of their higher education systems (2000). It grades states for the performance of their total system of higher education, public and private, and not the results of individual colleges and universities. The report card format garnered wide attention in the national and state media, which loves reports that grade enterprises into winners and losers. The Center sees the Report Cards as a policy tool for states. Its prospectus notes that potential students and their parents "can examine a wide range of institutional rankings and comparisons. But state leaders cannot now obtain meaningful comparative measures of their state's performance in higher education" (National Center for Public Policy 2000, p. 4). The Report grades the states against the best performers in the following areas: student preparation for college; participation or college going opportunities; affordability for students and their families; student persistence and degree completion; and educational gains and returns or the economic, civic, and social benefits for the state from a more highly educated population. A state's score on several quantitative indicators will determine its grade on each of the above categories. Significantly, it issued incomplete grades on student learning, because of the lack of valid and comparable data for all of the states.

This new spotlight on higher education is only likely to encourage the adoption of programs that link funding to results. Governments, including those of states, are reactive. They respond to media pressure. As Kingdon (1995) says, when the pressure of a problem forces a political issue, politicians look for a policy alternative that relieves the public pressure. The new pressure for performance by the State Report Cards on the results of higher education is likely to spur state interest in an accountability policy with the teeth of performance funding and budgeting for public colleges and universities.

Traditional Budgeting

State budgeting for public higher education resembles a family's attic. Everything is added but nothing is thrown away. Serban notes that budgeting objectives "evolved from adequacy in the 1950s, to distributive growth in the 1960s, to redistributive equity in the 1970s, to stability/quality in the 1980s, to stability/accountability/reform in the 1990s" (Burke and Serban 1998b, pp. 15-16). But Caruthers and Marks (1994) claim that that "each decade's new objective, to be served by the funding process, became an additional rather than a replacement purpose" (p. 1).

The funding process in traditional budgeting usually takes three basic forms: formula, incremental, and initiative funding. States used one or all of these forms for the budget stages of preparation, justification, and allocation. Although campuses, systems, and coordinating or governing agencies followed these forms for budget preparation and justification, available resources determined the actual allocations.

Formula budgeting considered complex ratios, such as enrollments by student levels and academic disciplines for calculating instructional budgets, the numbers of faculty lines and students for general staffing, and gross square feet of buildings for maintenance and operations. The calculations grew ever more complex in pursuit of adequacy and equity, the chief purposes of formula budgeting (McKeown 1996a). Incremental budgeting built base budgets on historical costs and then added additional moneys for enrollment growth, inflationary increases, and special initiatives, depending on the availability of state revenues. Although the two approaches appear different, in reality they reach much the same conclusion. Many states used formulas merely to set a base budget and then considered changes in enrollments and inflation. Layzell and Caruthers (1995) call the incremental budget "the traditional — and dominant — form of governmental budgeting..." (p. 2). The bottom line in state budgeting for public campuses usually reflects mostly current costs, student enrollments, and inflation.

The third budget approach, initiative funding, merely supplemented formula or incremental funding. It supported special projects that en- couraged high-quality programs in instruction and research, through competitive or categorical grants, such as Virginia's Fund for Excel- lence and Ohio's Selective Excellence program (Hines 1998). Initiative funding provided up front money to encourage a campus activity based on future promises rather than achieved results (Burke and Serban 1998b). In addition, these initiatives stemmed more from campus de- sires than state priorities, since the programs supported generally fol- lowed the resource and reputation model of institutional excellence.

The budget problems of the early 1990s eliminated nearly all of these initiative programs. Although campus leaders favored and often instigate these policies, when faced with budget cuts, they opted for their first priority — protecting their base budgets (Folger and Jones 1993). Special initiatives usually rewarded only selected campuses, while base budgets benefited all colleges and universities. Spreading the wealth among institutions and protecting their budget bases wins support not only from most campus leaders but also from legislators, who usually have a public college or university in their districts.

Whatever the budget approach, enrollments really drove state fund- ing for public colleges and universities. During the years of enrollment growth in all states, this type of budgeting brought increases, at least in times of rising state revenues. But by the 1980s, stable enrollments in some states no longer produced budget growth. In those states with bur- geoning enrollments, limited resources made it difficult to fully fund enrollment increases.

McKeown (1996b) claims that the budget crisis in the early 1990s produced "major shifts ... away from equity and adequacy ... toward goals of accountability and efficiency" (p. 15). She predicted a para- digm shift in budgeting based on the new accountability.

> ...Maintenance of the base may not be possible when the general public seems to no longer be a willing participant in its love affair with higher education.... Legislators have been calling for reform and accountability fueled by stories of how industries have been restructuring their budgets, rethinking their strategic plans, reorganizing, and reengineering the cor- poration to be more efficient and produce higher quality outputs. Cor-

porate leaders, long-time supporters of higher education, have called on institutions to reinvent themselves, to rethink their missions (and return to teaching as the primary mission)…, just as industry has done. The movement to accountability and performance suggests that a watershed may have been reached in the way in which higher education is funded. Perhaps it is time for a new paradigm (pp. 30-31).

McKeown leaves no doubt that the new paradigm would spur the popularity of somehow linking state resources to campus results. Such an approach would meet the efforts of state policy makers to establish "accountability with teeth" by linking funding to performance (Ruppert 1998, 3). In many states, performance reporting seemed a rest stop on the road to performance funding and budgeting. If governors, legislators, or coordinating or governing boards had information on the performance of public colleges and universities on priority statewide indicators, it seemed logical to consider such results in state allocations. State officials may have seen this development as a simple step, but campus leaders considered it a momentous move.

Performance Funding:
An Attractive Policy Alternative

By the early 1990s, the convergence of problems and politics made the linking of state resources to campus results an attractive policy alternative in state capitols as predicted by Kingdon's (1995) theory. The recession and the competition for funding by public schools, criminal justice, health care, and welfare had restricted the revenues available for higher education. Funding for performance also fit well with the popular movements of reinventing government and reengineering business. The drumbeat of criticism about performance and productivity, and costs and inefficiencies, had produced a negative reaction toward public higher education in state capitols. These resource and performance problems surfaced at the very moment when a conservative mood favoring cutting taxes and government spending spread throughout the states. Conservative Republicans captured many of the governorships and state legislatures on campaign pledges to cut spending for state programs. By the early 1990s, many of the new office holders considered public higher education as just another government program and educational leaders as one more interest group.

Following the Kingdon Theory, the now connected streams of problems and politics sent state leaders searching in the policy stream for a program that could satisfy their needs. They sought a policy that stressed improved performance, increased productivity, and contained costs. The policy had to conform to the new management mantra of centralized direction on the priority goals, objective measurement of performance results, and decentralized methods of goal achievement. Performance funding and budgeting seemed a ready-made policy for the problems and politics of the period. As a result, a program that Tennessee had launched in the 1970s, and states had largely neglected for two decades, became a popular policy in state capitols across the country. As a long-time legislator said:

> As long as I can remember, legislators financed higher education by poking money through a hole in the fence. Lately, they have started looking over the fence to see what was on the other side (Schmidt 1999).

Chapter 2

PERFORMANCE FUNDING AND BUDGETING: OLD DIFFERENCES AND NEW SIMILARITIES

Joseph C. Burke

Introduction

From the hindsight of history, state policy making seems to shift steadily from assessing, to reporting, to funding the performance of public colleges and universities. The popularity of performance assessment spread in state capitals from the mid-1980s but waned at the end of the decade from campus resistance and the inability to compare campus results. Performance reporting flourished in the early 1990s, but declined by mid-decade from lack of fiscal consequences and effective use by state and campus policy makers, although recently it seems to be making a recovery. Linking budgeting and funding to performance emerged as a popular phenomenon in the middle '90s. By 2000, the practice had spread to three quarters of the states (Burke, Rosen et al. 2000).

But history and policy making are never neat. Changes come but continuity continues. Elements of each initiative live on in their successors. Policy making often follows the Hegelian dialectic of moving from thesis, to antithesis, to synthesis. The faults of one policy father a second, which corrects its predecessor's errors at the cost of slighting its benefits. Finally, a third initiative emerges, which tries to borrow the best elements of both predecessors.

The growing demands for accountability — fueled by diminished tax revenues in the first half of the 1990s and the rising costs of public higher education — produced a political problem in state capitals. This problem pushed the issue of efficiency and effectiveness of public higher education toward the top of the political agenda in state capitals. The policy answers and alternatives had long existed. Tennessee had a program tightly tying state funding to campus results and Hawaii had a policy loosely linking state budgeting to campus performance since the 1970s. In a classic case of the Kingdon theory (1995) in practice, the converging streams of problems and politics made the policy alternatives of linking budgets and funding to performance politically attractive.

Traditional Budgeting

States traditionally budgeted public colleges and universities based largely on current costs, student enrollments, and inflationary increases. These input or resource factors ignored the quantity and quality of graduates and the range and benefits of services to states and society. This cost-plus budgeting also promoted inappropriate growth in expenditures, enrollments, and programs, even in states with declining demographics and decreasing student demands. Some states had previously provided front-end funding to encourage desired campus activities in research and instruction that promoted economic development.

Programs linking budgeting to performance differ from these earlier efforts by allocating resources for achieved rather than promised results. This practice shifts somewhat the budget question from what states should do for their campuses toward what campuses do for their states and their students. The shift is slight in all states, since the sums allocated to performance remain relatively small. Whatever the future of using campus performance in budgeting, the workload measures of current costs, student enrollments, and inflationary increases will —

and should — receive the lion's share of state allocations. The real issue is whether performance should count for something in state funding and budgeting.

Performance Funding and Performance Budgeting

Until recently, linking state budgeting to campus performance took two different forms, based on the connection of resources to results. Previous authors do not clearly define the differences between performance programs that directly impact or only indirectly influence budgeting. McKeown (1996a) cites only the growing use of performance indicators in state budgeting. Christal (1998) mentions direct and indirect effects on budgets but does not explain the differences. Albright (1998) deals mostly, and Layzell and Caruthers (1995) exclusively, with direct effect on funding. The lack of a clear definition that distinguishes programs by their direct or indirect effect on funding has confused state policy makers. They often use "performance budgeting" or "performance funding" as synonymous terms that cover both direct and indirect impact.

Beginning in 1997, the Higher Education Program at the Rockefeller Institute has tracked the current status and future prospects of what it has labeled "Performance Funding" and "Performance Budgeting." The tracking from 1997 through 2001 used annual telephone surveys of State Higher Education Finance Officers (SHEFOs) in the 50 States (Burke and Serban 1997, 1998a; Burke and Modarresi 1999; Burke, Rosen et al. 2000; Burke and Minassians 2001).

The Surveys sought to separate the two approaches to funding and budgeting by using the following definitions:

- *Performance funding* ties tightly specific resources to institutional results on each of the designated indicators. The tie is automatic and formulaic. If a campus achieves a set target on a designated indicator, it receives a specific amount of performance money for that measure. Performance funding focuses on the distribution phase of the budget process.

- *Performance budgeting* allows governors and legislators, or coordinating or system boards, to consider campus performance on the indicators collectively as merely one factor in determining the total allocation for a public college or university. The link is loose and discretionary. This approach usually concentrates on budget preparation and presentation and slights — or even ignores — budget distribution.

The advantages and disadvantages of each of these approaches are the reverse of the other. In performance funding, the tie between results and resources is clear but inflexible. In performance budgeting, the link is flexible but unclear.

The obvious relation of resources to results in performance funding provides a tangible incentive for institutions to improve performance. On the other hand, this automatic link to funding may punish campuses in cases where performance falls because of circumstances beyond their control. The tight tie of funding to each indicator and the small sums usually allocated to performance funding also limit the number of indicators, since too many measures would trivialize important objectives with trifling sums. This restriction excludes many of the critical objectives of colleges and universities.

In performance budgeting, the loose link of funding to results gives state governments or coordinating or system boards discretion over allocations based on performance, which allows consideration of campus circumstances. The absence of a direct tie of funding to each indicator also permits the use of a longer list of performance measures, which can include more of the many objectives of higher education. Using more measures in performance budgeting also diminishes problems of validity and reliability with individual indicators, in contrast to performance funding where each measure counts for money. On the downside, the loose link of resources to results in performance budgeting reduces the incentive for institutions to improve performance.

Despite these definitions, policy makers continue to confuse these two different concepts. Alabama offers a recent example of this confusion. Although the Coordinating Board labels its new program "performance funding," its finance officer, after hearing the above definitions, calls it performance budgeting (Alabama Commission on Higher Education, 2000).

Recently, the Hegelian dynamic is beginning to diminish the differences between the two funding approaches. Several innovations are blurring the boundaries between performance funding and performance budgeting. They borrow elements from both approaches to achieve the advantages and avoid the disadvantages of each policy. The future may bring a synthesis, which combines the best and corrects the worst elements in both programs.

Current Status and Future Prospects

Performance Funding

Performance funding exhibits the conflicting characteristics of popularity and instability. Forty percent of the states now have programs (Table 1) (Burke and Minassians 2001). While their number went from 10 to 19 since 1997 — a 90 percent increase — Arkansas, Colorado, Kentucky, Minnesota, and Washington abandoned their programs during the same period (Burke et al. 2000). These aborted efforts demonstrate that the desirability of performance funding in theory is matched by its difficulties in practice. It is easier to adopt than to implement and simpler to start than to sustain. On the other hand, Arkansas and Colorado have recently readopted performance funding and Kentucky planned to do so in the fall of 2001. In addition, some legislators in Minnesota are reconsidering the initiative.

SHEFOs say that 17 of the current programs in Performance Funding are likely to continue for the next five years, while those from Arkansas and California claim they cannot predict the future of their programs. Projections suggest some future growth, with seven states considered likely to adopt the program. But they also reveal the resistance to performance funding in state capitols, and especially on public campuses. Fourteen states seem unlikely to have the program in the next five years. Finance officers claim they cannot predict the program's future in 11 states. Actually, the "unlikely" projections have decreased and the "cannot predict" projections have increased since the 2000 Survey.

Performance Budgeting

Performance budgeting is even more popular and at least until this year more stable than performance funding. It expanded from less than a third of the states in 1997 to more than half by 2001 — nearly a 70 percent increase in just three years (Burke and Minassians 2001). Two-thirds of these programs for higher education appeared in states

Table 1. States with Performance Funding 1997-2001		
Year	Number (Percentage)	State
First 1997	10 states (20%)	Colorado, Connecticut, Florida, Kentucky, Minnesota, Missouri, Ohio, South Carolina, Tennessee, Washington
Fourth 2000	17 states (34%)	California*, Colorado**, Connecticut, Florida, Illinois*, Kansas, Louisiana, Missouri, New Jersey, New York***, Ohio, Oklahoma, Pennsylvania, South Carolina, South Dakota, Tennessee, Texas
Fifth 2001	19 States (38%)	Arkansas**, California*, Colorado, Connecticut, Florida, Idaho**, Illinois*, Kansas, Louisiana, Missouri, New Jersey, New York, Ohio, Oregon**, Pennsylvania, South Carolina, South Dakota, Tennessee, Texas

*   2-year colleges only
** New program
*** State University of New York System only

with performance budgeting for some or all of their government agencies. According to the SHEFOs, half of the states currently mandate performance budgeting for state agencies. Programs of performance budgeting that appear in earlier and not in later surveys stem from the perceptual problem of identifying the program's existence because of the loose link to funding, and not from policy decisions to end these initiatives.

Performance budgeting appears stable in the states where it exists, but its presence in over half of the states may limit future expansion. SHEFOs see nearly all of the current programs as likely to continue. Only those from Florida, Georgia, and Washington claimed they could not predict the program's future. However, only six states appear likely to adopt performance budgeting in the next five years; and 14 seem unlikely to accept the practice. Respondents from 11 states could not predict future action.

To identify the actual, as opposed to the potential, connection of resource to results in performance budgeting, the most recent survey asks SHEFOs to estimate the effect of their program on state funding for public campuses. The responses indicate that performance budgeting has a limited effect on institutional funding. None of the SHEFOs call the effect great. Three claim a considerable and ten a moderate impact.

Table 2. States with Performance Budgeting 1997-2001		
Year	Number (Percentage)	State
1997	16 states (32%)	Colorado, Florida, Georgia, Hawaii, Idaho, Illinois, Indiana, Iowa, Kansas, Mississippi, Nebraska, North Carolina, Oklahoma, Rhode Island, Texas, West Virginia
2000	28 states (56%)	Alabama, California, Connecticut, Florida, Georgia, Hawaii, Idaho, Illinois, Iowa, Kansas, Louisiana, Maine, Maryland, Massachusetts, Michigan, Mississippi, Missouri, Nebraska, Nevada, New Jersey, New Mexico, North Carolina, Oklahoma, Oregon, Texas, Utah, Virginia, Wisconsin
2001	27 states (54%)	Alabama, California, Connecticut, Florida, Georgia, Hawaii, Idaho, Illinois, Iowa, Kansas, Louisiana, Maine, Maryland, Michigan, Mississippi, Missouri, Nebraska, Nevada, New Mexico, North Carolina, Oklahoma, Oregon, Texas, Utah, Virginia, Washington, Wisconsin

In contrast, seven see minimal impact and three see no effect. Four could not assess the impact.

The loose link between performance and budgets in performance budgeting offers political advantages to policy makers that may explain its popularity in state capitals and its preference over performance funding. The latter achieves fiscal consequences at the cost of campus controversies. State legislators may champion, in theory, altering campus budgets based on institutional performance, but they often oppose, in practice, programs that may result in revenue losses to colleges or universities in their home districts. Performance budgeting offers a political escape from this troublesome dilemma. Governors and legislators can claim credit for considering performance in budgeting without the controversy of altering campus allocations. This program also protects a prized power of legislators — retaining control and discretion over state budgets.

At times, the link between performance and budgeting is so loose as to become almost invisible. A legislative staff member, commenting on Florida's Performance Based Program Budgeting for all state agencies, quipped: "the only connection between funding and performance was that the indicators and the allocations often appear on the same page in the budget bill (Anonymous, 1996). Although governors and legislators have the authority to alter allocations in performance budgeting, they seldom seem to use this discretion.

Dual Programs

Ten states currently have both performance funding and performance budgeting for public colleges and universities. At least in theory, having both programs allows a state to achieve the benefits, while offsetting the problems, of each approach. Performance funding provides the clarity of funding specific sums on each indicator. It automatically allocates designated amounts based on performance. Adding performance budgeting gives governors, legislators, and coordinating and system boards the discretion to consider additional allocations based on total campus performance. The first adds certainty; the second offers flexibility.

Components

Again, like a family's attic, governments add to, but seldom discard, elements of abandoned public policies. Performance Funding and Performance Budgeting are no exceptions. They include planning and fiscal ingredients borrowed from program planning budgeting, zero-based budgeting, management by objectives, and other initiatives that link managing, planning, and budgeting. Both also incorporate concepts from outcomes assessment and performance reporting. The differences of performance funding and, to a lesser performance budgeting, is their attempt to move beyond assessing and reporting performance and beyond budget preparation and presentation to at least consider distributing some resources based on campus achievements.

Performance funding and performance budgeting share some of the same components:

- *Program goals* include demonstrating external accountability, improving institutional performance, and meeting state needs. Increasing state funding often constitutes an unannounced goal for coordinating boards and campuses.

- *Performance indicators* identify the areas of anticipated achievement. (They run from as few as one in Connecticut to as many as 37 in South Carolina's original plan, with most of programs using around ten.)

- *Success standards* for the indicators use improved performance for each campus, comparisons with the results of state or national peers, or a combination of these criteria.

The remaining components apply only to performance funding:

- *Funding weights* assign the same or different values to the indicators, or allow some campus choice.

- *Funding levels* comprise a percentage, or a specified amount, of state support for campus operating budgets. The levels generally range from half a percent of state general fund support to about six percent and average around two percent.

- *Funding sources* involve additional or reallocated resources, or a combination of the two. Nearly all of the programs in performance funding call for some additional monies beyond base budgets.

- *Allocation methods* consist of base budget increases or annual bonuses based on performance. Most programs increase the budget base.

- *Funding plans* are competitive or noncompetitive. Most programs are noncompetitive, permitting campuses to earn only up to their assigned level of performance. A few permit high performing institutions to gain funds beyond their assigned levels from monies not earned by other campuses (Burke and Serban, 1998b).

Challenges

Despite important differences, performance funding and performance budgeting share some, but not all, of the same challenges. They affect performance funding more than performance budgeting because the tight tie to funding generates special concerns and controversies. The inputs of critical stakeholders, methods of initiation, and timing of program implementation affect the stability of performance funding more than performance budgeting. The same is true for the details of program design, the emphases on policy values, and the resolution of major difficulties.

Higher education has many stakeholders: state officials and opinion leaders; state coordinating officers and university system officials, campus administrators and faculty members; and students and alumni. Business leaders, K-12 educators, and the general public increasingly see themselves as stakeholders in the success of public higher education.

A proper start will not guarantee the longevity of either program, but success is unlikely without it. Three methods exist for initiating performance funding and budgeting. They appear below, from the least to the most effective.

- *Mandated/Prescribed*: Legislation mandates the program and prescribes the indicators and is initiated by governors or legislators.

- *Mandated/Not Prescribed*: Legislation mandates the program but allows state-coordinating agencies in cooperation with campus leaders to propose the indicators. Coordinating or system officers could initiate these programs, as well as governors and legislators.

- *Not Mandated*: Coordinating or system boards in collaboration with campus officials initiate and adopt the plan without legislation.

Mandates, and especially prescriptions, clearly undermine program stability, because they are imposed and ignore the importance of consultation with coordinating, system, and campus officials. No consultation means no consent. They also run counter to the dual directions of organizational decentralization and professional participation. Many of the early programs in both performance funding and performance budgeting ignored these maxims. Four of the five states that dropped performance funding mandated the program and three prescribed the indicators. In the fifth, the coordinating board in Arkansas adopted a plan designed to please the governor and to avoid a mandate (see Chapter 10). Of the 12 new or readopted programs since 1997, seven were not mandated and five mandated, but only one of the latter prescribed the indicators.

The recent move in performance budgeting also is away from mandates and prescription. Legislation mandated nearly 80 percent of the performance budgeting policies in place in 1997, but — of the sixteen programs launched after that date — ten were not mandated and only two prescribed the indicators. Most of the nonmandated programs came from coordinating boards, but in performance funding more college and university systems are launching programs on their own. University systems in New York and Pennsylvania, and Community College Systems in California and Illinois, recently adopted their own plans for allocating some resources based on campus performance.

Although coordinating and system boards are initiating programs on their own, it is done with an eye on the attitudes of governors and legislators. As noted above, Arkansas started its initial program in performance funding to please the governor, who threatened to impose a mandate. Tennessee's coordinating board, faced with an end to enrollment increases that had previously produced bigger budgets, started its program in the hopes of attracting additional allocations from state government by funding quality improvements. To many officers of coordinating and system boards, performance funding and performance budgeting appeared the best way — some would say the only way — to win increased state support, especially in states with stable enrollments.

Whatever the reasons or methods, all programs in performance funding and performance budgeting require continuing support from state, coordinating, system, and campus leaders. State officials can mandate and prescribe the program, but the initiatives cannot succeed without the cooperation of coordinating and system leaders who monitor the policies, and of faculty and administrators who produce the results. Coordinating and system officials can voluntarily initiate either program, but only governors and legislators can supply the funding.

The initiation of performance budgeting causes much less consternation on campuses than performance funding. The conflict varies based on the connection between performance and funding. The loose link in performance budgeting is less frightening to campus leaders. The tight tie of funding to performance causes controversy for performance funding. Campus leaders prefer the stability of base budgets built on current costs, enrollment levels, and inflationary increases. They also question the validity of assessing "good" performance, given the differences in campus types and missions, the complexity of higher education outcomes, and the difficulty — some would say the impossibility — of evaluating student learning in undergraduate education. Only the hope of additional allocations overcomes this opposition, and the rewards from either program seldom meet expectations in good economic times and really disappoint during economic downturns.

Both performance funding and performance budgeting, in varying degrees, must cope with conceptual and practical difficulties. Choosing performance indicators, assessing higher education results, and protecting mission diversity and campus autonomy present special problems. The multiplicity of objectives in higher education makes selecting a limited number of indicators a perplexing problem, especially in performance funding. In that program, restricted funding usually forces fewer measures, since specific sums are assigned to each indicator. Performance budgeting avoids this problem by considering performance on the indicators collectively and not individually for funding. Designing a funding program that not only covers but also fits a wide diversity of campus types and missions presents another difficulty. Finally, both programs must specify and support particular priorities for public colleges and universities without diminishing the campus autonomy required for institutional diversity and faculty creativity.

Practical problems also plague both programs. They include the timing of program planning and implementation, the costs of data collection and analysis, and the changes in state priorities and leaders. Performance funding also raises the specter of budget instability, because it automatically allocates specific sums based solely on performance, which can produce annual budget fluctuations. In addition, implementing complex and controversial programs takes time. Complexity of program design, controversy over critical components, consultation with multiple stakeholders, and collection of required data demand long periods for planning and implementation. Achieving results in higher education also takes time. State priorities and program requirements must continue long enough to allow campuses to produce and evaluate the desired and demanding results. Despite this need for continuity, state priorities fluctuate with changes in governors and legislators and with shifts in constituent interests and pressing issues. The costs of data collection and analysis for tracking and assessing institutional results add another burden to strained campus budgets and staffs.

Regional, Economic, and Political Relations

Although both performance funding and performance budgeting began with regional origins, they soon expanded into national programs. Performance funding in 1997 clustered mostly in the South (four) and Midwest (three). The East had only a small program with a single indicator on minority enrollment in Connecticut, while the West had only the programs in Colorado and Washington. By 2000, the policy had spread more evenly across the country. Although the South still had the most programs, the greatest rate of growth came in the East with three new programs. Performance Budgeting also found the most fertile soil in the South (seven) and the Midwest (five) in 1997. Again, the East had only one and the West two. By 2000, it too had become more national in scope. The South had ten and Midwest eight, but the West had six, and the East three programs.

The size of populations, economies, and higher education seem to have some relation to program adoption. Hines (1998) identifies nine Megastates, which have relatively large populations, well-developed industrial and business bases, and larger systems of higher education. He defines larger systems as those where states appropriate over a billion dollars for higher education. The Megastates include California, Florida, Illinois, Michigan, New York, North Carolina, Ohio, Pennsylvania, and Texas. In 1997, of the ten states with performance funding, only Florida and Ohio represented Megastates. By 2000, all of the Megastates, except Michigan and North Carolina, had performance funding.

Performance budgeting appears less attractive to Megastates. Four of them had Performance Budgeting in 1997. By 2000, only one more of the Megastates had adopted the policy, despite the addition of 12 more programs. The causes of the differences remain unclear. Perhaps the existence of larger and more costly systems of higher education makes the tight tie of resources to results in Performance Funding more attractive to states searching for a policy alternative than the loose link in Performance Budgeting.

Although politics always affects policy making, party politics appears to have little, if any effect, on decisions to start either performance funding or budgeting. Looking at the results from the 2000 SHEFO Survey, legislation initiated eight of the 11 earliest programs in performance funding. Five of those states had democratic governors, but that party controlled the legislature in only two. The other three had Republican governors, whose party also controlled the legislature. Democrats held sway in the governorship and the legislature in all three of the states with nonmandated programs of performance funding. In the programs started after 1997, Republicans held the governorship in all the states and the legislature in six. Control of the legislature split in five states, and the Democrats controlled two.

In performance budgeting, Democrats controlled the governorship and the legislature in seven states when the program began; the Republicans controlled the state house and the legislature in six. Eight Republican Governors had Democratic legislatures and four had split houses. One Democratic governor had a Republican legislature. One Independent had a Democratic legislature and one Republican had a nonpartisan legislature in Nebraska. Both parties supported the start of Performance Funding and Performance Budgeting and neither appears as the preferred champion of either program.

Impact on Institutional Improvement

Of course, the bottomline in assessing both performance funding and budgeting is the extent to which each has improved institutional performance. A realistic assessment is still premature, since nearly all of these programs are products of the mid to the late 1990s, and have been implemented for only a few years. Still, it is not too early to start a preliminary assessment of their effect on performance. The 2000 Survey asked SHEFOs, with performance funding and/or performance budgeting in their states, to assess the effect of each program on improving campus performance (Burke et al. 2000). Results confirm that it is still too soon to evaluate their effect, given the short history of both programs. They do suggest that performance funding has much more effect than performance budgeting and that the impact of both approaches increases in relation to the clarity and the level of fiscal consequences.

Forty percent of the SHEFOs say it is too early to evaluate the effect of performance funding on institutional improvement in their states, in large part because the programs were too recent to assess (Burke and Minassians 2001). But 25 percent claim that the program has improved performance to a great or considerable extent. They cite a great extent in Missouri and a considerable extent in Ohio, South Dakota, and Tennessee. SHEFOs from Connecticut, Idaho, and South Carolina believe performance funding has had a moderate impact on campus performance. Florida, Louisiana, and Oregon are assessed as having a minimal effect and New Jersey no effect.

Program duration and funding levels clearly affect these estimates. Tennessee, Missouri, and Ohio have had programs for some time and have supported them with considerable funding. South Carolina represents an exception, since it began in 1996 and at least for the last three years had sizeable funding, although far less than mandated in law. Although Florida's effort has existed for five years, its university sector has received only about $3 million annually for division among its ten institutions. Even respondents from states that give low ratings to the effect on program improvement say that performance funding has caused campus leaders to concentrate more on institutional performance as opposed to program objectives.

Although performance budgeting has a longer history than performance funding, still 22 percent of the SHEFOs consider it too early to assess its impact. Missouri, which also has performance funding, gets a rating of great extent. Respondents believe performance budgeting improved campus performance to a considerable extent only in Louisiana and Maine. A third of the SHEFOs say performance budgeting had a moderate effect on performance and the same percent claim little or no impact. It seems especially significant that most of the programs cited as having considerable or moderate effect on improving institutional performance also reported having coordinating or system boards that consider performance in campus allocation.

The effect of both programs on improved performance appears to depend on fiscal consequences, which is the rationale for both performance budgeting and performance funding. The loose link of performance to allocation in performance budgeting, as opposed to the tight tie in performance funding, seems to explain why the former appears to have a lesser impact on performance.

The Higher Education Program at the Rockefeller Institute also surveyed state and campus policy makers' attitudes toward performance funding in late 1996 and early 1997 (Serban 1997). The responses came from over 900 state and campus policy makers in nine states with performance funding in place at that time. A critical question asked the extent to which performance funding had achieved its avowed goals of increasing the accountability and improving the performance of public higher education.

The results reveal the division between state and campus policy makers. In general, state policy makers cite a more positive impact on enhancing accountability and improving performance than did campus leaders. Over 50 percent of the state officials saw a positive impact on both accountability and improvement, although slightly less for improvement. A majority of campus leaders believed the program had a positive impact on accountability, but most of them considered it too soon to assess the impact on institutional improvement.

Merging Models

Merging the models of performance funding and budgeting could perhaps achieve the advantages and avoid the disadvantages of each program. As noted earlier, the tight tie between results and resources in performance funding is clear but inflexible. Conversely, the loose link in performance budgeting is flexible but unclear. The key is to clarify the funding connection of performance budgeting, and to increase the flexibility of performance funding. The 2000 SHEFO Survey shows these changes are already occurring in some states.

The newer programs in performance budgeting are clarifying the connection of resources to performance. According to the 2001 SHEFO Survey, Alabama, California, and Missouri are now earmarking specified funds for performance. In addition, 48 percent of the SHEFOs from states with performance budgeting say that the program has considerable or a moderate effect on the actual funding of higher education, while only 37 percent claim little or no effect. Fifteen percent say they cannot judge the effect. The 2000 Survey also suggested that nearly 40 percent of the states with performance budgeting have coordinating or system boards considering performance in institutional allocations.

If the new initiatives in performance budgeting attempt to address its problem of uncertainty, several of those in performance funding try to reduce its inflexibility. Many of the early efforts at performance funding suffered from rigid mandates that sought radical reform of public higher education. They imposed long lists of statewide indicators that discouraged campus diversity and tied annual funding to institutional results that take years to improve. Of the nine comprehensive programs in place in 1996, legislation mandated six and prescribed the indicators in four. Six of these policies imposed only statewide indicators and gave no campuses choice on performance measures. Three of them imposed the same indicators for two- and four-year institutions — all three later dropped the program.

The newer programs reduce the rigidities of those earlier efforts. In the last two years, most of the initiatives came from coordinating and — especially — system boards rather than from legislative mandates. Community college systems in California and Illinois initiated their own programs, as did university systems in New York and Pennsylvania. Legislative prescription of performance indicators — found in several of the earlier programs — has become rare.

Many of the newer programs, including the renewed effort in Colorado, permit campuses to select an indicator or two related to their strategic plans. Only three of the first eleven programs in performance funding included this feature of campus choice. The Louisiana program goes even farther. It rejects statewide indicators and relies solely on institutional measures. The newer plans also tend to have more limited objectives and use fewer indicators than early performance funding programs. Most of the recent plans also permit lead-time for program development and campus consultation before implementation. This careful approach contrasts with the immediate or hurried implementation of most of the early programs. A classic example of the careful approach is the new effort in Arkansas. Its aborted program implemented immediately a rigid and uniform program on two- and four-year colleges and universities. Its new program asks one two-year and one four-year program to volunteer for an experimental program that would develop the approach to linking state funding to campus performance.

Several of the newer initiatives also link performance funding to multiyear plans. The Partnership for Excellence between California and its Community College System spreads consideration of performance over seven years. The System for Higher Education in Pennsylvania ties funding to institutional performance over four years. Louisiana's program has a five-year time line, with institutions presenting annual operational plans. A stalled effort in Virginia, which its SHEFO says is highly likely to receive future approval, involves "Institutional Performance Agreements" for six years, which include statewide and campus indicators linked to institutional strategic plans.

These changes certainly blur the differences between performance funding and budgeting. They may foreshadow the emergence of a merged model, with the advantages of both and the disadvantages of neither program. The link of state resources to campus results constitutes the major differences between the two policies. This distinction diminishes when performance budgeting commits more coordinating and system boards to consider performance in campus allocations. It almost disappears when programs earmark state funds for campus results.

Only one distinction remains. Performance funding ties specific amounts or percentages to each indicator, while performance budgeting considers the collective achievements on all indicators in funding decisions. Performance funding could close the narrowing gap with the performance budgeting programs that earmark funds, if it allocates funds collectively on the combined indicators rather than individually on each measure.

In any case, the new innovations in performance budgeting certainly blur or reduce the main distinction with performance funding. Meanwhile, the introduction of more flexibility in performance funding narrows its differences with performance budgeting. If these trends continue, they could produce a merged model for linking state resources to campus results that is more certain and flexible. Such a policy could become more effective in practice and more acceptable on campus.

Conclusion

Some conclusions about programs linking state resources to campus results are clear, while others are cloudy. The popularity in state capitols of finding some way to relate state resources to campus results is unmistakable. The expansion of legislation for performance-based budgeting for state agencies demonstrates this popularity. If the desirability is undeniable, the method remains debatable for higher education. Performance budgeting is the preferred program, although performance funding recently is showing a greater rate of increase. Fifty-four percent of the states have adopted this approach versus thirty-eight percent that have opted for performance funding. Both have exhibited remarkable growth in the last four years. The recent responses to the SHEFO Survey responses suggest that this rate of increase is unlikely to continue in the future (Burke et al. 2000). With programs in place in over half of the states, performance budgeting has less room to expand. Performance funding with programs in only thirty-eight percent of the states could grow but it has aroused opposition in some states. Continued campus resistance to performance funding could limit its growth.

The future of both programs may well depend on the adoption and the effectiveness of the new innovations recently introduced. Can the practice of earmarking funds and of considering performance in allocations clarify the uncertainty of performance budgeting without creating campus opposition? Can multiyear evaluations and funding commitments, institutional indicators, and emphasis on campus strategic plans gain the support — or at least diminish the resistance — of the leaders of colleges and universities to performance funding? Will the borrowing of elements from both programs create a merged model capable of attracting approval from both state capitols and public campuses? Whatever the answers to these questions, the similarities of performance funding and performance budgeting are likely to receive as much scrutiny as their differences.

Chapter 3

PERFORMANCE FUNDING INDICATORS: IMPERFECT NECESSITIES

Joseph C. Burke

Introduction

If what gets measured is what gets valued, what gets funded is what gets prized. The indicators picked for performance funding provide clues about the priorities of policy makers for public colleges and universities. This chapter seeks answers to a series of questions by analyzing the funding indicators in the study states of Arkansas, Colorado, Florida, Kentucky, Minnesota, Missouri, Ohio, South Carolina, and Tennessee. Did performance funding merely repeat the indicators commonly used for performance reporting; and if not, how did they differ? Did policy makers in the nine states select mostly common or mainly different indicators for their performance funding programs? What types of indicators did they favor; and what did their choices suggest about their concerns, values, and models of excellence for public colleges and universities? Finally, did they choose the same or different indicators for two- and four-year campuses; and what did these selections suggest about their attitudes toward these two types of institutions (Burke 1997)?

Our Surveys shows that both state and campus leaders consider selecting the indicators as one of the most difficult decisions in building performance funding programs (Chapter IV). Ewell and Jones (1994) describe an indicator as a "policy relevant" statistic that provides "a concrete piece of information about a condition or result of a public action that is regularly produced, publicly reported, and systematically used for planning, monitoring, or resource allocation..." (pp. 6-7).

Choosing indicators is always controversial, especially for statewide measures that cover all public colleges and universities. They seldom measure directly campus performance on the priority results of higher education or the actual impact on students, states, and society. Quality — the hallmark of higher education — is an elusive and subjective attribute that is seldom easy to assess objectively and always difficult to measure quantitatively. In addition, higher education is a complex enterprise with multiple goals, delivered by different types of institutions pursuing diverse missions and educating students with a broad range of natural abilities and academic preparations. Given the complexity and diversity of higher education and the subjectivity of educational results, performance indicators can offer only signs or signals that suggest the extent of institutional success in achieving priority objectives.

With so many problems and limitations, a reasonable question is: Why bother with indicators at all? The answer is simple. The difficulty of performance indicators is exceeded only by their necessity. Like democracy, they only become acceptable when compared to their alternatives. As imperfect as they are, indicators offer the only available and reasonable means of evaluating performance. Public higher education has become too important and too costly for states to assess campus performance only by antidotes or assertions. Indicators are needed to appraise the progress of public colleges and universities in reaching assigned objectives, for the new accountability no longer accepts public higher education as an unquestioned public good.

When precision is difficult in practice, the inevitable reaction is to rely on principles. To earn institutional acceptance and external support, experts say that performance indicators should pursue the following principles (Ashworth 1994; Board of Governors 1997; Ewell and Jones 1994).

1. Appear clear and credible;

2. Exhibit validity and reliability;

3. Show internal consistency;

4. Seem fair and equitable to all institutions;

5. Evaluate only performance influenced by institutional efforts;

6. Rely more on outcomes and outputs than on inputs or processes;

7. Produce measurable and auditable data, not subject to manipulation;

8. Use available, or economically collectable, data;

9. Relate to planning goals and strategies;

10. Allow differences in institutional missions and types; and

11. Remain stable long enough to give institutions time to respond.

Campus critics quarrel not with the validity of these principles in theory but with their difficulty in practice. The simplicity demanded for clear and understandable indicators conflict with the complexity required for validity and reliability. Some indicators, such as increasing student access and improving admission standards seem inconsistent. Critics also consider many outputs and outcomes — such as graduation rates and job placements — beyond campus control, since these results also depend on student effort and economic conditions. Outputs and outcomes, in their view, reflect mostly inputs of student quality and institutional resources. They prefer process indicators; in part, because improved student outcomes flow from improving campus practices. Measurable data, which favors quantifiable over qualitative indicators, appear incompatible with the accent of the academy on quality. Critics also charge that no list of statewide indicators could encompass — much less encourage — the diversity of campus conditions, missions, and types. The time, effort, and cost of data collection generate constant complaints. Most of all, critics claim that the unique nature of higher education makes assessing results difficult, if not impossible. Criticism of indicators also varies with their use, for campus leaders hold indicators for funding to a much higher standard than those for reporting (Borden and Banta 1994; Gaither et al. 1995).

Creating Comparative Core Indicators

This chapter analyzes the funding indicators used in nine states. They include five states that continue performance funding (Florida, Missouri, Ohio, South Carolina, and Tennessee), and four that later dropped the program (Arkansas, Colorado, Kentucky, and Minnesota), although Colorado has since started a new initiative, with different indicators. Comparing indicators of performance funding in nine states is challenging, since they differ in number, content, and wording. Some programs link different objectives in a single indicator, such as retention rates, graduation rates, and time-to-degree, whereas others list them separately.

This study constructs a common core of indicators where two or more states share similar items. These generic indicators combine related objectives that are separate measures in some states. For example, retention and graduation rates are joined, although some programs list them separately. Similarly, separate indicators — such as credits on graduation and time-to-degree — are linked to denote a common concern with the cost of students taking too many courses and too long to graduate. As a result of this comparative effort, the number of indicators listed for states on the table in Appendix A often differs from the actual number in their performance funding programs.

The indicators for two- and four-year institutions show significant differences among the programs. The nine states take five different approaches to developing indicators for their community colleges. Arkansas, Colorado, and Kentucky used the same indicators for both two- and four-year institutions, although Kentucky mandated some indicators for each of the sectors. Missouri and Tennessee adopt mostly common indicators, but add an alternate item for their two-year campuses. Minnesota had separate indicators for the University of Minnesota and for the Minnesota State College and University System, which included both campus types, although the two systems share some indicators. South Carolina applies many, but not all, of its prescribed indicators to its Technical Colleges, and to a lesser extent to its two-year branch campuses. Florida has separate indicators for two- and four-year institutions. So does Ohio, except that its access indicator also applies to a few baccalaureate campuses as well as to all two-year colleges. Despite these approaches, the small differences in indicators between sectors confirms the complaints of leaders of community and technical colleges that the measures fail to consider their unique missions, of short-term job training, local community service, and educating older, part-time, students.

Although the indicators for some programs distinguish between two- and four-year institutions, only Kentucky and now South Carolina differentiate between comprehensive campuses and graduate and re-search universities. Indeed, a common complaint charges that these funding programs seldom include an indicator on graduate studies, al-though many insert an item on research productivity, usually the dollar volume of sponsored research. Some programs try to address the prob-lem of encouraging mission diversity by including one or two campus specific indicators selected by institutions to emphasize their special missions. This concession fails to satisfy many campus critics, who see more differences than commonalities among institutions, even though they often grant the same degrees in the same majors.

Indicator Content

The list of indicators for performance funding parallel those selected for performance reporting, although a close comparison also reveals signif-icant differences. Both focus overwhelmingly on undergraduate educa-tion. However, programs of performance funding share far fewer indicators than those found in performance reporting. The former also exhibit declining concern with traditional issues and increased interest in emerging problems.

The move away from indicators on ethnicity and gender in student enrollment, so prevalent in performance reports, represents a signifi-cant shift in performance funding. None of the nine programs in the study states initially had a specific indicator on minority access, and only a single program included an item on minority retention or gradua-tion rates. Kentucky alone used an indicator on gender. On the other hand, three funding programs selected measures on the number of mi-nority graduates and on the diversity of faculty and staff — items gener-ally not found in performance reporting. Apparently, emphasis has moved from minority access to minority graduation. This abandonment of minority access and enrollment foreshadows the later effort to end af-firmative action in college admissions in California, Texas, and other states.

The stress on student access that appears in the indicators for perfor-mance reporting also diminishes in those selected for performance funding. Only Colorado — which anticipates huge increases in student demand — and South Carolina — which faces no such pressures — in-sert an access item for both two- and four-year colleges. Ohio includes access only for two-year and a few four-year campuses, but not for their main universities. Florida, with projected enrollment demands second only to California, omits student access for both categories of campuses, although an initial University System proposal had such a measure.

State officials pushed some of the performance-funding programs based on the perception that many four-year colleges and universities admitted unqualified students to increase their budgets. The South Carolina plan clearly reflects this belief. As a result, the funding indicators also place much less emphasis on total enrollments and credits hours than those used in performance reporting. Although only Colorado and Florida face large increases in enrollment demand, many of the other states do have comparatively low college-going rates.

Whatever the reasons, few programs could have been launched or even considered for public higher education in the 1970s and 1980s without stressing the goals of access and equity. Apparently in the 1990s, the new anxieties about efficiency and standards began to replace the old imperatives of equity and access. Only Kentucky and Ohio have an indicator on tuition and fees. Given the concerns that emerged in the late 1990s of access and affordability in a number of states across the country, it seems probable that new funding programs will add such indicators to their plans for performance funding.

If the funding indicators repeat many of the items in the performance reports, they also introduce new policy issues. New indicators appear on the use of technology and distance learning, administrative versus academic costs, and program productivity and duplication, which voiced more current concerns of state policy makers about efficiency in public higher education. State needs, especially in workforce training and economic development, also receive added attention. The performance-funding indicators exhibit more of a preference for efficiency and productivity measures than those in performance reporting. The funding indicators also begin to respond to the current criticism of remediation programs. Three programs have indicators on degree completion of at-risk students.

Critics charge that the indicators often used for performance reporting owe more to the availability of data and ease of measurement than to their importance as policy concerns (Ewell and Jones 1994). Although availability probably influenced the inclusion of many of the indicators in performance-funding programs, a number of items require substantial investment and effort to implement, such as satisfaction surveys of alumni and employers, tests for general education and majors, job placements, use of technology, and institutional cooperation. The heavy reliance on process indicators, where data are not traditionally collected, nor easily assessed, also counters this contention. Moreover, the limited number of indicators used in most states forced difficult decisions. Choosing indicators is like admission into heaven: "Many are called but few are chosen." The funding plans also omit some of the obvious indicators with available data — such as admission and enrollment information, which performance reporting commonly used.

Criticism of performance indicators — for reporting and even more for funding — inevitably center on their inability to capture fully the essential but elusive character of quality in higher education. The critics are correct that no limited set of indicators can capture completely the character of quality in higher education (Bogue and Saunders 1992). The assessment movement, which also concentrates on undergraduate education, evaluates quality by analyzing what graduates know and are able to do. Licensure test scores — selected by four funding programs — try to answer these questions. Three states have indicators that assess students' knowledge and skills through satisfaction surveys and test scores. Missouri and Tennessee had long experience with such standardized exams, and Arkansas only committed to implementing the appropriate tests as part of performance funding. With only three states opting for an indicator of standardized exams beyond those for licensure, fears that testing would dominate, as an indicator of quality for performance funding, appear unfounded.

Another surprise is that only two states include an indicator on assessment of student learning, given the reported popularity of outcomes assessment in colleges and universities. One explanation is that assessment has become a process used mostly by campuses for institutional improvement and not for external accountability. External program reviews also have support from only two states as a quality measure. Favored by campus groups as a guarantor of quality, this approach lacks the confidence of state policy makers who see it as self-serving. The same might be said for program accreditation, which only two states use.

Performance-funding programs pay scant attention to the several measures of quality long favored by the academy. Student academic preparation and sponsored research funds appear in only three states. Class size and post-baccalaureate education, as opposed to job placement, exist in only two programs, and the perennial, student/faculty ratios, in just one. Not a single program selects scholarly publications.

Few Common Funding Indicators

It is not surprising that the performance-funding programs share a common list of indicators with performance-reporting systems. After all, both programs evaluate the performance of public colleges and universities on priority objectives. The surprise comes from the lack of commonality among the states in their choices of funding indicators compared with those in the performance reports. More than half of the 62 generic indicators listed in Appendix A are found in only one program. Just four indicators appear in more than half of the programs in the nine study states and only three more in four states. Retention/graduation rates represent the most used indicator.

Aside from demonstrating the lack of commonality in indicator choices, the most used items suggest some differences in the indicators selected for two- and four-year colleges and universities. Eight programs require retention/graduation rates for baccalaureate campuses and six for community colleges. Such a slight difference is unexpected, given the complaints from community colleges that graduation rates are unfair measures for institutions with open admissions, more part-time enrollment, and a special mission in short-term job training. Conversely, six programs insert job placement for two-year colleges, but only two include it for four-year campuses — probably because of the

Table 1. Funding Indicators Selected by Four or More Programs		
Indicator	Baccalaureate Institutions	Community Colleges
Retention/Graduation Rates	8	6
Two-to-Four Year Transfers	5	7
Job Placement	2	6
Graduation Credits/ Time-to-Degree	5	3
Staff/Cost, Instructional vs. Noninstructional	4	4
Technology/Telecommunications/ Distance Learning	4	4
Test Scores, Licensure Exams	4	4

conviction that the two-year colleges should be tied more closely to the job market. The surprise is that all nine programs do not use this indicator for community colleges, since job training constitutes a primary mission for these campuses. The same could be said for two- to four-year transfers, which seven programs have for two-year campuses and five for their baccalaureate counterparts. One would expect that all community colleges would include a transfer indicator, since it constitutes one of their major missions. The same would apply to four-year campuses, which have a special responsibility of admitting transfers from community and technical colleges, especially at a time when more and more students start their baccalaureate programs on two-year campuses.

Indicator Types

Performance indicators fall into four types: *Inputs*, *Processes*, *Outputs* and *Outcomes*. Inputs are the human, financial, and physical *resources received* to support programs, activities, and services. Examples are student academic preparation, faculty salaries, and faculty credentials. Processes are the *methods* used to deliver programs, activities, and services. This type includes assessment of student learning, use of technology, and evaluation of faculty. Outputs involve the *quantity* of products produced, such as the number of degrees granted, retention and graduation rates, and the dollar volume of sponsored research. Outcomes represent the *quality* of the benefit or impact of programs, activities, and services on students, states, and society. Their indicators include test scores, job placements, and satisfaction survey results.

An examination of the 62 indicators in Appendix A shows a shift from inputs to outputs and — to a lesser extent — to outcomes, when compared to those used for performance reporting. The surprise is that both types of institutions devote 40 percent to process measures. The reliance on process indicators reflect in part the popularity of the quality movement, with its emphasis on improving processes to serve better the organization's customers (Seymour 1993). The heavy use of process measures also indicates increasing interest in "good educational practices," which stressed methods for improving teaching and learning (Ewell and Jones, 1993). Despite these influences, the preference for process indicators undoubtedly stems from the difficulty of identifying and evaluating the results of higher education. Consequently, process measures such as course availability, assessing student learning, and faculty evaluation become surrogates for quality in teaching and learning.

The indicator types for two- and four-year campuses show only small differences (see Figure 1). Baccalaureate institutions have a somewhat higher percentage of inputs and a correspondingly lower percentage of outputs. Most of this difference comes from the change of the single indicator on transfers, an output for two-year and an input for four-year institutions. Both sectors rely heavily on process indicators.

This overall picture of indicator types hides some differences, for baccalaureate institutions, especially on the use of process measures. A heavy reliance on process in Colorado, Kentucky, and South Carolina skews that statistic. Still, the other states evince considerable interest in process, except for Florida's and for Ohio's universities, which have no process indicators. The large number of these indicators in Kentucky stemmed from their intended use as initial and temporary measures. Kentucky planned to turn many of these process indicators into output or outcome measures by the Year 2000. Minnesota and, to a lesser extent, Arkansas spread their measures fairly evenly between processes, outputs, and outcomes. Florida has a high percentage of output indicators for four-year colleges and universities, and Ohio allocates all of its four indicators to that type. Missouri and Tennessee have some process indicators but stress outputs and outcomes.

Most of the shifts for two-year colleges arise from the change of the transfer indicator from an input to an outcome. A few changes occur in states with separate programs for the two types of campuses. The major

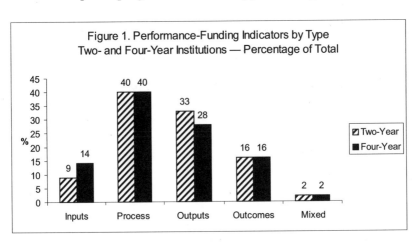

Figure 1. Performance-Funding Indicators by Type
Two- and Four-Year Institutions — Percentage of Total

shift comes in Ohio. Its single indicator on student access, mostly for two-year campuses, represents an input. The reliance on process remains in most programs for two- and four-year institutions, although somewhat diminished for the former. The categories of mandate and prescription appear to have little or no influence on the choice of indicator types.

External or Internal Concerns

Whether indicators express primarily the external concerns of state policy makers or the internal concerns of the academic community raises a significant policy question. Few students of the subject would deny that indicators reflect primarily either the external concerns of states and society or the internal concerns of the academy. Although all performance-funding programs claim both external accountability and internal improvement as goals, the indicators chosen imply a priority of one purpose over the other (see Figure 2). Appendix A designates each indicator as representing an external or internal concern, or in some cases a combination of the two. Retention/graduation rates, job placement, and faculty workload represent examples of external concerns. Student preparation, sponsored research funds, and program accreditation express internal concerns. External concerns clearly dominate the indicators for both four- and two-year campuses.

An analysis of whether indicators by states stem primarily from the external or internal concerns reveals some interesting differences and

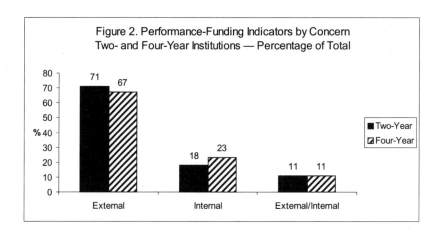

Figure 2. Performance-Funding Indicators by Concern
Two- and Four-Year Institutions — Percentage of Total

one intriguing deviation among three categories of program initiation: Mandated/Prescribed, Mandated/Not Prescribed, and Not Mandated (see Chapter 2). Legislation mandated performance funding in Colorado, Florida, Kentucky, Minnesota, Ohio, and South Carolina. Statutes also prescribed the indicators in Colorado, Florida, Minnesota, and South Carolina. Legislation mandated the performance funding in Kentucky and Ohio, but allowed their coordinating agencies, in consultation with campus representatives, to develop the proposed indicators. Arkansas, Missouri, and Tennessee comprised the Not Mandated States. Their coordinating boards, without legislation and with extensive consultation with campus representatives, initiated performance funding on their own.

One would expect that Mandated/Prescribed Programs would heavily favor measures reflecting external concerns, since state leaders prescribed them in legislation. Mandated/Not Prescribed programs would probably stress external concerns to reflect the mandate, but would also recognize internal concerns because of the consultative process with campus leaders. Conversely, Not Mandated Programs would show increased interest in internal concerns without neglecting external concerns, since funding required support from governors and legislatures. This hypothesis holds for nearly all of the states, especially for baccalaureate institutions, with one notable exception.

Four-year indicators in the Mandated/Prescribed States of Colorado, Florida, Minnesota, and South Carolina stress external concerns. The Mandated/Not Prescribed States of Kentucky and Ohio emphasize external without slighting internal concerns. The Not Mandated States of Missouri and Tennessee show considerably more interest in indicators reflecting internal concerns. Indeed, half of Tennessee's and 40 percent of Missouri's indicators stress internal concerns. The third Not Mandated State, Arkansas, breaks this pattern. It resembles a Mandated/Prescribed Program, with overwhelming emphasis on external and scant attention to internal concerns. Although a committee dominated by campus presidents designed the performance-funding program in Arkansas without legislation, it fashioned indicators to please the governor and to avoid a mandate (see Chapter 10).

The two-year institutions follow the same pattern by method of initiation. Ohio, a Mandated/Not Prescribed Program, constitutes an exception, for its single indicator on student access — mostly for two-year colleges — expresses an external concern. Arkansas, a Not Mandated

Program with the same indicators for both sectors, continues as an outlier, with overwhelming support for indicators of external concerns.

Policy Values

Roy Romer, former governor of Colorado and chair of the Education Commission of the States, declares that the states "need to be clear about what we value in higher education so we can act on those values" (Ewell and Jones 1995, p. v). "Higher education policies," claims Richardson (1994), "reflect the core social values of choice, equity, efficiency, and quality" (p. 132). The following definitions follow Richardson's descriptions. *Choice* represents the ability to select from a range of options. *Efficiency* calculates the resources used in relation to the results achieved. *Equity* represents the response to the disparities and diversity in human needs among different groups. *Quality* means achieving or exceeding high standards of performance. Some of the indicators exhibit two or more policy values.

This study designates each of the indicators as implying one or a combination of these four values (see Figure 3). Over half of them suggest either efficiency or quality, in nearly equal proportions. This result counters the contention that state policy makers have abandoned their interest in quality in favor of efficiency. A surprising statistic shows a sizeable percentage of indicators reflecting both efficiency and quality. Apparently, state policy makers view efficiency and quality as complementary, not conflicting, values. This belief has few followers on cam-

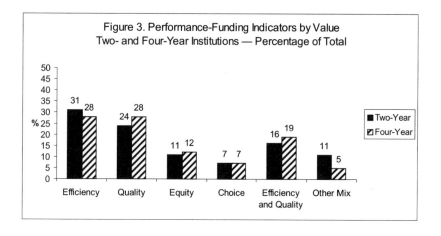

Figure 3. Performance-Funding Indicators by Value
Two- and Four-Year Institutions — Percentage of Total

puses, where businesslike efficiency is often seen as the enemy of educational quality.

The values implied by the indicators selected for two-year colleges and baccalaureate campuses reveal a similar pattern, with the former having a slightly higher percentage of efficiency. The two sectors have low percentages of equity indicators and relatively high percentages of indicators suggesting a combination of efficiency and quality. Choice and equity receives little support for either sector.

Data for the individual states tell a different tale. The projected pattern suggests that Mandated/Prescribed programs would emphasize efficiency; Mandated/Not Prescribed programs would show interest in both efficiency and quality; and Not Mandated initiatives would devote more attention to quality without neglecting efficiency. As projected, the strong interest in quality indicators comes largely from the nonmandated states. Even the perennial outlier Arkansas conforms. The Mandated/Prescribed programs exhibit more than twice as much interest in efficiency as in quality indicators. Surprisingly, South Carolina proves the exception to this projection, with nearly an equal percentage of indicators for each of these values. This result is astonishing, since a committee of legislators and business leaders in the Palmetto State determined the indicators with little input from educational leaders (Chapter 9). The Mandated/Not Prescribed state of Kentucky departs from the pattern by having more quality than efficiency indicators. Ohio, the other state in that category, follows the expectation for four-year campuses. Although it has no quality indicators, it uses an equal number of measures for efficiency and for its combination with quality.

The differences between two- and four-year institutions in all but one case conform to a similar pattern, although the former exhibit much more attention to efficiency indicators and diminished interest in quality measures. Florida shows a dramatic shift from the baccalaureate campuses to the community colleges. Though efficiency indicators rise only slightly, quality items fall to zero. The most startling change in Florida flows from the climb of indicators reflecting both efficiency and equity, due to measures on the number of degree completers from economically, physically, and academically disadvantaged groups. The combination of efficiency and quality also falls sharply in that state in the transition from four- to two-year campuses. The other programs follow fairly well the expectations. The exception is Ohio, with a single indicator on student access largely for two-year colleges that stresses equity.

Models of Excellence

The indicators imply — consciously or unconsciously — models of excellence for public colleges and universities. They signify the goals and objectives that policy makers perceive successful institutions should pursue. The diverse stakeholders of higher education — state officials and lay public, students and their parents, faculty and administrators — means multiple models. Astin (1991), Ewell and Jones (1994), and Richardson (1994) developed models of excellence for colleges and universities that reflected the interests and concerns of these stakeholders. Drawing on some of their concepts, this study uses three models of excellence for colleges and universities:

1. *The Resource/Reputation Model* represents a traditional faculty-oriented model, with indicators such as institutional choice, faculty credentials, and student academic preparation.

2. *The Strategic Investment/Cost-Benefit Model* constitutes a state-oriented model, with indicators such as graduation credits/time-to-degree, cooperation among campuses, and test scores in general education/majors.

3. *The Client-Centered Model* comprises a student and other customer-oriented model. Sample indicators included faculty availability to students, satisfaction survey results, and internships and cooperative education.

The first combines Astin's two models of resource and reputation into one, since he conceded that both produce similar results or ratings. The second uses Ewell's concept of Strategic Investment, which stresses the state's interest in seeing its funding of public higher education from a cost/benefit point of view. The third follows the customer or client-focus of the quality movement.

Indicators selected for performance funding in the study states show the declining attraction of the Resource/Reputation, the growing attachment to the Strategic Investment, and the emergence of the Client Centered Model. The appeal of a merged model of Strategic Investment and Client-Centered forms the most striking finding. Indicators for this mixed model include student access, graduation/retention rates, and job placement. The differences between two- and four-year institutions on the models implied by their indicators seem small but significant. Baccalaureate campuses have more indicators suggesting the Resource and Reputation Model, although perhaps less than expected, given its popularity in academic circles. They also have fewer indicators of the mixed model of Strategic Investment/Client Centered. Despite these small differences, the mixed model dominates the measures for both sectors.

In the 1990s, businesses, schools, citizens, and local communities clearly became clients, along with current and prospective students. During this period, policy makers increasingly saw states as customers as well as supporters. These developments tended to merge the Models of Strategic Investment and Client Centered, despite some conflicts in client interests. Community colleges had long considered their local communities as interested customers as well as financial supporters. The gap between the two models will probably close even more as constrained resources and competitive demands for tax dollars push states and counties to limit their support for, while increasing their demands for services from, public higher education. They are likely to see themselves less as the primary supporter, and more as a most favored client purchasing products and services.

The Client-Centered Model already is, and the Strategic Investment is becoming, a market model. On the other hand, the Resource/Reputation paradigm is a provider-driven type, out of step with the new emphasis on customer service in business organizations and increasingly in government agencies. One would expect that community colleges would reject the Resource/Reputation model, which favors graduate research universities and elite liberal arts colleges, and would adopt a client-centered approach, because of their traditional responsiveness to local students and community needs. But the indicators used for performance funding also push baccalaureate institutions away from the Resource/Reputation model.

The results reveal that both four- and two-year institutions did move away from the traditional Resource/Reputation Model, but not to a pure Client-Centered Model (see Figure 4). Comparison of community colleges with baccalaureate campuses identifies a slight fall in an already low percentage of indicators reflecting the Resource/Reputation Model coupled with a similar increase in the merged model of Strategic-Investment and Client-Centered. Given the community colleges' commitment to open admissions, emphasis on teaching rather than research,

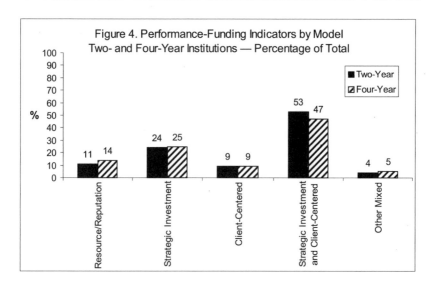

Figure 4. Performance-Funding Indicators by Model
Two- and Four-Year Institutions — Percentage of Total

and commitment to job training, the surprise is that their differences with baccalaureate institutions on the models of excellence are so small. Using mostly the same indicators for both sectors explains this similarity.

The shift from Resource/Reputation appeared in the absence of, or slight attention to, usual hallmarks of this traditional Model. Only faculty compensation dealt with the level of state funding, so fundamental to that model. The indicator list contains no item on expenditures per student; and only South Carolina included class size and student/faculty ratios. Just three programs used the traditional indicator of sponsored research; and not one included faculty publications. Three programs for baccalaureate campuses do use the hallowed indicator of student academic preparation, but it expresses more concern about admission standards than academic reputation.

Again, analysis by states reveals important differences. The method of initiation explained some but not all of these differences for baccalaureate campuses (see Figure 5). As expected, the Not Mandated states of Missouri and Tennessee show the greatest interest in the Resource and Reputation Model for baccalaureate institutions. Arkansas continued as an anomaly with few measures from this Model. The Mandated/Prescribed states also fit the anticipated pattern by having much lower percentages of their indicators devoted to the Resource and Reputation Model. Contrary to expectations, the Mandated/Not Prescribed states of Kentucky and Ohio evince little or no interest in this Model.

The mixed model of Strategic Investment/Client-Centered dominates the indicators for the Mandated/Prescribed programs and Arkansas. The Mandated/Not Prescribed States exhibit a balance between the Strategic Investment and its combination with the Client-Centered Model. Missouri looked more like one of those states. Only Tennessee slights the mixed Model. The pattern remains much the same for two-year colleges, except Ohio, whose single indicator reflects the mixed model (see Figure 5). For two-year campuses, states with separate or some different indicators all placed more emphasis on the model combining the Strategic Investment and Client-Centered (see Figure 6).

Conclusion

The performance-funding indicators in most of the nine states obviously respond to external complaints about public colleges and universities. They concentrated on undergraduate education and slighted graduate studies and research in an obvious effort to right a perceived imbalance in the priorities of state colleges and universities.

This study of the performance-funding indicators suggests the following conclusions:

- Despite selecting indicators from a list developed for performance reporting, the choices made by states show a surprising lack of commonality.

- The external concerns of state policy makers rather than the internal concerns of the academic community dominate the choice of performance funding indicators.

- The types of indicators selected display a declining interest in inputs, a growing attraction to outputs and — to a lesser extent — outcomes, and a surprising acceptance of process measures.

- The heavy use of process measures indicates a growing concern with institutional processes that flow from the movements for total quality management and good educational practices and from the difficulty of defining results in higher education.

- The policy values implied by indicator selections exhibit increased interest in efficiency, a continued concern with quality,

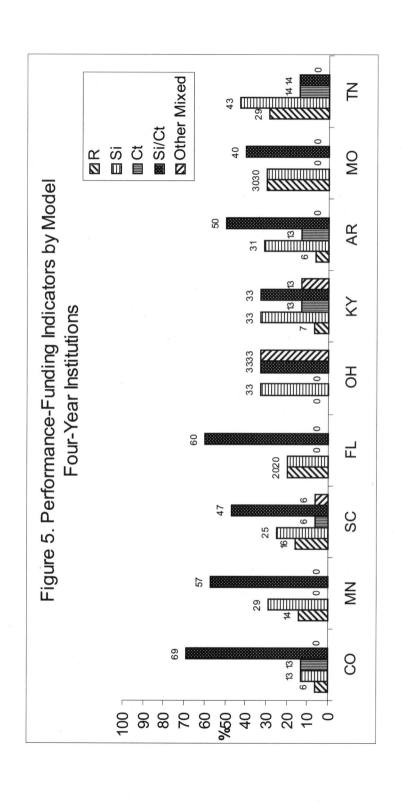

Figure 5. Performance-Funding Indicators by Model
Four-Year Institutions

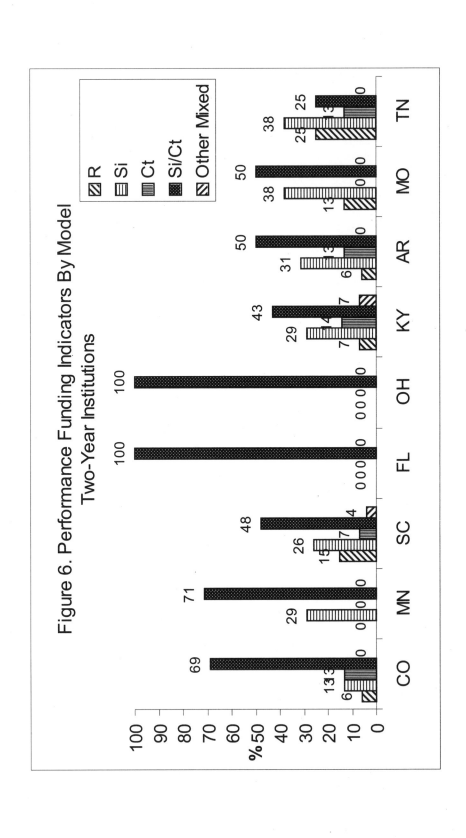

Figure 6. Performance Funding Indicators By Model
Two-Year Institutions

a diminished attention to equity and access, and a growing attraction to measures that combine efficiency and quality.

- The indicators refute the common contention that state policy makers had abandoned interest in quality, but they do suggest that state leaders defined quality differently from the traditional view in academia, since the former often couple it with efficiency.

- The models of excellence for public higher education implied by indicator choices reveal the decline of the Resource/Reputation, the rise of the Strategic Investment, and the surprising popularity of a combined Strategic Investment and Client-Centered Model of excellence for public colleges and universities.

- The performance-funding indicators seem designed to prod colleges and universities from provider-driven enterprises — motivated by the aspirations of administrators and faculty — into client-centered institutions, committed to meeting the needs of students, states, and society.

- The categories of Mandated/Prescribed, Mandated/Not Prescribed, and Not Mandated explain many, but not all, of the indicator selections and the concerns, values, and models embedded in them.

State and campus policy makers developing or revising performance funding indicators should consider the following:

1. The identification of preferred values and desired models for public higher education should always precede and consciously shape the choice of indicators.

2. The list of indicators should be long enough to include critical objectives, yet short enough to set clear priorities. (A minimum of about eight and a maximum of around twelve, depending on the level of funding.)

3. The indicators should give much more attention to part-time students and their special needs.

4. Two- and four-year institutions should have some common and some different indicators to reflect both their shared and their diverse missions.

5. Programs should reserve one or two indicators for campus choice to encourage mission diversity.

6. Indicators should promote a new notion of educational excellence-based performance not prestige, and on service to students and society rather than on resources and reputations.

7. State and campus leaders should design sets of indicators that reconcile quality and efficiency and reject the lingering notion on campus of an inevitable conflict between these two critical values.

8. When states mandate performance funding, they should set broad priorities and goals and use a representative group of external stakeholders and internal professionals to develop the indicators, under the leadership of state coordinating agencies, whose staff understand both perspectives.

9. When coordinating agencies or university systems initiate performance funding without a mandate, they should also use a representative group of external and internal stakeholders to propose the indicators and not neglect the external concerns of state officials, legislative leaders, and the general public.

10. Whatever the current political and social attitudes, access and equity are essential and enduring values for higher education, which are worthy of inclusion in performance-funding indicators.

Now that performance funding has moved from the "unthinkable" to the "fashionable," it is crucial that its indicators should be carefully and collaboratively chosen, encompass both external and internal concerns, reflect the policy values of efficiency, quality, choice, and equity, and emphasize the combined Strategic Investment and Client-Centered Models. They should flow from more inclusive models of excellence for public colleges and universities that reflect the diversity of institutional types and the demands of multiple stakeholders. Performance-funding indicators should encourage a new notion of quality based on performance and service — not prestige and resources. Although some indicators should stress the particular priorities of each state, surely a common core should recognize that what is most valued in higher education knows no boundaries.

Chapter 4

PERFORMANCE FUNDING: CAMPUS REACTIONS

Joseph C. Burke and Terri A. Lessard

Introduction

Campus reactions influence the fate of performance funding, since success depends on improving campus performance. Governors and legislators can pass mandates and coordinating and system boards can launch initiatives, but professors and professionals produce the programs and services that performance funding seeks to improve. Although reactions may not reflect the reality of program impact, perceptions do affect campus actions and state policies on performance funding.

Assessing campus reactions to performance funding requires answers to a series of questions. How familiar are campus officers with the programs in their states; and how extensively are performance results disseminated to internal units? Do campus leaders oppose or favor institutional performance as a factor in state budgeting? What purposes do they believe performance funding should pursue; and do they think the program has achieved these goals? Which groups seem to increase their influence through performance funding? How appropriate do campus leaders consider the indicators frequently used in funding programs? Do performance results influence campus decisions; and what impact have they had on institutional objectives? What do campus leaders see as the advantages and disadvantages of performance funding in their states? Which difficulties present the greatest obstacles to program success; and what changes could alleviate those problems? Finally, do campus leaders believe that the program will persist in their state?

The Survey

To answer these questions, the staff of the Higher Education Program at the Rockefeller Institute conducted a mail survey of campus leaders in late 1999 and early 2000. Questionnaires went to over 4,000 presidents, chief academic officers, senior business officials, academic deans, and department chairs at all public two- and four-year colleges and universities in Florida, Missouri, Ohio, South Carolina, and Tennessee. After three administrations of the survey, the response rate reached 45 percent, ranging from a high of 54 percent in Missouri and South Carolina to a low of 37 percent in Ohio. The returns reflect a reasonable representation of targeted positions and campus types (see Appendix). Use of similar questions in a survey of campus and state leaders in late 1996 and early 1997, including the five study states, allows some comparisons of opinions over time (Serban 1997).

The survey contains twenty-one generic questions, along with a few specific queries for each state. Most items use a five-point scale. Four questions include a "can't judge" category, which is not counted in calculating mean scores or percentages. The text, tables, and graphs often collapse response categories, such as "strongly agree" with "agree" and "strongly disagree" with "disagree." Throughout the analysis, rankings are based on mean scores. The term "senior officials," when used in comparing responses from holders of particular positions, combines responses from presidents, chief academic officers, and top business administrators.

The survey has two limitations. The preponderance of department chairs — 64 percent of the total — dominates the overall responses. In addition, sizeable percentages of deans, and especially chairs, say they "can't judge" or do not answer questions that fall outside their academic activities.

Familiarity and Dissemination

Respondents certainly had the opportunity to become familiar with the performance funding in their states. Nearly half held their positions for seven years or more, and two-thirds for at least four. Despite this longevity, they appear less familiar with performance funding than expected. Only half of the total respondents claim they are "very familiar" or "familiar" with the program in their state, although those from two-year campuses seem more aware than their four-year counterparts. Lack of familiarity appears even in South Carolina with its controversial program and in Tennessee, which started performance funding in the 1970s. Controversy and longevity clearly affected familiarity but not nearly as much as anticipated. State responses vary widely on familiarity, from highest in South Carolina to the lowest in Ohio. Overall, respondents in 1999-2000 say they are slightly less familiar than those who answered this question in the 1996-1997 Survey. Apparently, the passage of three years did little to enhance familiarity.

Performance funding becomes increasingly invisible on campus below presidents and vice presidents. Nearly 90 percent of the senior officers say they are familiar with the program, but over 40 percent of the deans and over 60 percent of the chairs admit little or no familiarity. Even in South Carolina, more than a quarter of the deans and over 40 percent of the chairs say they are only "somewhat," "slightly," or "not at all" familiar. Despite the longevity of the program in Tennessee, over a third of deans and more than half of the chairs give the same reply.

Figure 1. Familiarity with Performance Funding by State
Very Familiar/Familiar

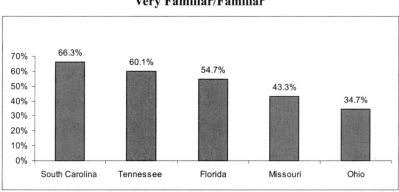

Nearly forty percent of the academic deans and almost two-thirds of the chairs in Missouri concede they are not fully familiar with the program. Florida does better, but still a third of deans and over half of the chairs admit little or no familiarity with performance funding in their state. Responses from Ohio, which launched its program later than the other states, shows that two-thirds of the deans and over 80 of the chairs admit little or no familiarity with the program.

This lack of familiarity is only partially explained by the level of dissemination of program details and results. Although statistically significant ($p < .01$), the connection between dissemination and familiarity has a low correlation ($r = .334$). Senior officers, who are responsible for dissemination, believe it is extensive, while deans and chairs, on the receiving end, call it only "moderate." Total replies from both two- and four-year campuses also consider it "moderate." Among the states, only respondents from South Carolina describe dissemination as "extensive."

Stakeholder Influence

About a quarter of the respondents — mostly deans and chairs — say they cannot judge the effect of performance funding on the influence of

Figure 2. Familiarity by Academic Position

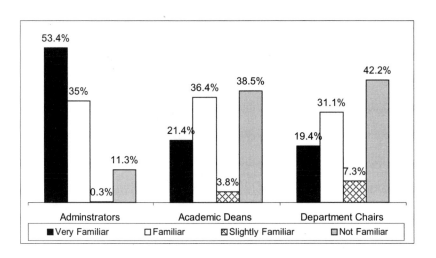

outside groups. Respondents giving definitive answers to the question believe that coordinating boards and staff clearly won the most influence, followed closely by legislators and staff. Senior campus officers run third, university system officials fourth, and governors and staff fifth. The earlier survey rated legislators first, coordinating boards second, and governors third. The shift from legislators and governors to coordinating boards flows from the move over time from initiation to implementation of performance funding. Legislators and governors may have started the program, but coordinating boards dominated the implementation phase and its continuing operation. Although unclear about external groups, respondents to the latest survey recognize that performance funding has increased the internal influence of presidents and vice presidents, but not that of academic deans, department chairs, and faculty leaders.

Campus leaders from Missouri, Ohio, and South Carolina see performance funding as increasing most the influence of coordinating boards. Those from Florida — without a coordinating board and with a mandated program — perceive the greatest increase in legislative influence. The collegial nature of performance funding in Tennessee is reflected in the belief that performance funding increased most the influence of senior campus administrators and university system officials, followed by coordinating boards. Although replies from most states claim enhanced influence for coordinating boards, they differ on the other groups. Those from Ohio and South Carolina indicate added authority for legislators and staff, while Tennessee places this group fourth. In Missouri, without a legislative mandate, senior campus officers run second to coordinating boards in added influence. Overall, the rankings by states seem fairly consistent for all positions, with a difference between sectors. At four-year schools, respondents believe university system officials gain more leverage. Replies from two-year colleges view deans as gaining more influence than those from four-year institutions.

Performance as a Budgeting Factor

Survey results counter the common complaint in state capitals that campus leaders reject performance as a component in state budgeting for public colleges and universities. A question asks: "How important should the following factors be in state budgeting: *campus performance, current costs, enrollment levels, inflationary increases, new programs*, and *special initiatives*." Campus leaders consider all these factors important, but with clear preferences. They place inflationary and salary increases first in importance, but see current costs second and campus performance third. Other factors receive slightly less support, with new programs fourth, enrollment levels fifth, and special initiatives sixth. The low rating for enrollment conflicts with the current concern for access and affordability. Rankings from the 1996-97 Survey place current costs first, student enrollment second, campus performance third, and inflationary increases fourth.

In the recent survey, leaders from all of the states, except Florida, pick campus performance as their second or third choice. It ranks second in Ohio; third in Missouri, South Carolina, and Tennessee; and fourth in Florida. Four-year officers rate campus performance third, while two-year leaders put it fourth place after new programs. Deans and chairs see campus performance as more important in budgeting than senior administrators. Performance rates second for deans, third for chairs, and fourth for presidents and chief academic officers. The last two groups consider new programs more important than campus performance. Chief business officers think only special initiatives are less important than institutional performance as a budget factor.

Despite these differences in ratings based on mean scores, overwhelmingly campus leaders from all positions and states agree on the importance of performance in state budgeting for public colleges and universities. Clearly, respondents believe that state budgeting for campus performance is desirable in theory, even though replies to later questions demonstrate that they think it is less desirable — and certainly more difficult — in practice.

Purposes of Performance Funding

The avowed purposes of performance funding usually include *external accountability* and *institutional improvement; and some programs* add *meeting state needs. Increased state funding* for public higher education often represents a tacit purpose for campus leaders, which encourages them to accept the program — or at least acquiesce to its adoption. Contrary to popular impressions, campus leaders appear to accept all four purposes, including external accountability, but they have decided preferences. They clearly favor institutional improvement, followed closely by increased state funding. Respondents see meeting state needs as trailing in third place and view external accountability as a distant

Table 1. Campus Performance as a Budgeting Factor			
State	Very Important	Important	Somewhat/Slightly/ Not At All Important
Florida	37.6%	45.4%	17.1%
Missouri	29.1%	49.9%	21.0%
Ohio	31.5%	48.3%	20.3%
South Carolina	30.5%	54.2%	15.2%
Tennessee	41.1%	46.7%	12.3%
Position			
Senior Campus Administrators	33.5%	50.6%	15.9%
Academic Deans	45.1%	39.9%	15.1%
Department Chairs	30.3%	50.9%	18.7%
Type of Institution			
Two-Year	29.5%	52.2%	18.4%
Four-Year	36.5%	46.5%	17.0%
Total	33.7%	48.8%	17.5%

fourth. Our earlier survey showed increased state funding as less important in third place. Apparently, over time, the failure of performance funding to produce the desired level of state appropriations elevated the importance of increased state funding as a program purpose.

On the latest survey, campus leaders in all positions — except financial officers — and both sectors endorse the overall order of preference. (Business officers rate external accountability before state needs.) Most of the state replies repeat the overall ranking. However, those from South Carolina rate increased state funding even above institutional improvement; and Tennessee places external accountability before state needs.

Policy Values

Consideration of the policy values of *quality, efficiency, equity,* and *choice* in performance funding underscores the dichotomy between theory and practice in performance funding. Responses to our 1996-97 survey insisted that performance funding should stress quality over efficiency but believed that the reverse occurred in practice (Serban 1997). The current survey shows that the great majority of respondents agree that performance funding should emphasize all of the policy values, but the levels of agreement exhibit decided differences. Quality easily wins the battle of values, with choice, equity, and finally efficiency falling far behind. Replies from two-year colleges show more support for efficiency, while those from baccalaureate institutions exhibit more interest in quality, but both clearly put the latter first. The latest survey results reveal more agreement on policy values than our earlier findings. They also indicate more interest in equity and choice than our 1996-97 Survey.

Returns from all of the states reiterate the overall ratings of policy values. Leaders in all positions place quality first by far, but vary in their placement of choice, equity, and efficiency. Business officers endorse quality as their first choice, but with less fervor than the other leaders. As befits their job, they favor efficiency as their second value. Department chairs show much less support for efficiency than other campus leaders. Indeed, endorsement for this policy value descends from the highest support by presidents though the administrative chain to the lowest by chairs.

Table 2. Policy Values by Position				
Position	*Quality*	*Equity*	*Choice*	*Efficiency*
Presidents	99.1%	89.5%	75.9%	86.0%
Chief Academic Officers	96.6%	81.2%	81.0%	80.3%
Chief Business Officers	88.0%	77.1%	73.5%	80.7%
Academic Deans	96.2%	77.1%	77.4%	78.0%
Department Chairs	92.8%	71.7%	70.4%	67.5%
Total	93.9%	74.8%	73.0%	72.2%

Indicator Preferences

A majority of the total respondents consider appropriate all of the indicators frequently found in performance-funding programs, except *time-to-degree* (see Table 3). This rating of indicators repeats the 1996-97 results, except that *job placement* then ranked second rather than fifth. The division between the indicators favored by campus leaders and those prized by government officials demonstrates the differences between academic concerns and capitol desires. Some of the indicators thought least appropriate on campus in both surveys are those often desired in state capitals. Governors and legislators tend to push for *undergraduate access, K-12 linkage, two-to-four year transfers, faculty workloads, new student preparations, standardized tests,* and *time-to-degree.* Unfortunately, the relatively low rankings of indicators on *diversity of students, faculty, and staff* show shared attitudes on college campuses and in state capitols.

The ratings from 1999-2000 refute the common contention of a sharp conflict on indicators between leaders of two- and four-year campuses. Despite some difference in rankings, respondents from both sectors jointly favor nine of their top ten indicators. They also share low ratings of four measures: *time-to-degree, diversity of faculty/staff,* and *standardized test scores.* Mean scores suggest that leaders of both sectors give low ratings to the indicator on two- to four-years transfers. Surprisingly, almost a third of the respondents from two-year colleges call this indicator inappropriate, as do slightly more than half of those from baccalaureate institutions. The approval of *retention and graduation rates* by two-year respondents and their less than full support for student transfers run counter to popular perceptions. The shared views on indicators of leaders from both two- and four-year institutions may suggest that position as a department chair — which dominates the total response — is more important than sector in determining indicator preferences.

Senior administrators, deans, and chairs share their dislikes of indicators but differ in their preferences. Deans and chairs give top ratings to accredited programs and peer reviews, but senior administrators seem to see these as self-serving. Senior officers favor two-to-four year transfers, student satisfaction surveys, and K-12 linkage more than deans and chairs. Not surprisingly, governors and legislators also consider these items important. Deans and chairs naturally support admin-

Table 3. Performance Funding Indicators			
Indicators Ranked by Total Mean	*Total Mean*	*Two-Year Rank*	*Four-Year Rank*
1. Accredited Programs	1.72	3	1
2. Professional Licensure Exams	1.87	4	3
3. External Peer Review	1.92	9	2
4. Employer Satisfaction Survey	1.93	1	7
5. Graduate Job Placement	1.93	2	6
6. Alumni Satisfaction Survey	2.03	7	5
7. Retention/Graduation Rates	2.04	8	4
8. Student Satisfaction Survey	2.06	5	9
9. Undergraduate Access	2.10	6	11
10. Administrative Size/Cost	2.12	10	8
11. Faculty Workload	2.19	14	10
12. New Student Preparation	2.25	12	12
13. K-12 Linkage	2.29	11	16
14. Diversity of Students	2.31	16	13
15. Standardized Test Scores	2.32	15	14
16. Diversity of Faculty/Staff	2.34	17	15
17. Two-to-Four Year Transfers	2.42	13	18
18. Time-to-Degree	2.58	18	17
Scale: 1. Very Appropriate, 2. Appropriate, 3. Inappropriate, 4. Very Inappropriate			

istrative size/cost and new student preparation more than the former. Unexpectedly, higher percentages of deans and chairs, than senior administrators, favor faculty workloads as a funding indicator. Probably the deans and chairs from comprehensive and two-year institutions, which compose a majority of the total responses, believe their heavy faculty workloads would bring increased funding. A majority of senior officers, deans, and chairs dislike time-to-degree. All three groups also give less than enthusiastic support to standardized tests and diversity indicators.

Success Standards

Of the three standards for assessing success on the performance indicators, *institutional improvement* achieves by far the most approval. *Comparison with peers* receives strong but less enthusiastic support, while just half of the respondents endorse *targeted external standards*. All of the states follow this overall pattern. Leaders of four-year institutions are more favorable to peer comparisons than their two-year counterparts. The latter often complain that peer comparisons fail to recognize their wider range of sizes, missions, and locations than comprehensive and research institutions. Choosing peers also presents problems for four-year campuses. Their leaders usually want aspirational peers for determining funding but not for evaluating performance, while state officials often favor the reverse.

Campus Use of Performance Results

The survey asks respondents to assess the use of performance results in decisions on nine campus activities, often targeted in performance funding. The overall averages indicate "moderate" rather than "extensive" use in all areas, except *faculty workload*, which gets only "minimal" use. *Institutional planning* receives the most use, followed by *student outcomes assessment* and — surprisingly — by *internal budget allocation*. Most experts think that internal budgeting for schools and departments usually ignores performance in favor of the traditional factors of student enrollments and faculty salaries (Meisinger 1994; Mortimer 1986; Moore 1994; Layzell and Lydden 1990; Seagren 1993; and Vandament 1989). Conversations with knowledgeable observers in the study states — including the authors of the case studies — confirm the conclusion that performance results are rarely used in internal institutional budgeting. Indeed, one of the flaws cited in performance funding is the failure to include performance in internal campus budgeting for schools and departments (Burke and Serban 1998b).

Respondents from two-year colleges suggest significantly more use of performance results in campus activities than those from four-year colleges and universities. This response probably reflects more administrative control of campus activities in community and technical colleges. Leaders of two-year institutions rate the use of performance results in institutional planning as "extensive" and even claim "moderate" use in faculty workload. They place *curriculum and planning* second, *student outcomes assessment* third, and *internal budget allocations* fourth. Senior campus officers also perceive more use of performance results than deans and chairs in campus decision making. On the other hand, deans see less use than chairs.

Responses by states reveal some differences. Leaders from South Carolina claim to use performance results in more areas than any other state, while Ohio apparently uses them the least in campus decisions. Those from Florida say that their institutions consider performance re-

Table 4. Use of Performance Results			
Campus Activity Ranked by Total Mean	*Total Mean*	*Two-Year Mean Score*	*Four-Year Mean Score*
1. Institutional Planning	2.66	2.46	2.80
2. Student Outcomes Assessment	2.98	2.79	3.13
3. Internal Budget Allocations	3.05	2.95	3.12
4. Curriculum & Planning	3.08	2.77	3.32
5. Admissions	3.32	3.36	3.28
6. Administrative Services	3.34	3.09	3.54
7. Student Services	3.39	3.20	3.55
8. Academic Advising	3.48	3.24	3.66
9. Faculty Workload	3.54	3.48	3.58
Scale: 1. Very Extensively, 2. Extensively, 3. Moderately, 4. Minimally, 5. Not At All			

sults extensively in institutional planning. They give a moderate rating to all the other activities, including faculty workload — and place the use of results for internal budgeting second behind institutional planning. Returns from Missouri and Tennessee rate student outcomes assessment first before institutional planning, which reflects the incorporation of assessment into their funding indicators. Despite this ranking, their estimate of moderate use of performance results for assessment appears low, given its emphasis in their performance programs. Returns from neither state claim extensive use for any activity including student outcomes assessment. This result is surprising, since they are generally considered two of the most successful programs in performance funding (Burke and Modaressi 2000).

Ohio's respondents rank internal budget allocation second after institutional planning, followed by student outcomes assessment, and curriculum and program planning. All of these areas get a moderate rating, but the other five activities involve only minimal use. Those from South Carolina give a moderate rating to use of performance results in all activities, except institutional planning, which is considered extensive. Internal budget allocations come second, and administrative services runs third. With its initial 37 indicators that even include faculty workload, the moderate rating in almost all activities seems understandable, although lower than expected for a state that has placed so much emphasis on performance funding. Replies from South Carolina two-year campuses give a more favorable evaluation of the use of performance results than those from four-year institutions.

Impact on Campus Performance

Respondents believe that performance funding has only a minimal impact on most of the goals often set in performance-funding plans. Overall, they think that the program has a moderate impact only on *mission focus* and *administrative efficiency*. Significantly, performance funding has the most impact on the objectives largely controlled by senior administrators and a minimal effect on outcomes mainly dependent on faculty activities. *Inter-institutional cooperation* — which senior officers do control — did receive only a minimal rating, but this objective is generally not a favorite goal of top administrators. Both sectors and most positions give moderate rankings only to mission focus and administrative efficiency. Business officers and chairs include only mission focus in that category. Although mission focus and administrative efficiency constitute important objectives, they hardly represent the only desired goals. State officials and the general public are also concerned about *faculty performance, faculty-student interaction, job placements,* and the *quality and quantity of student learning.*

It is probably too early to evaluate the campus impact of performance funding, since most programs have been fully implemented for only a few years and performance improvements take considerable time (Burke and Serban 1998b). However, Tennessee, with an official program in place since the late 1970s, offers more than enough time for evaluation. Despite this longevity, the average of the replies from Tennessee suggest a moderate impact only on *mission focus.* Moreover, their mean scores fall below the average for all five states on all goals, except *job placements* and the *quality and quantity of student learning.*

Table 5. Impact of Performance Funding on Campus Goals						
Campus Goals Ranked by Total Mean	*Total Mean*	*FL Rank*	*MO Rank*	*OH Rank*	*SC Rank*	*TN Rank*
1. Mission Focus	3.21	1	1	1	2	1
2. Administrative Efficiency	3.47	2	5	2	1	2
3. Quality & Quantity of Student Learning	3.64	3	2	4	5	3
4. Faculty Performance	3.65	4	3	5	3	4
5. Inter-Institutional Cooperation	3.86	6	6	3	4	6
6. Faculty-Student Interaction	3.91	7	4	7	6	5
7. Research Funding	4.03	6	7	6	7	8
8. Graduates' Job Placement	4.06	5	7	8	9	6
9. Graduates' Continuing Their Education	4.14	8	8	9	8	7
Scale: 1. Very High, 2. High, 3. Moderate, 4. Minimal, 5. No Effect						

Despite Tennessee's emphasis on student learning, its mean score is just one tenth of one percent better than the five state average. Responses from deans and chairs caused this relatively low rating in the Volunteer State, since they rank the impact of performance funding on student learning third, while senior administrators place it first. Tennessee's rating on this goal is considerably below that of Florida, whose plan did not accent student learning. Replies from Florida add student learning to mission focus and administrative efficiency as objectives receiving a moderate impact from performance funding.

Missouri, which also stresses student learning, has a much better mean score on that goal than Tennessee and includes it along with mission focus in the moderate category. Despite having indicators on all of the objectives listed in the survey, respondents from South Carolina claim that performance funding has a moderate impact only on mission focus. Those from Ohio reach the same conclusion. Despite dissimilar programs of different durations, response from the five states rate performance funding as having a moderate impact on only one or at most three of the traditional goals in performance funding.

Achievements of Performance-Funding Purposes

A critical question asks campus leaders the extent to which performance funding in their state has achieved its four purposes. As noted before, campus leaders rate *improved institutional performance* first in desirability, with *increased state funding* a close second, and show much less interest in *meeting state needs* and *increasing external accountability*. Only achievement of external accountability — the purpose least preferred by campus leaders — wins agreement from a majority of the total respondents. About a third believe that the program improved institutional performance and increased responsiveness to state needs, but just 15 percent think that it increased overall state funding. In other words, a majority of the respondents believe that performance has achieved only accountability, which they view as the least important purpose. On their favorite items, achievement is far less than desired on improving institutional performance, and nearly disappears on increasing state funding. This pattern persists for positions and sectors.

Table 6. Achievements of Performance Funding Purposes

Achievement	Agree	Neutral	Disagree
Increased Accountability	54.6%	24.9%	20.5%
Increased Responsiveness to State Needs	33.0%	36.1%	30.8%
Improved Performance	33.1%	30.7%	36.3%
Increased State Funding	15.4%	26.3%	58.3%

Half or more of the respondents from all of the states, except Ohio, agree that performance funding has increased accountability. Only 44 percent of those from Ohio support this conclusion. Achievement of improved institutional performance receives support from sizeable minorities in Florida, Missouri, and Tennessee, while replies from Ohio and South Carolina indicate much lower levels of agreement. Strong minorities in Florida and Missouri also agree that performance funding has increased responsive to state needs, but agreement on achieving this purpose falls considerably in Ohio, South Carolina, and Tennessee. Respondents by states seem most disappointed with the achievement of increased state funding. Aside from Missouri, where a third agree on the achievement of this purpose, the percentages ranges from a high of 14 percent in Ohio to a low of 7 percent in South Carolina.

The high value placed on the prospect of increasing state funding and the low rating of its perception of achievement may explain some of the negative assessments of performance funding. Actual state appropriations dashed the hope of increased funding in most of the study states (Palmer 2000). Only Florida (10.4%) and Missouri (7.7%) experienced annual average increases in state appropriations over the last five years that exceed the national average of 5.8 percent. Ohio gained only 5.6 percent, South Carolina 4.5 percent, and Tennessee just 1.9 percent. Despite funding increases far above the national average, only 12 percent of the survey replies from Florida and 33 percent from Missouri agree that the performance funding increased overall state funding. Reactions by states to the achievement of the goal of increased state funding suggests that performance funding gets the blame for scant increases and no credit for improved appropriations.

Difficulties of Performance Funding

The difficulties posed by performance funding help to explain the perception of its limited impact. Overall, campus leaders consider *choice of performance indicators*, followed by *inappropriate criteria for institutional success, measuring the results of higher education*, and *changing state priorities* as the greatest problems. Smaller majorities cite other difficulties, such as *insufficient time for implementation*, and *frequent changes in program requirements*. Again, the major difficulties arise mainly in the academic area, such as choice of indicators, criteria of success, and measuring the outcomes of higher education. The averages for sectors are similar, except that two-year colleges seem more concerned about frequent changes of program requirements and insufficient time for implementation. Senior officers cite the problems of choice of indicators and frequent changes of program requirements, while deans complain of too little money for performance funding. Department chairs see more difficulties with performance funding than the holders of other positions. They cite as problems: inappropriate criteria for institutional success, measuring the results of higher education, and changing state priorities.

Responses from most states repeat the overall rankings. Surprisingly, Tennessee, which has a nonmandated program, places changing state priorities before inappropriate criteria. Recent initiatives by the Governor and the Legislature to improve accountability and productivity may explain this response. Missouri's replies identify measuring the results of higher education as the top difficulty. Those from Florida rate choice of indicator first, changing state priorities second, and inappropriate criteria for institutional success third. Replies from Ohio pick choosing indicators as the first and measuring education results as the second difficulty. In South Carolina, leaders see inappropriate criteria for institutional success as slightly more of a difficulty than choice of indicators.

Advantages of Performance Funding

Campus leaders rate the following items as moderate advantages in their *states: emphasis on results and performance, increased external accountability, identification and prioritization of goals for higher education, campus discretion over performance-funding money, improved higher education performance,* and *increased response to state needs.* They view *increased efficiency* and — significantly — *increased state funding* as only minimal advantages. Over 20 percent of the total respondents claim that increased state allocations represents no advantage of performance funding. Although campus leaders differ in ranking the advantages, all place increased state funding last.

Two- and four-year sectors show the same rankings. Few differences also appear in the ratings by positions or states. Leaders from all positions, except presidents, view emphasis on results and performance as the top advantage. Presidents place it second after increased external accountability. Senior officers view all of the items as more advantageous than do deans and chairs — and deans tend to see more advantages than chairs. Respondents from four states see emphasis on results and performance as the chief advantage, but those from South Carolina favor increased external accountability. Leaders from Missouri make discretion over performance money their second choice and push external accountability to third.

Disadvantages of Performance Funding

Although respondents rate all of the disadvantages listed in the questionnaire as moderate, the mean scores suggest a greater awareness of the disadvantages than the advantages of performance funding. Campus leaders perceive the *high cost of data collection and analysis* as the most serious disadvantage, followed by *budget instability, erosion of institutional autonomy, unhealthy competition among campuses,* and *erosion of institutional diversity.* Little difference appears between two- and four-year colleges and universities on nearly all of the listed disadvantages. Department chairs consider all of the items as more of a disadvantage than those in other positions, except for the high cost of data collection. Although less critical than chairs, the same applies to academic deans versus senior administrators. Responses from Florida and Missouri follow the overall pattern. Those from South Carolina put the erosion of institutional autonomy second and push budget instability to fourth. The South Carolina response undoubtedly reflects the move in that state from funding based entirely on performance to a limited performance pool. Campus leaders from Tennessee view budget instability as the biggest problem, probably because it is the only one of the five states without increased appropriation as a component of performance funding.

Desired Changes

A majority of respondents agree in recommending *more institutional choice on indicators*, followed by *increased funding for performance*, as changes that would most improve performance funding. The item of *fewer indicators* comes close to winning a majority. All of the states endorse these changes. Respondents from South Carolina, with 37 indicators, naturally pick fewer indicators as their first change, followed by institutional choice among indicators, while taking a divided stance on increased funding for performance. Leaders from the two- and four-year sectors rate more choice of indicators first, but the former favors fewer indicators as an additional change, while four-year leaders seek increased funding for performance. Respondents from all positions support increased institutional choice of indicators. Senior officers also want fewer indicators, but chief academic and business officers strongly support increased funding for performance, while only about half of the presidents endorse this view. Deans advocate increased choice of indicators and increased funding for performance, while chairs approve both but are less enthusiastic than the deans about the second change.

Program Future

Despite their critical critique of the use of performance results and the impact of performance funding, respondents from all positions, both sectors, and every state overwhelmingly consider performance funding as likely to continue. Ohio is the least optimistic about the future of performance funding, although a solid majority of its respondents believe it will persist. Missouri is less supportive than expected, given its reputation for a stable program (Burke and Modarresi 2000b). Leaders from South Carolina and Tennessee are the most confident of continuance. Occupants of all positions overwhelmingly see a likely future for performance funding, although senior officers are more positive than deans and chairs. Clearly, the belief in continuation comes from support in state capitals rather than from campus preference, since campus leaders seem critical of the program and doubtful of its use in campus activities

State	Likely	Uncertain	Unlikely
Table 7. Program Future by State, Position, and Type of Institution			
Florida	72.6%	24.8%	2.6%
Missouri	65.6%	32.9%	1.5%
Ohio	58.0%	38.5%	3.5%
South Carolina	81.8%	16.2%	2.0%
Tennessee	81.0%	18.2%	0.7%
Position			
Senior Campus Administrators	82.1%	14.8%	3.0%
Academic Deans	73.2%	23.5%	3.3%
Department Chairs	66.8%	31.6%	1.6%
Type of Institution			
Two-Year	70.5%	26.6%	2.9%
Four-Year	71.1%	27.1%	1.7%
Total	70.8%	26.9%	2.2%

and its impact on institutional objectives. The appraisal of program continuance differs from the 1996-97 Survey, when more campus leaders saw the future of performance funding in their states as uncertain, although majorities in all states predicted program persistence (Serban 1997).

Findings

The survey findings confirm some, but conflict with other, common beliefs about performance funding.

- Performance funding is considered desirable in theory but difficult in practice.

- The program becomes increasingly invisible on campus below the presidents and vice presidents.

- Contrary to popular beliefs, campus leaders accept institutional performance as a factor in state budgeting.

- They support all four purposes of performance funding, but clearly favor institutional improvement and increased state funding over meeting state needs and external accountability.

- Despite these preferences, campus representatives believe that the program achieves only external accountability, the least desired purpose.

- Quality remains by far the most desired policy value, but results reveal more endorsement for equity, choice, and efficiency than earlier findings.

- Although equity is endorsed as a policy value in theory, campus leaders give only lukewarm approval to diversity in students and staff as performance indicators in practice.

- Responses on funding indicators by leaders of two- and four-year campuses show commonalities that refute the usual assumption of their conflicting views.

- Although performance results are used moderately in decision making on most relevant campus activities, they have a moderate impact only on the goals of mission focus and administrative efficiency.

- Areas with the most impact are those controlled largely by senior administrators, while those with the least effect involve mostly faculty activities.

- Despite a critical assessment of the use and impact of performance funding, campus leaders overwhelmingly conclude that the program will continue in their states.

Conclusion

The survey results suggest that the choice is not whether performance funding will continue in the five states. The choice that confronts campus and state leaders is what to continue and what to change. Campus leaders are clear on the desired changes, favoring more institutional choice of indicators and increased funding for performance. The survey suggests that money is the heart of the matter. Institutional leaders see increased funding for performance as a desired change and increased state appropriations for public higher education as a desired purpose that proved most disappointing in practice.

The effect of performance funding on campus performance may have been better than the survey respondents believed. The State Higher Education Finance Officers in four of the five study states certainly thought so. In a recent survey, Finance Officers from South Carolina and Tennessee claim that performance funding had a "great effect" on improving campus performance in their state, while those from Missouri and Ohio cite a "considerable effect." Only the Finance Officer from Florida concludes that performance funding had little effect (Burke et al. 2000). These conflicting views between state and campus leaders raise the conundrum of whether the objectivity derived by distance or the knowledge produced by proximity provide a better perspective. The case study chapters attempt to estimate the actual effect of the program in each of the states. Whatever the reality, the attitudes of campus leaders provide an important perspective on performance funding.

Appendix

Table 8. Population and Respondents				
State	Percent of Total Respondents	Sent	Received	Response Rate
Florida	21.7%	1,045	414	39.6%
Missouri	19.4%	685	370	54.0%
Ohio	24.9%	1,295	475	36.7%
South Carolina	18.6%	663	355	53.5%
Tennessee	15.5%	603	296	49.1%
Position				
Chief Executive Officer	6.1%	184	116	63.0%
Branch Campus Director	1.2%	62	22	35.5%
Chief Academic Officer	6.2%	168	118	70.2%
Chief Business Officer	4.5%	159	85	53.5%
Academic Dean	18.7%	666	357	53.6%
Department Chair	63.5%	3,052	1,212	39.7%
Type of Institution				
Two-Year	39.8%	1,688	761	45.1%
Four-Year	59.6%	2,603	1,139	43.8%
Other (Unidentified)	0.5%	—	10	—
Carnegie Classification				
Research	21.4%	975	408	41.8%
Doctoral	14.9%	733	284	38.7%
Masters	18.5%	700	353	50.4%
Bachelors	2.9%	115	55	47.8%
Associates	39.8%	1,688	761	45.1%
Specialized	2.0%	80	39	48.8%
Other (Unidentified)	0.5%	—	10	—
Total	100.0%	4,291	1,910	44.5%

Chapter 5

TWENTY YEARS OF PERFORMANCE FUNDING IN TENNESSEE: A CASE STUDY OF POLICY INTENT AND EFFECTIVENESS

E. Grady Bogue

Representatives from higher education and state government in Tennessee began exploring the technical and philosophic feasibility of performance-funding policy in 1974, and Tennessee was the first state to formally implement a performance-funding policy in 1979-1980. For Tennessee, performance funding, then and now, involves the allocation of a modest portion of state appropriations to public campuses based on a small number of performance indicators.

Tennessee applies this policy to its 23 public colleges and universities: 9 four-year universities and 14 two-year institutions. Two multicampus governing boards, The University of Tennessee (3 universities) and the Tennessee Board of Regents (9 universities and 14 two-year colleges), operate the 23 public institutions. There is a rich tradition of private higher education in the state, with 60 private colleges, although these institutions are not involved with performance funding. The Tennessee Higher Education Commission serves as the coordinating board with responsibilities for mission planning, finance and facility recommendations, new program approval, and the conduct of policy studies related to higher education, although it does not have program termination authority.

Anticipating the Call to Accountability: Policy Heritage

The primary intent of the pilot and development work on performance funding in Tennessee during the 1970s was "To explore the feasibility of allocating some portion of state funds on a performance criterion" (Bogue and Troutt 1980, p. 1).[1] The purposes were to demonstrate the initiative of the Tennessee higher education community in engaging performance issues and to forestall the imposition of performance measures and assessments by political action. The policy could be considered a success, since there are no legislative mandates for assessment in higher education in Tennessee. The program was also built on the tacit expectation that government decision makers would see this in a favorable light, which would encourage increased financial support of higher education.

The leadership initiative for development of performance funding in Tennessee came from the Tennessee Higher Education Commission (THEC), the state's coordinating agency for higher education and the agency having responsibility for developing policies for the equitable distribution and use of public funds. Under the direction of its initial Executive Director, Dr. John Folger, a staff was assembled at THEC in the fall of 1974 under project director Dr. Grady Bogue, who came to THEC in 1974 as an American Council on Education Fellow. Between 1974-76, approximately $500,000 in grants was secured from the Fund for the Improvement of Postsecondary Education, The W. K. Kellogg Foundation, The Ford Foundation, and one anonymous Tennessee foundation. These funds supported five years of pilot and developmental work on performance-funding policy during the years 1974-1979.

The five-year developmental work involved (1) the creation of pilot projects at ten campuses; (2) the advice and review of a state-level advisory committee composed of campus, governing board, and government officials; and (3) input from a national panel of higher education scholars and experts on fiscal policy.

Performance funding in Tennessee has been revised every five years. Each revision has produced a variety of policy shifts, the last occurring in Spring 2000. They included changes in (1) the nature and number of performance indicators; (2) acceptable measures and evaluation standards for several of the performance indicators; and (3) the proportion of stated appropriation.

These five-year revisions constitute a form of periodic peer evaluation, in which a panel of institutional, governing board, and coordinating commission representatives examine the policy and make suggestions for improvement. The increased percentage of state appropriations dedicated to performance funding – from 2.0 to 5.54 percent — offers additional evidence of policy success. The program has also worked in times of diminished as well as increased appropriations to higher education. It has also survived two Republican governors and one Democratic governor.

During the decade of the 1990s, funding for Tennessee higher education has not reflected the financial commitment of earlier years. The state has slipped in both regional and national position on indicators such as percentage of high school students attending college, percent of population holding a four-year degree, and faculty salaries. A recently commissioned Governor's Council on Excellence in Higher Education (1979-99) recommended that the state needs to spend an additional $100 million per year on higher education to bring its system anywhere close to parity with most other states. This cannot happen without serious change to revenue policy, since Tennessee has no income tax and depends heavily on sales tax revenues. As of late 2000, the governor and the legislature have not developed consent on political partnership for revenue reform.

The structure for funding public campuses has evolved due to performance funding. Over the past 30 years, Tennessee has employed formula funding as the basic instrument for the equitable and objective allocation of state appropriations to its colleges and universities. While satisfying the public policy criteria of equity and objectivity, this enrollment-driven formula funding involves no consideration of performance or quality. In other words, the emphasis is on the educational question of "how much" and not "how good." Tennessee's performance-funding policy modifies the appropriation recommendation based on enrollment by institutional performance on prescribed indicators.

An important characteristic of the Tennessee policy is that the performance amount is not an "add-on," and does not require additional appropriations. The appropriation recommended for a campus has effect or "grip" regardless of the level of state funding. Thus, the performance feature is in effect whether state appropriations are increasing, decreasing, or remaining stable. A second distinguishing feature is that the program does not pit one campus against another in a "zero-sum" competition for funds. Essentially, campuses are competing against their own record, where one campus is not advantaged by the poor performance of another.

Evolution of Indicators and Standards

The performance indicators and standards changed over the twenty-year history in the following ways:

- The number of indicators grew from five to ten.

- The indicators moved from a common set for all campus types to a list that allows some differences based on campus missions.

- The evaluation shifted from standards that focused largely on institutional improvement to one that also considered performance compared to similar institutions outside Tennessee.

Indicator weights have also shifted from uniform to differential values that reflected the relative importance of each measure. Later cycles also added alternate indicators for two- and four-year institutions to emphasize their different missions.

These changes reflected primarily the values and interests of higher education representatives from campuses, governing board staffs, and coordinating commission staff, and did not emerge from political interests or pressures.

The initial performance indicators included five items, whereas current policy includes four standards with ten measures (see Table 1). Some of the indicators remained stable while others varied over time. The item on "Program Accreditation" remained stable, but the one on assessing general education has experienced the greatest change. The pilot phase used the power of fiscal policy to call institutions to more assertive performance assessment efforts, without the state specifying or

Table 1. Performance Funding Standards	
Performance Standards, Pilot Cycle (1979–80)	*Points Awarded*
Standard 1 — Program Accreditation	20 Points
Standard 2 — Graduate Performance in Major Fields	20 Points
Standard 3 — Graduate Performance on General Education	20 Points
Standard 4 — Evaluation of Institutional Programs/Services by Students/Alumni	20 Points
Standard 5 — Peer Evaluation of Academic Programs	20 Points

Performance Standards, Fifth Cycle (2000–04)	*2-Year Campuses*	*4-Year Campuses*
Standard 1 — Academic Testing and Program Review		
A. Foundation Testing of General Education Outcomes	15	15
B. Pilot Evaluations of Other General Education Outcome Measures	5	5
C. Program Accountability		
1. Program Review	5	10
2. Program Accreditation	10	15
D. Major Field Testing	15	15
Standard 2 — Satisfaction Studies		
A. Student/Alumni/Employer Surveys	10	10
B. Transfer and Articulation	NA	5
Standard 3 — Planning and Collaboration		
A. Mission Distinctive Institutional Goals	5	5
B. State Strategic Plan Goals	5	5

Performance Standards, Fifth Cycle (2000–04)	2-Year Campuses	4-Year Campuses
Standard 4 — Student Outcomes and Implementation		
A. Output Attainment		
1. Retention/Persistence	5	5
2. Job Placement	15	NA
B. Assessment Implementation	10	10
Total Points	100	100

mandating an instrument. The policy later became more prescriptive and now authorizes: the California Critical Thinking and Skills Test, the College BASE test, and the Academic Profile Assessment. The initial ACT COMP has gone out of existence.

The item on "Alumni Survey" began by merely funding efforts to obtain graduates' opinions. Present policy calls for a common instrument and surveys of alumni, current students, and employers. The latest cycles also add measures recognizing campus performance in achieving institutional and state strategic goals. This feature began to tie campus performance to state goals, and also allowed campuses some flexibility in their own strategic planning.

In the 1997-2002 cycle, as originally conceived, campuses were permitted to choose two performance indicators, one related to their own educational interests and one directed to state strategic goals as specified in the 1996-2000 THEC Master Plan for Higher Education — Higher Education Uniting to Serve Tennesseans. The Master Plan contains thirteen goals organized in these five areas:

- Increasing Performance in Higher Education
- Using Information Technology to Serve Tennesseans
- Enhancing Partnerships with K-12
- Enhancing Partnerships with Business, Industry, and Government
- Extending Inter-Institutional Partnerships and Cooperation

The framing of institutional goals also required the development of benchmarks by which goal achievement could be measured. Obviously, the individual nature of campus goals does not yield a statewide or comparative indicator profile beyond points awarded.

Technically, the Tennessee performance-funding policy was not due for review and evaluation until the end of the latest five-year cycle in 2002. However, in response to informal suggestions arising in the 1999 legislative session, THEC decided to undertake a re-evaluation of the entire Tennessee funding formula and included a revision of the performance-funding policy in that review. Legislative interest centered primarily on simplifying the basic formula. The change added academic program review along with program accreditation to the category of program accountability, because only a limited number of programs were eligible for national accreditation. Another feature asked not only what an institution found from its assessments, but also how their findings affected campus decisions. This change can reduce cosmetic responses to assessment results and encourage educational application of performance data.

Institutional History of
Points and Dollars Earned

Following the "shakedown" years of the initial pilot cycle, most institutions begin to perform at higher levels, and some achieved 100 percent of their performance goals. Performance funding does not appear to favor particular types of institutions, as all Carnegie classifications show high and low scores. The policy attempted to honor institutional equity from its earliest stages of planning (Bogue and Troutt 1980). The University of Tennessee at Knoxville, the state's public research university, was high scorer in one cycle, but community colleges achieved the best rating in others. Table 2 furnishes a twenty-year summary of institutional points and dollars earned from performance funding.

Evidence of Policy Impact and Effectiveness

A reasonable question is whether the program has improved the performance of Tennessee's public colleges and universities. This issue is approached from several perspectives, using the concept of triangulation

Table 2. Twenty Year History of Performance Points and Dollars

Institution	1978-79/1981-82		1982-83/1986-87		1987-88/1991-92		1992-93/1996-97		1997-98/1998-99	
	Pts	Dollars	Pts	Dollars	Pts	Dollars	Pts	Dollars	Pts	Dollars
APSU	56.0	$352,428	93.8	$2,592,534	77.8	$3,263,365	90.4	$5,189,253	92.0	$2,182,790
ETSU	43.8	$568,984	85.6	$4,632,841	81.0	$6,811,325	84.8	$8,570,113	92.0	$3,706,955
MTSU	60.5	$878,976	90.0	$5,948,048	76.4	$8,181,453	90.2	$12,788,952	91.0	$5,599,720
TSU	45.0	$521,661	83.8	$3,592,708	51.2	$2,978,562	80.2	$5,622,167	86.0	$2,549,006
TTU	71.8	$789,099	98.2	$5,136,264	83.8	$6,525,823	92.6	$8,050,890	94.0	$3,324,818
UM	61.3	$1,578,081	91.4	$10,743,739	80.0	$14,238,431	89.8	$18,502,259	90.0	$7,419,482
Subtotal		$4,689,229		$32,646,134		$41,998,959		$58,723,634		$24,692,771
UTC	62.8	$560,278	86.8	$3,557,180	78.8	$4,670,112	92.2	$6,533,513	96.0	$2,837,793
UTK	74.8	$3,261,881	99.0	$19,137,613	84.2	$23,710,066	89.0	$28,970,873	95.0	$12,392,866
UTM	64.5	$477,541	91.0	$2,925,204	77.2	$3,470,876	87.4	$4,751,459	92.0	$2,041,926
Subtotal		$4,299,700		$25,619,997		$31,851,054		$40,255,845		$17,272,585
CSTCC	50.0	$193,008	91.2	$1,627,585	84.4	$2,685,522	87.0	$3,694,427	95.0	$1,652,619
CLSCC	57.3	$161,246	90.0	$1,013,639	72.8	$1,129,126	88.2	$1,674,507	92.0	$701,611
COSCC	62.0	$125,458	93.4	$813,589	84.8	$1,424,127	96.4	$1,922,715	97.0	$857,492
DSCC	26.8	$30,097	94.4	$527,284	82.2	$725,757	86.4	$980,122	92.0	$444,246

Institution	1978-79/1981-82		1982-83/1986-87		1987-88/1991-92		1992-93/1996-97		1997-98/1998-99	
	Pts	Dollars	Pts	Dollars	Pts	Dollars	Pts	Dollars	Pts	Dollars
JSCC	69.0	$146,442	97.2	$891,125	76.2	$1,131,219	85.6	$1,614,382	82.0	$646,410
MSCC	67.0	$114,264	95.2	$704,247	85.2	$1,055,179	95.0	$1,576,937	94.0	$631,947
NSTCC	12.0	$14,700	88.4	$637,644	84.2	$948,277	90.2	$1,584,319	91.0	$869,291
NSTI	58.0	$191,770	100	$1,455,401	82.2	$1,633,040	85.4	$1,910,020	91.0	$700,892
PSTCC	34.3	$58,493	84.2	$695,753	81.0	$1,759,759	89.4	$3,089,343	94.0	$1,358,153
RSCC	64.0	$166,456	97.2	$1,209,117	92.0	$2,120,846	89.8	$2,797,022	91.0	$1,154,515
SSCC	60.3	$286,733	96.4	$1,726,959	81.6	$2,056,157	87.4	$3,219,541	76.0	$1,101,673
STIM	38.5	$182,910	98.2	$2,006,850	79.8	$2,601,385	87.4	$3,643,838	99.0	$1,645,199
VSCC	72.0	$175,103	100	$1,069,624	88.6	$1,572,782	93.6	$2,547,349	94.0	$1,197,530
WSCC	47.5	$136,710	94.4	1,198,726	92.4	$1,920,956	91.2	$2,644,351	95.0	$1,218,347
Subtotal		$1,983,390		$15,577,543		$22,764,132		$32,898,873		$14,179,925
Grand Total		$10,972,319		$73,843,674		$96,614,145		$131,878,352		$29,439,495

School abbreviations include: APSU is Austin Peay State University; ETSU is East Tennessee State University; MTSU is Middle Tennessee State University; TSU is Tennessee State University; TTU is Tennessee Technical University; UM is University of Memphis; UTC is University of Tennessee at Chattanooga; UTK is University of Tennessee at Knoxville; UTM is University of Tennessee at Martin; CSTCC is Chattanooga State Technical Community College; CLSCC is Cleveland State Community College; COSCC is Columbia State Community College; DSCC is Dyersburg State Community College; JSCC is Jackson State Community College; MSCC is Motlow State Community College; NSTCC is Northeast State Technical Community College; NSTI is Nashville State Technical Institute; PSTCC is Pellissipi State Technical Community College; RSCC is Roane State Community College; SSCC is Shelby State Community College; STIM is State Technical Institute of Memphis; VSCC is Volunteer State Community College; and, WSCC is Walters State Community College.

(Worthen, Sanders, and Fitzpatrick 1997). The policy's persistence for twenty years — four five-year cycles — may be accepted as partial evidence of its effectiveness, although longevity is not an infallible indicator of merit. The periodic evaluation and revision conducted by campus, board, and coordinating commission staff offers evidence of its robustness, and the increase in funding percentage represents endorsement of its effectiveness.

When work on the policy began, only two public institutions in Tennessee were involved in assessment of general education. Today, all institutions have accepted methods of evaluation. Table 3 shows recent trend data for universities.

While these data suggest a small downward trend in performance, the variations are modest. On the other hand, the universities have consistently scored above the national norm on the College BASE, although below it on ACT COMP, except for the first year.

Campuses have raised the national accreditation of eligible academic programs from 65 to nearly 100 percent. Community colleges in Tennessee have become fully accredited in all eligible program fields and the universities are approaching this goal.[2] Accreditation is, for academics, one of the most distinctive symbols and indicators of quality in American higher education. Even those who argue its liabilities are usually not willing to remove "bragging" rights from their college catalogs when programs are accredited. Thus, the academy would consider the results on this indicator as evidence of both educational improvement and meeting a quality criterion. The Tennessee plan includes program review at both undergraduate and graduate levels, but the nature of the standard is such that evidence beyond the points earned is qualitative.

Data available from THEC gives the satisfaction index on the "Enrolled Student Survey" for 1995 and 1997 (see Table 4). For this indicator, all campuses use the ACT Student Opinion Survey. The "financial

Table 3. General Education Outcome Average and Comparison					
Assessment Instrument	*1994*	*1995*	*1996*	*1997*	*1998*
ACT COMP	183.1	181.6	180.8	180.4	180.6
NORM GROUP	180.1	181.9	181.9	181.9	181.9
COLLEGE BASE	308.0	310.3	309.4	309.3	305.6
NORM GROUP	300.0	304.0	306.0	305.0	303.0

Table 4. Enrolled Student Survey — Overall Satisfaction Scores		
Institution	*1995*	*1997*
Austin Peay State University	16.73	17.19
East Tennessee State University	16.28	16.88
Middle Tennessee State University	17.93	17.35
Tennessee State University	17.31	17.56
Tennessee Technology University	18.17	17.78
University of Memphis	16.08	15.89
University of Tennessee at Chattanooga	16.78	17.15
University of Tennessee at Knoxville	16.81	18.07
University of Tennessee at Martin	17.65	17.80
University Norm	17.13	17.36
Chattanooga State Tech Community College	18.16	18.56
Cleveland State Community College	17.81	18.07
Columbia State Community College	17.73	17.78
Dyersburg State Community College	17.84	17.99
Jackson State Community College	17.79	18.12
Motlow State Community College	18.57	18.89
Northeast State Technical Community College	18.84	18.59
Nashville State Technical Institute	17.73	18.10
Pellissippi State Technical Community College	17.26	17.71
Roane State Community College	18.01	20.70
Shelby State Community College	16.66	17.54
State Technical Institute at Memphis	17.77	18.94
Volunteer State Community College	18.16	18.83
Walters State Community College	18.90	18.76
Community College Norm	*18.00*	*18.38*

Note: Scores are scale scores composed of clustered response items with a maximum score of 20.

Table 5. Persistence-to-Graduation Rates					
Sector	*1988-94*	*1989-95*	*1990-96*	*1991-97*	*1992-98*
Universities	44.5	46.1	45.4	44.2	44.9
Two-Year Colleges	26.3	25.3	25.1	22.3	22.2

bite" and importance of this indicator is obvious. In 1995, for example, the enrolled student satisfaction scores for the University of Tennessee at Knoxville earned it only one point on a ten-point scale. As a result, the University's funding fell approximately $500,000 below its potential award of $6,000,000 from performance funding. Even on a very large budget, a half million dollars is enough to get attention. Table 5 indicates that nearly all the universities and community colleges show some improvement in student satisfaction.

Table 5 presents Persistence to Graduation for public universities and two-year colleges. Evaluation on this standard is based on the extent to which institutions achieve statewide goals set for persistence to graduation. The state goal for universities is 51 percent persistence to graduation rate, and for two-year schools 35 percent. Universities are achieving approximately 88 percent of their goal and two-year colleges 62 percent. The overall statistics suggest slight improvement for universities, but a sharp decline for two-year colleges. Both types fall far below their targeted goals.

Job placement rates for two-year colleges, based on a survey of graduates over a one-year period after graduation, appear in Table 6. Evaluation on this standard is based on performance in each career field. The number of programs with job placement rates higher than 75 percent earn points. Statistics for individual campuses show both stable and high employment rates, but overall the rate has remained relatively stable.

Table 6. Job Placement Rates for Two-Year Colleges				
1993-94	*1994-95*	*1995-96*	*1996-97*	*1997-98*
90%	92%	92%	92%	91%

Survey and Case Study Evidence

During the 1999-2000 year, five doctoral students at the University of Tennessee conducted case studies to explore the impact of performance-funding at a research university, a doctoral university, a comprehensive university, and two community colleges. A sixth student conducted a qualitative study of major educational and civic leaders concerning the policy. These case studies were designed to probe more deeply the influence of performance-funding policy at the campus level and to furnish data complementary to the five-state survey data results given in Chapter 4.

In interviews of some thirty executive-level college administrators and government officials in Tennessee, Margaret Russell (2000) found that respondents attributed the long life of the Tennessee Performance Funding policy to its original and continuing "ownership" by both campus and government officials. The Tennessee responses to open-ended questions to the five-state survey also applauded this accent on involvement and collaboration. Both the interviews and the survey responses cited constructive impacts of the program, such as improvement in assessments and accreditation, but they also noted cosmetic reactions and game playing as problems. Despite this complaint, educational and government leaders believe performance funding remains robust and is likely to persist for the near future.

Kimberley Hall's (2000) case study of the University of Tennessee, Knoxville, found that interest in performance funding had waned over the twenty-year history, that awareness of policy intent and method centered primarily at the executive level (vice chancellor and above), and that a decade of modest financial support for higher education in Tennessee had caused administrators to concentrate on points and dollars rather than on instructional improvement.

Hall concluded that those interviewed ". . . felt that the basic philosophical foundation of the performance funding policy is valid — institutions of higher education must and should be held accountable to the state and its citizens" (p. 106). Weaknesses included the belief that incentives were not shared with colleges and departments; that funding of the performance feature had not helped maintain adequate funding levels in the 1990s; that some mechanics of the indicators and scoring needed revision; and that the policy caused considerable additional work with little noticeable results. The Tennessee responses to the open-ended questions in the survey reported in Chapter 4 also reflected these weaknesses. Despite these complaints, only one of twenty-eight persons interviewed at UT suggested that the policy should be discontinued.

The interviews also indicated the lack of linkage between the performance results and educational decision making — a shortcoming also noted in the five-state survey. For example, the University of Tennessee has required in recent years that a sample of its graduating seniors take the College Base general education assessment in response to the long-standing indicator in the Tennessee performance-funding policy. However, no decisions related to the academic diagnosis, progress, or degree certification of any student is based on this assessment, and no general education requirement appears based on the test results. In this case, assessment is used to satisfy the policy requirement and achieves no serious educational benefit. Although this weakness at UT represents another "cosmetic" response, other campuses that linked their assessment to practice affirm that this is an institutional decision rather than a consequence of the policy.

Latimer's (2001) case study of the University of Memphis, a doctoral research university, also discovered the lack of awareness of the details of performance funding at levels other than the senior administration. One dean of a college of the University briefed department chairs each year on performance-funding results; and a department chair reported looking at the data as a source for improving performance. These exceptions highlight the importance of leadership for implementing policy. The attitudes and actions of academic administrators influence the perceptions and use of policies on campus, although these policies cannot compensate for the lack of caring and communication on the part of academic leaders.

Unlike some other campuses, one respondent from this doctoral campus claims that performance funding had been influential in program decisions, at least in the early years of the policy.

> ...I know that colleges and departments really didn't like it when we terminated programs because of their performance. Academia has a tendency to carry dead wood for a long time. This (performance funding) was the trigger to do something about it (Latimer 2001, p. 4).

In more recent years, the administration of the University of Memphis has held the performance-funding allocation as an incentive fund for building program strength and as start-up for new programs.

Jeffrey Lorber (2001) examined the impact of the Tennessee Performance Funding policy at Tennessee Technological University (TTU), one of the eleven pilot institutions involved in the original developmental work on the policy. He found few significant educational policy changes had occurred at TTU as a result of performance funding. But the campus respondents suggested that the policy had prepared the University for the accent on effectiveness and outcomes assessment that emerged in recent years from both regional and program accreditation agencies. In addition, some campus representatives contended that the policy might have encouraged the University to pay close attention to peer review advice related to the consolidation of majors and new program needs.

Lorber (2001), as well as Hall (2000), found some interest in "revenue sharing," allowing some of the performance-funding money to flow to departments doing strong assessment and improvement work. The three presidents who served TTU over the past quarter century have all been supporters of quality assurance and this may constitute a reason for TTU's consistently strong scores since the inception of the policy. As with all five case studies, there was serious differentiation of awareness of the program between executive level administrators and department chairs and faculty; and indeed, the need to improve communication of the purpose, operation, and results of the policy. The interests in revenue sharing may suggest one reason for the lack of awareness of performance funding is that departments see no relationship between their performance and their funding.

In a study of performance-funding impact at Volunteer State Community College, Michelle Freeman (2000) also found that executive level administrators were more aware of the policy than division chairs and faculty, and that faculty members did not perceive a close link between the data derived from various assessments and their needs in instruction. Still, none of those interviewed suggested dropping the policy. Most also seemed pleased that Tennessee had taken a lead role in this accountability and assessment effort. Freeman also found that in recent years, as state funding lagged, administrative concern centered more on maximizing dollar return on the policy. As one administrator commented:

> I think the policy and the intent of the policy is to ... reward excellence and encourage campuses to take hard looks at academic programs, student services, and all the things we do. But ... the focus at a campus

level on occasions may become more of trying to get those points to get your five percent appropriation rather than really using it for improvement (Freeman 2000, p. 81).

Some participants pointed to the ethical challenge involved in setting improvement goals that are relatively easy to meet and more certain to earn increased funding rather than challenging targets less certain to gain financial reward. As one interviewee noted

> I do think that its greatest weakness is it does encourage game playing and manipulating ... I don't think there has been any dishonesty, but I do think that after you work with things like performance funding you become an expert in knowing it and knowing how to ... manipulate it (Freeman 2000, p. 90).

Volunteer State Community College was one of eleven institutions originally participating in the pilot trial of the policy, and its president has been in office for almost thirty years. For more than half of the twenty-year history of the project, Volunteer State Community College has had a total score at or higher than the highest institutional score in the state and, except for one year, higher scores than the average score for all institutions in the state.

Thomas Shaw (2000) undertook the second case study involving a community college, Walters State Community College (WSCC). This campus has probably experienced the deepest penetration (as defined by awareness and decision utility) of any of the five campuses studied. The performance-funding policy is part of a larger campus effort to build a culture accenting continuous improvement, and the institution's president, who has been in office for more than a quarter century, emphasizes this culture. There is a forty-six member Strategic Planning and Continuous Improvement Council on the WSCC campus. One of the findings of this case study echoed findings of other case studies. Early participation in the Tennessee performance-funding venture prepared WSCC well for the change in regional accreditation standards of the Commission on Colleges of the Southern Association of Colleges and Schools, which shifted from process-oriented standards to standards accenting assessment of educational outcomes and applying the results for institutional improvement. As with other case studies, faculty members and division chairs appeared much less aware of the policy than senior officers.

Reconciling Improvement and Accountability:
A Summary

Over its twenty year history, the Tennessee performance-funding policy has reflected the inevitable tension between improvement and accountability; between the use of quality assurance exercises to improve programs and their use to demonstrate that public monies have been applied effectively and efficiently. The original pilot indicators clearly accented improvement. In later years, the indicators featured comparative evaluations based on national or peer norms that stressed accountability. In the last policy iteration, the comparative feature remains, but it also acknowledges the importance of institutional improvement of student outcomes.

What conclusions may be derived from this descriptive and evaluative tour of the twenty-year history of the Tennessee performance-funding policy? The presence of an important accountability system is not necessarily a guarantor of enhanced financial support for higher education. In the decade in which the policy was developed in Tennessee (1970s) and in the first decade of the policy's operation (1980s), financial support for higher education was reasonably strong and at least regionally competitive. In the decade of the 1990s, however, Tennessee's financial support of its higher education system has seriously slipped relative to both the region and the nation.

It might be argued that America's investment in its educational systems has always been as much faith-based as fact-based. This lack of coupling between the presence of accountability systems and level of financial support is not so surprising, since other obvious factors influence financial support for higher education. These include the economic condition of the state, the architecture of its revenue system, the commitment of a state's governor to higher education, and the ability of a governor and state legislature to create a political partnership supporting public colleges and universities. The record suggests that, at least in later years, performance funding has not fulfilled the hope for increased state funding for higher education in Tennessee.

On the other hand, the record supports more affirmative conclusions about performance funding in Tennessee. First, the policy has been in operation for twenty years, which suggests continuing support from a succession of political and educational leaders. The program has persisted through periodic reviews and evaluations. Second, these reviews by panels of campus, governing board, and coordination commission representatives have added new ideas and encouraged a sense of ownership that contributed to its longevity. Third, state policy makers endorsed the initiative by raising the budget percentage based on performance from 2.0 to 5.45 percent. Fourth, all of the parties believe that performance funding will remain a public policy for Tennessee in the near future.

Tennessee now has in place an extensive array of performance indicators and trend lines not present in 1980, furnishing the state and its higher education community an important source of operational and strategic intelligence of performance on both campus and state goals. While some of the direct performance assessments — general education assessments as an example — do not reveal improvement in student performance, they do reveal favorable results when compared to national norms. On at least one other measure considered central as an indicator of both institutional and program quality, program accreditation, virtually 100 percent of community colleges and universities have achieved this goal. Given this success, policy makers are now considering modifying or dropping that indicator in favor of others that might continue to move the state forward. From few campuses doing any educational assessment in the beginning of performance funding, now most institutions have active assessment programs. For example, only three campuses assessed general education outcomes in 1979–80; now all campuses are conducting some assessment of general education.

Some important liabilities exist that suggest the need for improvement. Many of these were identified in the open-ended responses to the project survey reported in Chapter 4, and were affirmed in the six case studies reported in this chapter. Some assessments are clearly conducted mostly to satisfy the policy and have little or no relation to program decisions. The policy does not penetrate to the department and program level, for performance results are often not used for decisions on program improvement or for student placement and progress. This shortcoming represents an important disappointment on the impact of performance funding. Recent trends suggest more campus emphasis has been on maximizing points and dollars and not on increasing performance and effectiveness. The 2000-2004 policy revision addresses this liability by rewarding campuses for applying assessment results to improve institutional performance.

Given the depressed funding for higher education for Tennessee, it is not too surprising that campus executives are more interested in maximizing dollars earned than emphasizing educational improvements. As one of the university presidents interviewed commented:

> "We would get together each year and say prayers that the legislature would do what they're supposed to do and, of course, they would always disappoint you... At least we had performance funding we could put forth, because people would say, 'Well, where were you putting it? Are you putting it where people are really performing?' The answer is, 'No!' We're putting it just to survive" (Lorber 2001, p. 71).

Wildavsky (1993) believes one way to assess a public policy is to ask what problems are being addressed before and after the policy is implemented. The problems being addressed by the Tennessee higher education community now are certainly not about whether there are any assessments in place or any performance intelligence available. Nor is the problem whether Tennessee educational programs bear the well-recognized imprimatur of accreditation. The problem now turns on using more fully the impressive assessment effort for campus decisions.

No single indicator of quality in American higher education is without flaws. There is no system of quality assurance, whether accreditation or total quality management, that cannot be criticized on some philosophic or technical basis. There is no policy, especially one of quality assurance, that does not depend upon the values and skills of those administrators and faculty who implement the initiative. Policies are limited in their ability to compensate for a lack of caring, competence, or courage at any level in an institution. Occasionally, therefore, criticisms lofted at policies might be more properly directed to the values and skills of those who implement policy. As the comic strip character Pogo once observed, "We have met the enemy and he is us."

The possibilities of these and other liabilities of performance funding were not ignored as the Tennessee higher education community crafted the original policy twenty years ago. As William James reflected in his work, *The Will to Believe*, one stands immobilized in the mist on the mountain or decides to move and risk. "Acting on the possible while awaiting perfection" was the motto adopted by those framing the original program (Bogue and Troutt 1980, p. 57). Tennessee has pioneered two major educational accountability policies in the nation, the value-added assessment for its elementary and secondary schools and the performance-funding policy for colleges and universities. That both of these initiatives have enjoyed public affirmation and assault is not surprising, given the complexity of framing public policy in general and the special complexity of any effort that engages questions of educational quality and accountability. For these two pioneering policy ventures, Tennessee continues to warrant its nickname as the "Volunteer" state.

Appendix

Exhibit One: General Education Standard — Pilot Cycle 1979

1. The institution has assessed the performance of a represen-
    tative sampling of its graduates for its major degree — asso-
    ciate or bachelors — on a measure of general education
    outcomes at least once during the last four years.

2. The institution has, during the last four years, assessed the
    general education performance of a representative sampling
    of its graduates by major field and has begun a program of
    inter-field or inter-college analysis.

3. The institution has an ongoing program to assess the general
    education performance of its graduates on a measure of gen-
    eral education outcomes and has data available, preferably
    on the same measure, for representative samples of two or
    more classes of graduates during the previous four years.

4. The institution meets the requirement of standard 3 and can
    further demonstrate for the most recent assessments that the
    development of its graduates — that is, the change in perfor-
    mance from freshmen to graduation — is equivalent to or
    greater than the development of students for at least one in-
    stitution whose freshman performance is on a comparable
    level.

Note: Meeting each standard results in progressively more points
awarded. An institution meeting standard 1 receives 5 points, meeting
standard 2 10 points, standard 3 15 points, and meeting standard 4 20
points.

Endnotes

1   The developmental story of the Tennesse Performance Funding Policy is told more
    fully in a project monograph by Bogue and Troutt (1980) and in a *Harvard
    Business Review* article by Bogue and Brown.

2   For a treatment on the merits and limitations of accreditation, readers will find
    work by Bogue and Saunders (1992) informing.

Chapter 6

INTEGRATING BUDGET, ASSESSMENT AND ACCOUNTABILITY POLICIES: MISSOURI'S EXPERIMENT WITH PERFORMANCE FUNDING

Robert Stein

Introduction

It is not surprising that Missouri, the "Show Me" state, located in the country's heartland, should produce a unique version of performance funding. Differences in the "feel" of Missouri's cities and towns emphasize the state's diversity. Missourians are known to be strong-willed, often resisting popular trends in favor of homegrown initiatives. Throughout its 179 years, the 24th state to enter the union has served as a public battleground for dialogue about national issues. In the early 1990s, before most other states, Missouri developed a new approach to funding public colleges and universities — funding for results.

A highly decentralized system of higher education evolved in Missouri. In most cases, separate boards govern each of Missouri's ten public four-year colleges and universities (13 campuses), 12 public community colleges (17 campuses), 1 public two-year branch campus, 1 public two-year technical college, and 25 major independent institutions. Total full-time equivalent undergraduate enrollment in fall 2000 at public and independent two- and four-year institutions reached an all-time high of 204,121. The public sector accounted for over two-thirds of this enrollment, with the great majority in four-year institutions.

The current Missouri Coordinating Board for Higher Education (CBHE), a constitutional body established in 1972, has both advisory and governing powers. The governor appoints its members to six-year terms, and the Commissioner of Higher Education serves as a member of the governor's cabinet. Missouri's bipartisan higher education board has statutory authority for recommending a unified budget to the governor and the General Assembly for public two and four-year colleges.

State Economic Conditions and Revenues

Despite a strong economy, competing demands for other state services have affected higher education's share of state resources, which fell from an all-time high of 17 percent in FY 1989 to a low of 12.6 percent in FY 1995. Ranking 47th in state expenditures per capita, Missouri historically had to struggle to balance public resistance to increasing taxes with the need to provide its citizens with the higher education services they expect (Holden, 2002). In addition, with the passage of the Hancock Amendment to Missouri's Constitution in 1980, limits were placed on state revenue growth (Article X, Section 23, Missouri Constitution). In the late 1990s, Missouri's revenues exceeded the terms of the Hancock Amendment, thereby requiring the state to issue tax refunds. To date, these refunds total over one billion dollars. Although Missouri had a robust economy for most of the 1990s, tax cuts, credits from past years, and substantial increases in mandatory programs (e.g., health care costs in Medicaid), have placed additional stress on an already tight state budget (Holden 2002). As in other states, tight revenues led to new approaches to budgeting for public higher education.

A Commitment to Assessment

In Missouri, assessment served as a precursor to performance funding by encouraging a systematic approach to measurement. By the 1980s, Northeast Missouri State University (now Truman State University) became a national leader in value-added assessment, leveraging state funding for an improvement plan that emphasized performance (Hutchings and Marchese 1990; McClain and Krueger 1985). By the mid-1980s, Missouri Governor John Ashcroft assumed a leadership role as chairman of the Task Force on College Quality, sponsored by the National Governors' Association. In the Task Force's report, "Time for Results," Ashcroft declared: "… [t]he public has a right to know what it is getting for its expenditure of tax resources; the public has a right to know and understand the quality of undergraduate education that young people receive from publicly funded colleges and universities" (Ashcroft 1991, p. 3). Missouri, like many states, now began to question budget policies driven by inflation and enrollment formulas.

A commitment to assessment began to be fostered by the initiation of the Missouri Student Achievement Study (MSAS), now in its 14th year. Student-level data from all of Missouri's public colleges and universities are collected and analyzed annually. As a result of this effort, state-level reports on student and institutional performance using a single database with standardized definitions has become common practice (Stein 1996).

As interest in assessment increased both locally and nationally, Missouri's state educational leaders, with the support of Missouri's governor, challenged all of Missouri's public higher education institutions "to develop campus assessment programs [that] could be used to improve quality and demonstrate effectiveness" (Stein 1996, p. 36). From the beginning, assessment in Missouri was designed as a public policy initiative that would serve two functions: improvement and accountability. By avoiding legislation, educational and political leaders hoped to provide a "safe environment," where institutions could experiment with assessment without fear of negative consequences and design assessment programs that acknowledged differences in mission and clientele served. Although campus leaders proclaimed commitment to assessment activities, data reported to the CBHE suggested that assessment was not fully penetrating institutional culture or faculty behavior. While Missouri's colleges and universities used their involvement with assessment as a "bragging right," key policy makers began to question the utility of assessment as currently practiced.

The creation of the Missouri Assessment Consortium (MAC) in the summer of 1991 also served as precursor of performance funding. At their own initiation, assessment coordinators from public four-year institutions began to hold informal meetings with CBHE staff members. Initially, presidents and chancellors, as well as chief academic officers, were concerned about the formation of a state-level informal group that would have direct access to state policy makers. Although their fears subsided, this direct link between CBHE staff and institutional personnel represented a major break with tradition, which had tended to be more formal and hierarchical.

Effectiveness Indicators

The late 1980s saw the emergence of yet another precursor of regular and systematic measurement of performance within Missouri's higher education system. In response to declining state financial support, state policy makers expressed concern that the quality of student performance would erode unless either substantial new resources were located or institutions underwent reorganization to do more with less (Stein 1996). The CBHE urged the development of indices of effectiveness that "could be used to inform public policy and build support for increased funding of higher education" (Stein 1996, p. 37). A significant obstacle to be addressed was the tendency for institutional leaders to recommend a massive data system as a way to ensure that everything of value would be measured. While Missouri's initial attempt at designing state-endorsed indicators was not fully implemented, it helped to focus campus discussions about the importance of assessment.

Performance Funding Emerges as a Major Missouri Initiative

In 1989, the CBHE directed its staff to explore the concept of performance funding with all public-sector institutions, and the General Assembly and Governor established the Missouri Business and Education Partnership Commission (MBEPC 1991). While a high-powered, highly visible, statewide committee debated the future of higher education, CBHE staff began working with institutions to develop guiding principles for performance funding in Missouri. In his speech at the fourth annual Governor's Conference on Higher Education, Governor John Ashcroft issued six challenges to Missouri's educational leaders, including rewarding institutional performance by allocating state resources (Ashcroft 1989).

The report of the MBEPC in January 1991 recognized the value of allowing institutions flexibility in methods and strategies, so long as results became the driver of a structured reward system.

> In order to focus on goal achievement while freeing the institutions to find creative ways to produce the intended results, we recommend that performance funding mechanisms — mechanisms that reward institutions for results rather than pay them for programs designed to produce those results — be utilized to the maximum extent feasible" (MBEPC 1991, p. 6).

Dubbed the Economic Survival Act of 1991, Senate Bill 353, which included many of the MBEPC's recommendations, represented a new covenant between political and educational leaders. In exchange for increased allocations to colleges and universities, higher education agreed to establish a statewide higher education plan, with goals and objectives, focused statutory mission statements, and an accountability system involving both student and institutional performance data. At the same time, the state clearly avoided mandating specific approaches to assessment. Though the bill required use of standardized tests, flexibility in an institution's design of assessment programs was endorsed. In addition, use of performance data common to all institutions and some institution-specific data was promoted.

While Missouri educators wanted a major influx of state funds, politicians desired increased accountability in the use of those funds. In his testimony before the legislature concerning Senate Bill 353, Commissioner of Higher Education Charles J. McClain stressed the importance of linking funding with results.

> "[A]ny ACT you consider must assure significant results and measurable outcomes on the key issues ... so Missourians will have evidence that change truly has occurred. Without such assurances, there is the risk that Missourians will be left with paying a higher tax bill for 'more of the same'" (McClain 1991, pp. 3 – 4).

First Performance Funding Budget Recommendation

In October 1991, the CBHE's first recommendation for funding results appeared, without much fanfare, in its FY 1993 Budget Request. Commissioner McClain recommended to the Board that "additional resources (6.8 million) be appropriated . . . for success in achieving desired results," solely for public four-year institutions and only for three productivity measures. McClain cautioned that in future years, the reward structure should be revised to ensure that "we are not just rewarding degree productivity but rather degrees for which student learning has been appropriately assessed" (CBHE Board Book 1991).

During this period, Proposition B, a state referendum that outlined substantial reforms for higher education and included tax increases for $190 million in additional resources for colleges and universities went to the voters. Its overwhelming defeat on November 5, 1991, sent one clear message: Higher Education's commitment to be held accountable for results was not sufficient to raise significant new funds for higher education. In his keynote address at the annual Governor's Conference on Higher Education in December 1991, Governor Ashcroft acknowledged the defeat of Proposition B and challenged institutions to engage in planning and accountability reforms. In his budget recommendations to the General Assembly, the governor indicated that significant reforms would be necessary prior to gaining approval for new resources (Ashcroft 1993, p. 3-1). The CBHE responded by calling for an implementation plan for the future that would guide the development of higher education for the remainder of the decade, which would include performance funding as a major initiative (CBHE Board Book, April 1992).

By March 1992, the Task Force on Critical Choices had been appointed to help design the plan for higher education. Put on a fast track, the Task Force issued its report three months later. By involving campus chairs of trustee boards as members, the CBHE hoped "to facilitate [the plan's] acceptance at the institutional level" (CBHE Board Book, April 1992, p. 2). Requiring an annual accountability report put institutions on notice that they would have to provide evidence of success in attaining agreed-upon goals. Through the new plan, the concept of integrating planning priorities with funding policies was firmly established.

At a September 1992 public hearing, campus leaders generally expressed support for the new plan. While all stressed that success in achieving excellence required additional resources, they chose not to comment about the appropriateness of using performance funding. Either they believed that the governor and the General Assembly would continue to withhold their support for this new funding initiative or they thought that the amount of funding for this new initiative would be insignificant.

By October 1992, the CBHE officially approved the Critical Choices Report and asked its staff to develop and begin an implementation process. With the approval of the FY 1994 budget request, a performance-funding recommendation for four-year institutions again went to the governor and the General Assembly. Based on legislators' comments suggesting that results funding should not "inadvertently encourage institutions to lower their standards and become 'quasi-degree mills,'" the Board modified in its funding initiative to promote assessment (CBHE Board Book, October 1992, p. 2).

In December 1992, the Board clarified its approach to performance funding. In addition to acknowledging that many goals would take time to achieve, the CBHE reiterated a critical principle: "[F]uture performance funding programs [would] provide rewards for both improvement as well as [for] the attainment of specific goal objectives" (CBHE Board Book, December 1992, p. 5). The Board also indicated its expectation that additional measures, mutually agreed upon by institutions and the CBHE, would emerge.

State Commitment to Fund Results

In January 1993, Mel Carnahan became the first Missouri governor to support the allocation of state resources for performance funding. This coincided with the Governor's initiative to promote results-oriented funding for state services. Although the governor's recommendation of approximately $3 million represented only 44 percent of the CBHE's request and less than half a percent of the appropriation to higher education, it demonstrated a symbolic commitment to fund results.

In response, CBHE staff began working with institutions to design standardized reports that could be used both as an accountability system and as a trigger for funding recommendations based on results. Annual performance indicator reports tied to the board's 24 major goals and strategic initiatives began to be issued. Performance-funding elements were subsumed within the state's performance indicator system. Implicit in this approach was the assumption that only a portion of the state's major goals and strategic initiatives would be identified for performance funding.

The Board invited presidents and chancellors to share how their institutions' planning efforts aligned with the Board's strategic initiatives. The receipt of only one presidential comment on performance funding suggested that campus leaders did not consider it a priority. The presidents and chancellors appeared unaware of the level of commitment by Missouri's political leadership for this initiative or of the potential long-term impact performance funding on state appropriations for their institutions.

By the next October, the CBHE recommendation for performance funding included rewards for both two- and four-year institutions. The initial number of elements for public two-year colleges was also kept to a minimum, starting with productivity measures. The Commissioner of Higher Education forewarned the two-year sector — as he had the four-year sector — that in future years, outcome measures would not just reward productivity, but would include quality measures (CBHE Board Book, October 1995).

In January 1994, Governor Carnahan made performance funding more visible by placing funding for results under a separate budget heading, "Requiring Performance and Rewarding Success." His summary stated that he and "the CBHE believe that a portion of funding for higher education should be directly tied to the results they produce" (Carnahan 1995, pp. 2-3).

Although the amount of money remained relatively small, precedents were set. First, performance funding evolved without a legislative mandate for all public campuses. Second, modest annual changes in performance dollars and in the number of performance indicators were expected. Third, it was assumed that a collegial process would be used in identifying changes. Finally, performance funding represented discretionary base increases in contrast to "one-time" money. This budget approach seemed to ensure that institutional budgets would not change drastically in any given year. A grant from the Fund for the Improvement of Postsecondary Education (FIPSE) in 1995 helped to develop and emphasize these critical elements in Missouri's program.

Missouri's approach to performance funding had the advantage of using a simple funding model based on easy-to-quantify measures. Funding was directly linked to previous planning priorities, was developed in consultation with institutional groups, and required only limited funds. Missouri avoided an avalanche of extreme reactions, either negative or positive, from institutions. Although performance funding was on the map, it received minimal attention from state and campus policy makers. Chancellor Charles Kiesler of the University of Missouri-Columbia proved the exception. He urged reconsideration of the whole approach, which he labeled "basically flawed." (Kiesler, 1994).

Commissioner McClain replied: "I do not agree that the imperfect nature of measuring performance creates a flawed system that precludes the incorporation of performance in major public policy initiatives." McClain cited assignment of student grades, merit-pay systems, and processes used in grant competitions as evidence of the use of high-stakes assessments in academia (McClain 1994).

Labels help to sell programs. Missouri chose to call its program "Funding for Results" (FFR). Although the acronym "FFR" took a while to catch hold, it provided consistency as Missouri's version of performance funding gained state and national visibility. Beginning in October 1994, CBHE staff also started to provide regular reports about the status of the performance-funding initiative at each board meeting. By establishing an FFR Advisory Council, with a member from each public campus, the governor's office, and both houses of the Missouri legislature, the visibility and the sense of ownership of the program was expanded. An FFR Teaching and Learning Committee also engaged a group of professors and students in regular discussions about the relation of FFR to improvements in teaching and learning. A subgroup of the Advisory Council served as a steering committee, which included key legislative leaders. Although most legislators had limited familiarity with FFR, these few but powerful legislators became champions of FFR during budget hearings in the General Assembly. During the FIPSE years, Missouri worked extensively to refine and expand its FFR Program by making formal presentations and holding focus groups.

The potential for additional funding peaked institutional interest, but it also created tension. Policy makers questioned paying additional money for results that the core budgets should fund. Representative Steve Gaw, a member of the FFR Steering Committee and a strong proponent of performance funding, insisted that FFR should result in "improvement of the quality of higher education in the state of Missouri. If increases in the funding accomplish that goal..., then it is an appropriate means.... But I do not believe [increased funding] should be stated as a goal itself" (Gaw 1995).

Once it was apparent that the governor and legislature were committed to FFR, the academic community began to raise questions about its appropriateness as a change strategy. Some educational leaders saw increased financial support as an entitlement, associated with inflation. Some campus critics viewed FFR as an intrusion on institutional autonomy although most conceded that the public needed more information on institutional performance.

With support from the governor and key legislative leaders, the CBHE maintained its resolve to continue with FFR. In April 1995, the CBHE requested $2.8 million in state funding to support a voluntary campus-level FFR program. To be eligible for funding, public colleges and universities were required to submit a letter of intent, evidence of faculty involvement, and an abstract that summarized at least one major teaching/learning improvement project. Institutions were also expected to include anticipated outcomes, reward structures, and a commitment to collect baseline data.

CBHE staff continued working with institutional representatives from both two- and four-year institutions to identify modifications to FFR. Although not enthusiastic supporters, the leaders of four-year institutions appeared to accept FFR as evolving to include more quality assessments. In contrast, two-year representatives wanted to remove all assessment components from FFR. Commissioner McClain insisted that rewarding only productivity would not be sufficient and that the state's intent to reward performance on quality assessments would not disappear (McClain, May 17, 1995).

Withstanding a Change in Leadership

In September 1995, Kala M. Stroup became the new Commissioner of Higher Education. A former president of a Missouri institution, Commissioner Stroup was familiar with FFR. She not only supported the FY 1997 FFR budget recommendations that had been developed previously, but succeeded in garnering board approval for the continuation and expansion of FFR rewards to institutions for achieving state-level goals and for designing and implementing faculty-driven teaching/learning improvement projects. Participation by all public institutions in the voluntary campus program suggested support for at least that portion of the program.

Sparked by the new commissioner's leadership, the Board began a major planning process that engaged large numbers of people in the review of Missouri's key strategic initiatives. Funding for Results was one of a limited number of initiatives included in the *Blueprint for Higher Education,* issued in 1996. The governor and the General Assembly endorsed the program by supporting approximately 80 percent of the board's FY 1997 FFR recommendations.

The FY 1997 budget approved 100 percent of the request for the campus portion of FFR. A brochure designed by the CBHE's Committee on Teaching and Learning included recommendations about institutional commitments, characteristics of excellent teaching and learning, assessment practices, and assumptions about campus-level FFR models. The brochure addressed a major flaw in performance-funding programs by encouraging campuses to "reward departments, colleges, deans' offices, and the campus as a whole, by working with the institution to redesign its approach to the flow of money" (Stein 2000, p. 213).

This campus program faced several challenges. It had to overcome faculty perceptions of FFR as another bureaucratic burden. CBHE presentations stressed that FFR should not be seen as an add-on, but as a commitment to improving teaching and learning. Another challenge involved creating a standardized reporting format that not only streamlined the process but held institutions accountable for campus FFR dollars. Institutions began reporting annually about their FFR teaching/learning improvement projects. In June 1996, the Presidential Advisory Committee reflected the popularity of this program when it agreed to work toward a goal of increasing campus FFR appropriations to one percent of planned expenditures on instruction.

In his FY 1998 budget summary, the governor commended FFR and its objectives. "Missouri's public institutions are demonstrating their commitment to quality education and innovative programs by making progress in achieving these goals" (Carnahan 1998, p. 3). Changes in the FFR budget recommendations for FY 1999 involved modifications to definitions and allocation formulas, in addition to other elements. For the first time, FFR recommendations also included rewards for the state's new technical two-year college. The governor's FY 1999 budget proposal also unveiled a major shift in the treatment of FFR funds within the total budget. It combined FFR funding with inflationary increases, since both represented unrestricted dollars (Carnahan 1998, pp. 3-4). The General Assembly approved this change. While still providing new money, this approach did not sit well with institutions. Presidents and chancellors thought that the state should fully fund inflation before considering performance dollars. Although FFR was not designed to replace inflationary increases, the alteration announced a change in philosophy: Inflationary increases would no longer be automatic. Using this approach, 100 percent of the CBHE's state- and campus-level FFR recommendations were appropriated in FY 1999.

Funding for Results Principles

In February 1998, in response to questions about driving principles, the CBHE adopted the following nine FFR Principles as guides for further revisions to Missouri's FFR program: 1) emphasize priorities established by previous planning efforts, 2) be concise and easily understood, 3) involve only a limited number of measures, 4) make maximum use of existing data sources, 5) promote and acknowledge results, 6) include sector- and mission-specific elements, 7) establish assurance of quality graduates from Missouri's public colleges and universities, 8) FFR should represent a relatively small proportion of an institution's total state appropriation, and 9) motivate institutions to engage in continuous quality improvement (CBHE Board Book, February 1998).

Approval of these principles settled a long-standing debate about sampling student outcomes. By emphasizing the assessment of all graduates, the Board reinforced that sampling of student performance outcomes, while permitted, would not be encouraged by the allocation formulas used.

Increased Attention

In February 1998, chief academic officers of four-year institutions recommended a major overhaul of FFR. "Institutional goals [were] to be customized to fit the institution's mission" and more emphasis would be placed on improvement in reaching targeted goals. The plan would allow each institution to retain/gain two percent of its budget based on performance ("Four-Year Public Institution Chief Academic Officers' Plan," January 1998). In receiving the plan, the four-year presidents and chancellors "expressed support for the concept of FFR and agreed that the program should continue to be refined." They did not, however, pressure the board to make significant changes in its approach. Since decisions about the FY 2001 budget coincided with Governor Carnahan's last term in office, it was especially difficult to garner support for redesigning FFR. CBHE recommendations for the FY 2001 budget sent to the governor, therefore, involved no changes from the previous year.

A Shift in Dialogue About FFR

Clearly, conversations with institutional representatives had changed. Rather than argue about the advantages and disadvantages of performance funding, dialogue began to focus on better ways to evolve designs for FFR. Institutional representatives discussed, and made recommendations about, the number and types of indicators, their connection to campus missions, the size of the FFR budget, the definitions and allocation formulas, and improved communication of perspectives on teaching/learning improvements. Although the level of FFR appropriations varied depending upon the availability of resources in a given year, the governor and the General Assembly continued to support the program. During the budget process, legislators would raise questions about a particular measure, e.g., "Success of Underrepresented Populations," but the coalition of support between the CBHE, the governor, and key legislative leaders withstood opposition.

FFR Funding

Table 1 provides a summary of the FFR budget progression from FY 1994, when it was first introduced, through FY 2001. Public four-year institutions have received an addition of $56.6 million to their core budgets; community colleges $9.6 million; and the state's technical college $207,049. These totals include campus-level FFR funds of $3.3 million for four-year institutions, $1.5 million for community colleges, and $63,792 for the state's technical college. Although the total annual appropriation remained under 2 percent of higher education's funding from general revenue, it represented a substantially larger percent of new money available, averaging 17.0 percent for four-year institutions,

15.4 percent for community colleges, and 11.9 percent for the state's technical college.

Changes in FFR Elements

From the outset, Missouri sought to implement performance in the least threatening way to institutions. Collaboration with campus leaders in the selection of performance indicators represents a key feature of FFR. Table 2 provides a brief description of each FFR element. The initial FFR indicators emphasized productivity and efficiency values. As the institutions became more comfortable with FFR, new elements stressed quality and state policy goals. The program abandoned only two measures, although others were refined to establish more meaningful measurements. Some elements are common to all institutions; others are sector-specific. In some cases, a per capita headcount of students meeting a minimal threshold generates FFR dollars. In others, more complicated formulas that considered differences in institutional mission, size, and/or percent of expenditures on instruction were used. Throughout, FFR continued the initial commitment to a limited number of measures.

In Year One of implementation for both four-year and community colleges, FFR had only three elements. For the FY 2002 budget request, the community colleges had six; the state's technical college seven; and the public four-year sector eight elements. In addition, recommended increases to the campus teaching/learning core have been included each year for selected institutions in support of the statewide goal of dedicating one percent of planned expenditures on instruction to this effort.

Institutional representatives agreed with the deletions. "Graduates in Selected Disciplines" was eliminated because no clear criteria had been developed for what constituted a "critical discipline." The only other element to be deleted was "Assessment of Graduates." Institutional representatives agreed that assessment of student performance, both in general education and in the major, had become normative and that rewarding merely the accomplishment of an assessment process was no longer needed. It is important to note that the elimination of this element does not imply that assessment at Missouri's institutions is no longer valued. Assessment now accents student performance rather than an evaluation process.

The FFR element "Success of Underrepresented Groups" underwent significant change after the *Hopwood* case, when the measure shifted from minorities (African-Americans) to "Underrepresented Groups" (including Hispanics and Native Americans). "Underrepresented Groups," by definition, include graduates who are in the top quartile of Pell Grant eligibility at point of entry or who are from a minority group whose graduation distribution for a given year is less than the minority group's distribution of 18-year-olds or older in Missouri's population.

Another FFR element, "Freshman Completion Rates," provoked extensive debate. This element rewards institutions for meeting targeted goals concerning the percent of full-time degree-seeking freshmen who completed 24 hours with a 2.0 GPA or higher. Goals vary by institutional admissions category. Presidents and chancellors, primarily from open-enrollment institutions, requested changes in the targeted goals, which they claimed were too high. In addition, they wanted to lower the number of hours students would be required to complete. The Board agreed to lower the goals to a more realistic level, but refused to reduce the number of hours.

"Successful Transfer" also underwent significant change. At first, FFR rewarded two-year colleges for transfer students regardless of the credit hours taken at the two- or four-year institutions. With this change, students are now required to complete at least 12 hours at a two-year college and a baccalaureate degree at a four-year institution. Eventually, this provision also became a four-year element for transfer students completing associate degrees.

Impact of FFR on Institutional Behavior

The addition of substantial state dollars to the base budgets of Missouri's public institutions through FFR raises questions about whether the program's goals for continuous quality improvement are being realized. While the degree of penetration into the culture of institutions varies, conversations among a select group of campus leaders are clearly changing, and a new culture of accountability is emerging.

FFR elements are tracked through annual performance reports. Although FFR elements were introduced over several years, performance is reported for most elements from FY 1993 forward, since it corresponds to the adoption of the Board's major public policy goals. Through FFR, the CBHE seeks to improve, as well as sustain, performance in key areas. While it is not possible to demonstrate causality, the reports show the following results.

- **Assessment:** The percent of graduates assessed has increased significantly: General education assessment of baccalaureate graduates has increased from 71.5 to 83.7 percent; assessments in the major, from 63 percent to 83.5 percent; and associate graduates, from 20.3 percent to 81.8 percent.

- **Minorities:** From FY 1993 to FY 1999, the number of minorities completing degrees and certificates at Missouri's public institutions has increased from 10.2 to 11.9% for Certificates; from 10.6 to 11.3% for Associate Degrees; from 7.0 to 11.4% for Baccalaureate degrees; from 7.5 to 10.3% for Master's Degrees; and from 12.7 to 14.4% for Doctoral and First Professional Degrees (Figure 4.)

- **Performance in General Education and the Major:** In FY 1999, 59% of teacher education graduates in Missouri who took a national exit exam exceeded the national average, an increase of 2 percent from FY 1993. While the number of graduates assessed in the major has increased, the percentage of graduates scoring above the 50th percentile decreased from 63.2 to 56.6 percent from FY 1993 to FY 1999.

- **Freshman Completion Rates:** Institutional goals vary by the preparation level expected of entering students. In FY 1999, while the state's technical college surpassed the target goal of 55 percent for open-enrollment institutions by having 69 percent of its students meet the standards, community colleges reached only at 37 percent. The two open-enrollment public four-year institutions demonstrated increases between FY 1993 and FY 1999, but fell short of their target goal. Although all moderately selective institutions increased performance, only two met the target goal of 70 percent. Similarly, all selective institutions demonstrated increases, but only two met the target goal of 80 percent. The one highly selective institution also showed an increase, but fell two percentage points below its target goal of 90 percent (Figure 6).

- **Successful Transfer:** The number of students who began their studies at a public community college and completed their baccalaureate degrees at a public four-year institution increased by 25 percent between FY 1995 and FY 1999. The proportion of baccalaureate degrees at public four-year institutions conferred on students with 12 or more hours from a Missouri community college increased from 13 percent in FY 1995 to 18 percent in FY 1999 (Figure 8).

- **Quality of New Undergraduates:** The proportion of Missouri's first-time full-time degree-seeking freshmen entering public four-year institutions with the 16-unit high school core curriculum increased from 46 percent to 93 percent between FY 1993 and FY 1999 (Figure 5).

- **Quality of Prospective Teachers:** The CBHE's target goals for both entry and exit standards are higher than the state minimum. Between FY 1993 and FY 1999, the percentage of certificated teachers meeting the CBHE entry standard declined from 74 percent to 67 percent, while the percent meeting exit standards increased from 57 percent to 59 percent.

- **Quality of Incoming Graduate Students:** While the number of graduate students submitting entrance scores at the University of Missouri increased from 74 percent to 84 percent between FY 1994 and FY 1999, the percentage of those scoring at or above the 50th percentile on those examinations increased only from 82 to 85 percent. During the same time period, graduate students submitting entrance examination scores at the state's other master's degree-granting institutions increased from 55 to 57 percent, and those scoring above the 50th percentile went from 53 to 61 percent.

- **Graduation Rates:** Target graduation goals vary by institution as follows: 45 percent for open-enrollment institutions, 55 percent for moderately selective institutions, 65 percent for selective institutions, and 75 percent for highly selective institutions. The overall graduation rates at Missouri's public four-year institutions have increased from 47 percent for students in the 1989 cohort to 50 percent for students in the

1993 cohort. However, only one of Missouri's public four-year institutions met its target goal (Figure 7).

- **Critical Disciplines:** The number of students completing programs of study in critical high-skills trades or disciplines at four-year institutions increased 57 percent from FY 1993 to FY 1997.

- **Degree/Certificate Productivity:** The number of certificate and degrees conferred by public two-year institutions decreased by three percent from FY 1993 to FY 1999.

- **Job Placement:** Successful job placement of graduates from two-year institutions in technical areas increased from 64 percent to 76 percent from FY 1993 to FY 1998.

- **Campus-Level FFR:** All 32 public campuses are involved in designing and implementing campus teaching/learning improvement projects. Annual accountability reports on campus-level FFR projects suggest, "institutions are very much engaged in efforts to improve teaching/learning and that FFR provides the impetus, as well as a significant portion of resources allocated, for many new initiatives."

Conclusion

Missouri began discussing performance funding in the late 1980s. Based on a strong commitment of government and educational leaders, the CBHE developed its FFR program without legislative mandate. While not strong proponents, presidents and chancellors of public institutions provided validation by involving institutional representatives in ongoing dialogue about the program. A grant from FIPSE helped to promote, refine, and expand Missouri's program. Resistance from institutional leaders has transformed, over time, into more constructive discussions about ways to improve Missouri's approach to performance funding, including suggestions for additional FFR elements.

External consultants evaluating FFR have commended Missouri for shifting the dialogue around performance funding to teaching and learning and for building money into each institution's base budget. In addition, Missouri's commitment to use consensus through dialogue in evolving its program is often cited as one of its strengths. Suggestions for change have stressed the importance of rewarding institutions for demonstrating improvement toward achievement of absolute standards, for continuing to move from measures of quantity to measures of quality, for more fully recognizing institutional missions, and for better aligning FFR and new statewide initiatives (Albright and Jones 1996).

Between FY 1994 and FY 2001, FFR has resulted in an increase of $66 million in funding to institutional core budgets. While perceptions vary about the impact of FFR, the performances of institutions and students are improving. Missouri has found that by systematically reporting and funding results, change is occurring, albeit slowly.

An indication that a commitment to FFR remains strong has been demonstrated by Missouri's experimentation with the design of an FFR performance efficiency index. In short, Missouri is asking the question: "How much FFR money have institutions left on the table by the results that have not been achieved?" This index will allow Missouri to analyze the success each public institution has had in maximizing its FFR potential in any given year and will provide useful information for evaluating the overall impact of FFR. In addition, the CBHE established a precedent in October 2000, by agreeing to use an FFR performance efficiency index as a corrective factor in base adjustments recommended for selected community colleges. This occurred when their overall success in FFR fell below 85 percent of the median statewide levels for all community colleges.

In working with new political leaders, there are also positive signals that performance funding will not be eliminated although it does face challenges. Missouri's new governor, who was elected in November 2000, inherited fiscal stresses created by increases in mandatory costs and shortfalls as a result of tax cuts and credits. As a result, Governor Holden's budget recommendations for higher education for FY 2002 included neither inflationary nor FFR dollars. This marked the first time since the FY 1994 budget that FFR dollars were not recommended in a Missouri governor's budget recommendations. Despite his inability to support new state dollars for FFR for FY 2002, Governor Holden, in his budget summary, expressed his dedication to "managing state government to achieve the results Missourians expect" (Holden 2002, Legislative Financial Report p. 1). While the specifics of FFR will undoubtedly change, it is likely that once resources become available, performance funding will be maintained as a strategy to bring about systemic change within Missouri's higher education system.

In preparing for the future, the CBHE is working to design a new Coordinated Plan for Missouri Higher Education, a plan that will continue to foster a results-oriented budget policy. The Coordinated Plan will replace the *Blueprint for Missouri Higher Education* and will serve as "the seminal document from which future planning and budgeting processes will come to ensure . . . a thriving system of quality higher education" (CBHE Board Book, February 2001, p. 1). A draft of the Coordinated Plan, which was shared with the academic community in February 2001, addresses Student Success, Institutional Strength, and Public Service. Included within each of these three themes are goals, as well as measures of success, that will continue to reinforce the willingness of higher education to be held accountable and to use results to drive budget recommendations.

Table 1 FFR Budget Progression				
Community Colleges	Amount Requested	Amount Received	% Received of Request	FFR as % of New Money
FY 1995	$1,506,200	$ 500,000	33.2%	5.2%
FY 1996	$1,656,300	$ 799,690	48.3%	5.1%
FY 1997	$2,511,680	$2,083,760	83.0%	16.5%
State Level	$1,711,680	$1,283,760	75.0%	
Campus Level	$ 800,000	$ 800,000	100.0%	
FY 1998	$2,513,385	$1,513,440	60.2%	18.5%
State Level	$1,999,890	$ 999,944	50.0%	
Campus Level	$ 513,495	$ 513,496	100.0%	
FY 1999	$2,278,296	$2,278,296	100.0%	30.8%
State Level	$2,112,810	$2,112,810	100.0%	
Campus Level	$ 165,486	$ 165,486	100.0%	
FY 2000	$2,330,323	$1,165,162	50.0%	19.4%
State Level	$2,282,121	$1,141,061	50.0%	
Campus Level	$ 48,202	$ 24,101	50.0%	
FY 2001	$2,520,360	$1,260,184	50.0%	49.5%
State Level	$2,408,333	$1,204,166	50.0%	
Campus Level	$ 112,027	$ 56,013	50.0%	
Totals	$15,316,544	$9,600,532	62.7%	15.4%
State Level	$13,677,334	$8,041,431	58.8%	
Campus Level	$1,639,210	$ 1,559,096	95.1%	

Table 1
FFR Budget Progression

4 Year-State Institutions	Amount Requested	Amount Received	% Received of Request	FFR as % of New Money
FY 1994	$ 6,785,000	$ 3,021,849	44.5%	18.4%
FY 1995	$11,623,956	$ 4,272,131	36.8%	11.6%
FY 1996	$13,171,600	$ 7,010,000	53.2%	13.7%
FY 1997	$13,526,497	$10,644,874	78.7%	20.7%
State Level	$11,526,497	$ 8,644,874	75.0%	
Campus Level	$ 2,000,000	$ 2,000,000	100.0%	
FY 1998	$11,744,891	$ 6,112,446	52.0%	16.1%
State Level	$11,264,891	$ 5,632,446	50.0%	
Campus Level	$ 480,000	$ 480,000	100.0%	
FY 1999	$11,037,468	$11,037,468	100.0%	18.7%
State Level	$10,837,468	$10,837,468	100.0%	
Campus Level	$ 200,000	$ 200,000	100.0%	
FY 2000	$13,126,280	$ 6,563,140	50.0%	15.7%
State Level	$12,942,274	$ 6,471,137	50.0%	
Campus Level	$ 184,006	$ 92,003	50.0%	
FY 2001	$15,948,642	$ 7,974,324	50.0%	20.5%
State Level	$14,814,642	$ 7,407,321	50.0%	
Campus Level	$ 1,134,000	$ 567,000	50.0%	
Totals	$96,964,334	$56,636,232	58.4%	17.0%
	$92,966,328	$53,297,226	57.3%	
	$ 3,998,006	$ 3,339,003	83.5%	

Linn State	Amount Requested	Amount Received	% Received of Request	FFR as % of New Money
Table 1 **FFR Budget Progression**				
FY 1999	$ 110,125	$ 110,125	100.0%	17.8%
State Level	$ 60,125	$ 60,125	100.0%	
Campus Level	$ 50,000	$ 50,000	100.0%	
FY 2000	$ 82,469	$ 41,234	50.0%	8.9%
State Level	$ 71,885	$ 35,942	50.0%	
Campus Level	$ 60,584	$ 55,292	91.3%	
FY 2001	$ 111,379	$ 55,690	50.0%	8.5%
State Level	$ 94,379	$ 47,189	50.0%	
Campus Level	$ 17,000	$ 8,500	50.0%	
Totals	$ 303,973	$ 207,049	68.1%	11.9%
State Level	$ 226,389	$ 143,256	63.3%	
Campus Level	$ 77,584	$ 63,792	82.2%	

Table 2
FFR Elements Common to Both Sectors

Assessment of Graduates
Initially only national assessments in both general education and the major. Refined to include both national and local assessment and restricted to general education only. Allocation is based on a per capita headcount of graduates who were assessed.

Success of Underrepresented Groups
Initially only African-American graduates at baccalaureate level. This element was expanded and now includes financially at-risk students as well as minorities with a graduate distribution lower than their representation in the Missouri population 18 years old or older. Allocation is based on a per capita headcount.

Freshmen Success Rates
Includes first-time full-time degree-seeking freshmen completing 24 hours with a 2.0 or higher by the end of their first year. Goals vary by institution selectivity. Allocation based on percent of cohort meeting institutional goal multiplied by .15 of funding recommendations for on-campus instruction

Performance of Graduates
Based on graduates who score at or above 50th percentile on a nationally normed assessment in general education or in the major, or passed a national licensure, certification, or registration examination, or received an award in a field that does not have a national assessment. Allocation based on a per capita headcount for graduates who meet performance standard. Teacher education students treated separately.

Successful Transfer
Initially only for two-year institutions included any four-year student with some community college credit. Redefined to include baccalaureate graduates with a minimum of 12 hours at a community college. Expanded to include four-year institutions but only for those baccalaureate graduates who complete an associate degree prior to transfer. Allocation is based on a per capita headcount for each transfer who met the standard.

Degrees in Critical Disciplines
Includes degrees awarded in foreign languages, health, nursing, life and physical sciences, mathematics, and graduate engineering. Al-

location is based on a per capita headcount for each student graduating from one of the targeted disciplines. Element was deleted after FY 1996.

FFR ELEMENTS FOUR-YEAR ONLY

Quality of Prospective Teachers
Target goals set above state's minimum for both entry and exit standards based on performance on state-required assessments. Allocation initially based on a per capita headcount, redefined as percent of graduates meeting entry and/or exit standards multiplied by .15 of the funding recommendations for on-campus instruction.

Quality of New Graduate Students
Based on number of new graduate students who score at or above the 50th percentile on national entrance examinations. Allocation is based on a per capita headcount of students who met the standard.

Quality of New Undergraduate Students
Number of entering freshmen who completed a 16-unit high school core curriculum. Allocation is based on percent of new freshmen meeting standard multiplied by .15 percent of funding recommendations for on campus instruction.

Attainment of Graduation Goals
Based on a cohort analysis including students who graduate within six years from any Missouri institution. Goals vary by institutional selectivity. Allocation uses a formula based on percent of success in meeting graduation goals multiplied by .15 percent of the funding recommendations for on-campus instruction.

FFR ELEMENTS TWO-YEAR ONLY

Degree/Certificate Productivity
Includes all certificates of one-year or greater and associate degree graduates. Allocation is based on a per capita headcount

Successful Job Placement
Based on number of graduates in technical fields who are successful in locating a job-related or military-related position. Allocation is based on a per capita headcount.

Appendix

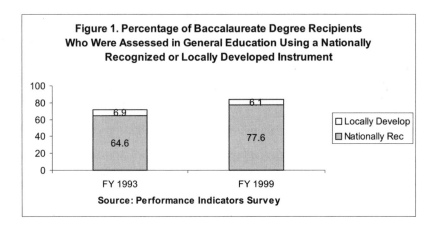

Figure 1. Percentage of Baccalaureate Degree Recipients Who Were Assessed in General Education Using a Nationally Recognized or Locally Developed Instrument

Source: Performance Indicators Survey

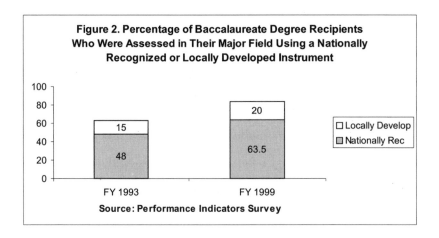

Figure 2. Percentage of Baccalaureate Degree Recipients Who Were Assessed in Their Major Field Using a Nationally Recognized or Locally Developed Instrument

Source: Performance Indicators Survey

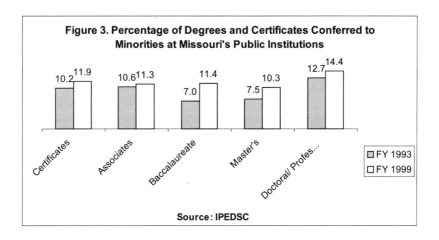

Figure 3. Percentage of Degrees and Certificates Conferred to Minorities at Missouri's Public Institutions

Source: IPEDSC

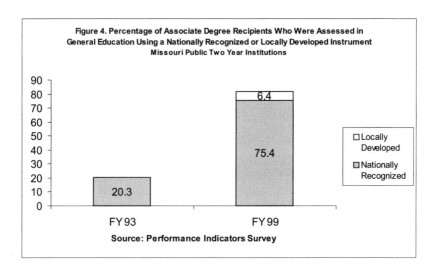

Figure 4. Percentage of Associate Degree Recipients Who Were Assessed in General Education Using a Nationally Recognized or Locally Developed Instrument
Missouri Public Two Year Institutions

Source: Performance Indicators Survey

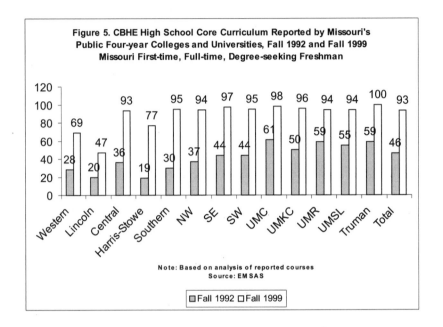

Figure 6

Three- and Six-year Graduation Rate of the 1993 (4-year) or 1996
(2-year) Freshman Cohort Who Graduated from Any Missouri
Public Institution as of Spring 1999

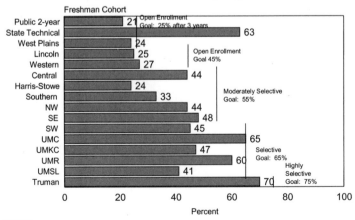

Source: EMSAS

Table 3. Freshman Success Rates by Admission Selectivity		
	FY 1993	*FY 1999*
Open Enrollment Goal 55%		
Public Two-year	37	37
Linn State	N/A	69
Lincoln	43	48
Western	41	52
Moderately Selective Goal 70%		
Central	56	71
Harris-Stowe	18	38
Southern	62	64
Northwest	62	76
Southeast	48	60
Selective Goal 80%		
Southwest	59	69
UMC	78	80
UMKC	70	76
UMR	78	83
UMSL	53	65
Highly Selective Goal 90%		
Truman	84	88

Chapter 7

READY, FIRE, AIM: PERFORMANCE FUNDING POLICIES FOR PUBLIC POSTSECONDARY EDUCATION IN FLORIDA

David L. Wright, Patrick H. Dallet, and Juan C. Copa

Introduction

Performance funding in Florida is a story of scattered shots of legislative policies that tried to tie state funding to campus performance. The state legislature fired several shots in the direction of performance funding, but its aim often appeared random and erratic. Mixed messages, added initiatives, and evolving requirements for existing programs confused the system and campus leaders charged with implementing performance funding in the Sunshine State. The decade of the 1990s began with a statute mandating that both the community college and state university systems report performance.

Later, a second law required both to submit annual budget requests based on performance, and the appropriations bill provided limited incentive funds for performance. The end of the decade saw the arrival of a third statute related to performance funding, which tied the largest percentage of incentive funds to date to the performance of community colleges and school districts in workforce development programs.

Now, landmark legislation in education governance, enacted in 2001, requires each sector of public higher education to develop an entirely new plan over the next few years that makes ten percent of its state funds contingent on system performance. The legislation leaves two open questions. Will it simplify and streamline the process by superseding the overlapping approaches to performance funding currently in place? Or will it become another point in an ever-growing scatter plot of legislative programs and policies?

Florida Background

Demographics and Enrollments

Florida's public higher education system comprises the 28-member Community College System of two-year institutions and the 11-member State University System (SUS) of four-year universities. Senate Bill 1162, passed during the 2001 Legislative Session, designated New College of Florida as the eleventh member of the SUS (Florida Statutes, Section 240.2011(12)). The public universities enrolled some 214,000 students in 1999-2000, public two-year colleges 320,000, and private colleges and universities 122,000 (*Almanac* 2000). The two-year colleges registered nearly 50 percent of all the college students in Florida. The state's "two plus two" system of articulation promotes the recognition and utilization of the public community colleges as a primary point of entry into postsecondary education, and the statewide Articulation Agreement guarantees entry to the SUS for transfer students with the Associate in Arts (AA) degree. The independent sector of postsecondary education includes 27 regionally accredited four-year, nonprofit colleges and universities, as well as some 500 other institutions licensed by the State Board of Independent Colleges and Universities.

State Economic Conditions
and Education Appropriations

Increasing enrollments and competition for state resources heralded greater accountability for higher education. Nationally, governors and legislators have been reducing the state investment in higher education since FY1979, as state tax fund resources have shifted to other budget priorities. In Florida, higher education appropriations have generally followed suit, although they have bucked the trend recently. Overall, state appropriations for Florida higher education per $1,000 of personal income dropped 34 percent from FY1975 to FY2000 (Mortenson 1999). The enrollment increases predicted for higher education in Florida exacerbated the problem of diminishing resources. The Postsecondary Education Planning Commission (PEPC), a higher education advisory agency, projected an increase in total enrollment of 258,000 or 41 percent, between 1995 and 2010 (PEPC 1997).

Education overall has received a shrinking share of state funding, declining from 30.8 percent of state appropriations in 1990-91 to 26.3 percent in 1999-2000 (see Table 1 in Appendix). Community colleges' share of the education total fell from 7.0 percent in 1990-91 to 4.3 percent in 1999-2000, while the state universities' portion increased from 17.0 to 18.4 percent over the same period (see Table 2 in Appendix). These differences may begin to explain why the Community College System responded more favorably to the idea of performance funding than the SUS, which had fared better under the traditional "base plus" funding approach.

Government and Governance

A divided governance structure diminished the capacity to restructure budgeting for public higher education. Florida's Constitution limited the governor's authority by dividing executive powers among elected and appointed cabinet officers, giving the legislature — especially its appropriations committees — extensive power over agency budgets and even administrative matters. Although responsible for annually submitting a comprehensive budget request, the State Board of Education composed of the governor and cabinet officers traditionally exercised little influence on higher education funding policies and outcomes. But recent action radically alters the Board's role and composition.

In 1998, Florida voters adopted Amendment 8 to the State Constitution, which established an appointed, rather than elected, Board of Education effective January 2003. The Commissioner of Education's Blue Ribbon Committee on Education Governance developed recommendations that became the basis for House Bill 2263. Passed during the 2000 Session, the bill provided for a new education governance model to oversee a seamless continuum of kindergarten through graduate education and consistent education policy across all educational delivery systems. In 2001, Senate Bill 1162 established the Florida Board of Education to govern the "K-20" education system. It abolished the state-level coordinating board for the community colleges and the Board of Regents that had governed the SUS. The Act authorized local boards of trustees, which had already been a feature of the Community College System, for each of the public universities.

Precursors to Performance Funding

Initiative Funding

Linking academic results to special funding for higher education was not new to Florida. The state had a long history of initiative funding, which advanced moneys to colleges and universities for specified activities in the hopes of encouraging the desired results. Initiative funding began in the 1970s and continues today. In 1974, Florida started the first of these initiatives with Programs of Distinction, later revised as Centers of Excellence. In 1979, it expanded this initiative into a Quality Improvement Program and launched a matching fund for an Eminent Scholars endowment. In 1986, the state created a High Technology and Industry Council that funded competitive grants for collaboration with industry and matching funds to foster private giving. The state started similar but smaller programs for the community colleges. From 1979 to 1989, initiative funding brought more than $200 million to the SUS and from 1983-89 more than $10 million to community colleges (PEPC 2000, p. 5).

Initiative funding depended on two conditions: rising revenues for state government and high credibility for higher education. The willingness of elected officials to fund initiatives — which the academic community generally wanted with few strings attached — depended on these fortuitous circumstances. By the late 1980s, many state officials believed that the institutions had used the special funding for what they wanted without improving performance in areas of state priorities. This perception — combined with a decline in revenues in the face of an impending demographic boom, and competing demands in the areas of criminal justice, health care, and social welfare — presaged a legislative mandate for increased accountability in areas of public concern.

Accountability Reporting

Florida officially joined the "accountability movement" in 1991 by establishing in statute a mandatory process for the systematic, ongoing evaluation of improvement in the quality and efficiency of the State University and Community College Systems. Each system would report annually on prescribed performance indicators.

About the same time, the Postsecondary Education Planning Commission released *Outcomes Assessment in Postsecondary Education*, which found that Florida had no established goals to determine if postsecondary education was fulfilling its mission. The report also confirmed that systematic and comprehensive assessment for the purpose of continual improvement in institutional effectiveness had not been a priority for all colleges and universities (PEPC 1992, p. 28). The Commission's follow-up report, *Accountability in Florida's Postsecondary Education System*, identified access, diversity, productivity, and the quality of undergraduate education as common statewide priorities for higher education and asserted that accountability should serve the dual purposes of providing information to state-level policy makers while fostering improvement at the institutional level (PEPC 1994, pp. 19-20).

The Government Performance
and Accountability Act of 1994:
The Arrival of Performance Budgeting

In 1994, at the initiative of Governor Lawton Chiles, the legislature passed the Government Performance and Accountability Act, a far-reaching initiative that required all state agencies to submit performance-based program budgets (Chapter 94-249, Laws of Florida). PB[2], as the law came to be known, attempted to relate state funding to outcomes on indicators closely associated with an agency's mission. It required state agencies, on a prescribed schedule, to present budget requests to the governor and the legislature, based on the results achieved on an approved list of performance measures (Florida Statutes, Section 216.023). Funding would follow rather than precede results. It appeared that at least a portion of higher education funding would be contingent, either directly or indirectly, upon demonstrated outcomes. The Act also established the Office of Program Policy Analysis and Government Accountability (OPPAGA) to consult with state agencies in identifying programs for performance-based program budgeting, evaluate proposed performance measures for their reliability and validity, and conduct a thorough performance evaluation, or "justification review," during the second year of an agency's operation under a performance-based program budget (Florida Statutes, Section 11.513).

This Act sought to shift budgeting from consideration of current and required resources toward the actual benefits conferred on the state and its citizens. It stressed effect rather than effort and carried "incentives" and "disincentives" (Florida Statutes, Section 216.163). However, the Act left more questions than answers for state and campus policy makers. The Law mandated the program but permitted the state agency to propose the indicators. It allowed both qualitative and quantitative indicators but demanded outcome measures that demonstrated "the actual impact or public benefit of a program" or output measures that exhibited "the actual service or product delivered by a state agency" (Florida Statutes, Section 216.011).

The law treated higher education, which had long been afforded special status and autonomy, the same as other government functions. Yet state policy makers soon learned that higher education was different. The divided nature of state government and academic governance in Florida hampered cohesive leadership on performance budgeting. In addition, the Act's incentives that granted increased autonomy for improved performance meant little to higher education, since public colleges and universities already had much more flexibility in managing budgets and personnel than state agencies.

The law set a seven-year schedule for introducing performance-based budgeting in each of the state agencies or state-funded organizations. The implementation schedule required that the Division of

Community Colleges (DCC) submit a performance-based budget request in the fall of 1995 for implementation in FY 1996-97 (Florida Board of Regents 1996). The State University System would get its turn the following year. As the first educational agency to come under PB^2, the Community College System bore the brunt of much of the disagreement and confusion over how the program would be applied to higher education. Would the submission of performance-based budgets merely justify the budget request for the Community College System? Or would the program set aside performance funds that institutions could earn by achieving the targeted outcomes? Would PB^2 place a percentage of campus budgets at risk? If so, how much of the funding would it cover?

Community Colleges and Performance Budgeting

By beginning with community colleges, the process started with the sector of higher education most worried about the impact of performance-based budgeting, and the one least capable of meeting its mandates. Without the sophisticated data base of the SUS and with a more diverse clientele and a broader mission, the community colleges were less certain of their results on the output, and especially the outcome, measures demanded by the Accountability and Performance Act. The performance plan prepared by the staff from the Division of Community Colleges in consultation with campus presidents appeared to follow the rule: If you must comply, go as simply, slowly, and as safely as possible.

The plan did not use existing Accountability Report indicators on retention and success rates for Associate in Science (AS) graduates and substituted simply the number of degree and certificate completers. It eliminated pass rates on the College Level Academic Skills Test (CLAST), and lowered the benchmark for grade point averages of AA degree transfers in their upper-division work in the SUS from 2.5 to 2.0. The plan dropped the success or graduation rates for AS students, because of the contention that many community college students never intend to obtain degrees. The performance of AA grads in the SUS was lowered because of the common complaint that the community colleges should not be held responsible for the performance of their transfers at the university level. Controversy over the CLAST as a rising junior exam for admission into upper-division programs — especially its possible impact on minority students — had already led to legislation allowing students to exempt the examination requirement by alternative means.

The standards for the indicators seemed to ensure success by promising relatively small improvements (Florida Community College System 1996). The plan was cautious but perhaps no more than might have been expected, given the diversity of the community colleges, the scarcity of outcomes data, and the unclear requirements and uncertain consequences of the Statute. Going first down an uncharted course called for caution.

Though the measures proposed by the Division of the Community Colleges lacked the desired emphasis on long-term outcomes, officials in the Governor's Office apparently concluded that demanding major revisions would probably be futile and could be politically dangerous. State officials obviously considered the clout of the 28 campuses with local legislators and the strong support for community colleges, especially in the Senate. Instead of insisting on a more ambitious plan, the governor's budget recommendation for 1996-97 actually reduced the number of indicators, including its outcome measures.

A Difference of Opinion

The legislature, particularly the Senate, insisted that performance budgeting be implemented at the institutional rather than the system level for community colleges, since the campuses, not the System, produced the performance. The governor's budget office argued for application to the system, not campuses. In the months that followed submission of the governor's budget, in meeting after meeting between officials from the governor's Planning and Budget Office and staff from Senate Ways and Means, each side clung to its position. Toward the end of the legislative session, the deadlock broke when the Senate traded an item on K-12 education important to the House and the governor to win approval for a Performance-Based Incentive program for the community colleges.

The Performance Incentive Funding approved during the 1996 session appropriated $12 million for community colleges, tied to the following measures (1996-97 General Appropriations Act, HB 2715, Specific Appropriation 172A).

- Measure 1: $5 million for AA degree, AS degree, and certificate completers;

- Measure 2: $5 million for completers from Measure 1 who were economically disadvantaged, disabled, Non-English speakers or English as a second language students, passed a state job licensure exam, or were placed in jobs in targeted fields; and

- Measure 3: $2 million for AA completers who graduated with fewer than 72 total attempted credit hours.

Passage of incentive funding in 1996 meant that Florida now had two approaches to performance funding in place — performance-based program budgeting and performance incentive funding. Both sought to relate funding to results. The former looked at the overall system performance when shaping total budget allocations, while the latter linked specific objectives to special allocations. Performance-based budgeting, which presumably affected an organization's total allocation, demanded a comprehensive set of indicators capable of assessing long-term benefits. Incentive funding used a limited number of output measures and tied small sums directly to specific results.

Legislative reluctance to implement performance budgeting for community colleges and the introduction of incentive funding caused confusion about the differences in the two programs. It also raised doubts about the future of performance budgeting for higher education. Robert Bradley, Budget Director for then-governor Lawton Chiles, conceded the resulting ambiguity at a Joint Meeting of the Board of Regents of the SUS, the State Board of Community Colleges, and the Postsecondary Education Planning Commission in June of 1996. Despite what he viewed as a common commitment to performance funding, disagreement persisted on whether performance-based budgeting should serve as a method of budget justification or a means of allocating funds tied to specific indicators. He explained that the budgeting process in Florida included policies to conserve, to justify, and to allocate funds. Since 1970, performance measures had been integrated into the budgeting process, although budgets had not been allocated on the basis of performance. Performance budgeting did allocate appropriations based on performance, said Bradley, but the key question debated in the legislature and in the sectors of higher education was, "How closely should the allocation of funds be tied to performance?"

Bradley believed this question could be seen from two perspectives — one stressed accountability, the other management. It was the appropriate balance between these two perspectives that remained at issue in the discussions between the governor's office and the Senate. Bradley stated that the Ways and Means Committee of the Senate, from an accountability perspective, wanted to make results the basis of allocating money. The governor, from a management perspective, continued to view performance measures as part of the budget justification process. Bradley concluded his remarks with the comment: "we will get this process right, or we will get out of it" (PEPC June 12, 1996, p. 3).

A Proposed Compromise

Although differences between the executive and legislative branches are inherent in budgeting, deadlock defeats the interests of both parties. When the two branches of state government champion different initiatives, the classic political solution is a compromise that approves both proposals. The Postsecondary Education Planning Commission's *Accountability Review,* issued in October 1996, foreshadowed such a compromise. It described performance-based budgeting and performance incentive funding as complementary rather than conflicting programs. The Commission's analysis of the strengths and shortcomings of each approach suggested that the two shored up and supported each other.

Since initiation of the accountability procedures in 1991, increased attention has been given to performance funding. Increasing pressure for access to postsecondary education coupled with growing demands on available state resources will continue to invite public examination of how these funds are allocated and spent. Performance-based program budgeting (PBPB) represents a natural evolution from the legislative demands for accountability. While PBPB can serve as a useful approach in providing a context for the overall budget, linking every dollar provided to a specific output or outcome would be burdensome effort with questionable benefits. Incentive funding can play a complementary role by focusing a limited amount of state funds based upon the achievement of results identified as high priorities (PEPC October 1996, p. 8).

The PEPC report went on to outline a rationale for combining the two approaches:

> The Commission supports performance based program budgeting and incentive funding as complementary concepts. Performance budgeting should continue to be followed by the State Board of Community Colleges and the Board of Regents in the development of the budgets for

their respective systems. This approach should be based on a standard set of measures with necessary variation due to differences in the missions of the two sectors. The focus should be on system goals and measures, not individual institutions. Performance incentive funding should be maintained as a tool for rewarding desired institutional behavior related to established priorities. It should serve as the basis for allocating a limited share (between two and five percent of new money) of overall funding to individual institutions (PEPC October 1996, p. 9).

The Commission report also stressed the need to integrate the information systems required for accountability reporting, performance-based budgeting, and incentive funding.

The 1997-98 Budget: An Incomplete Compromise Takes Hold

The following year, the Executive Budget recommended both performance-based budgeting and performance incentive funding. It kept both the program and the indicators vague, because the Senate, especially its Ways and Means Committee, opposed performance-based budgeting for the community colleges. The Division of Community Colleges and the college presidents had urged including adult education and nondegree completers in the program for Performance Incentive Funding. This plea echoed complaints by community colleges across the country that plans for performance funding tended to reflect traditional degree programs and full-time students and neglected the nontraditional students and the job-training mission of the two-year colleges. The community colleges would get what they wanted not in the performance incentive funding found in the appropriations bill, but in the Workforce Development Act of 1997. This law created a new performance-funding system for adult and vocational education for school districts and community colleges, but delayed implementation until 1998.

Community Colleges Under PB² Today

Despite the interest in a totally new workforce program, the legislature did continue a performance incentive funding portion of PB^2 for the community colleges, and a dual system of performance budgeting and incentive funding remains today. In the Community College System, incentive funds to be earned under PB^2 in 2000-01 amounted to $8.3

million, or just under one percent of the System's $848 million state budget (see Table 3). Funding for each of the System's 28 colleges is based on its *pro rata* share of the number of points earned in each of five funding pots, putting colleges in competition with each other for the limited resources associated with this program.

Community College PB² Measures and Success Criteria

For the community colleges' incentive funding portion of PB^2, there were five measures that determined the funding distribution for 2000-01. Table 3 contains a historical summary of the incentive dollars allocated under PB^2 from 1996-97 to 2000-01. A fuller explanation of those measures and the associated criteria for success follows.

Completers. Prior to 1999-2000, about forty percent of the funding was distributed among the colleges based on each college's *pro rata* share of the total absolute number of AA and AS degree completers and one half of the total number of certificate completers for the prior academic year. Beginning in 1999-2000, the disbursement was based solely on each college's *pro rata* share of AA degree completers. In 2000-01, the disbursement associated with this measure also considered the number of "dual enrollment" credit hours generated in the prior academic year divided by sixty, the number of credit hours required for an AA degree. The Florida Division of Community Colleges defines dual enrollment courses as courses where credits earned by a secondary school student are applicable to both the high school and postsecondary program (Florida Community College System 2001a, p. 101).

Special Categories. Prior to 1998-99, about forty percent of the funding went to a college based upon its *pro rated* share of the number of completers who: (1) required remediation based on the College Placement Test results (one point for each subject area requiring remediation); (2) qualified as economically disadvantaged under federal guidelines; (3) were reported as disabled under federal guidelines; (4) tested into English for Non-Speakers or English as a Second Language; (5) passed an occupational licensure exam; and (6) were placed in a job identified as critical for Florida's future workforce needs. Colleges received one point for each special category met by the student. Beginning in 1998-99, this measure's share of the overall funding fell to twenty percent. Also beginning in 1998-99, one category was added (whether or not the completer was an African-American male), and categories (5) and (6) were dropped.

Time to Degree/AA Degree Efficiency. From 1996-97 to 1997-98, about twenty percent of the funding went to institutions based on their share of the number of AA degree completers who graduated with fewer than 72 total attempted hours. Although not used from 1998-99 to 1999-2000, this criterion reappeared beginning in 2000-01 and accounted for ten percent of the funding.

Placements, SUS Transfers, and Partial Completers. Beginning in 1998-99, forty percent of the funding (reduced to thirty percent in 2000-01) was distributed among the colleges based upon their share of the number of completers or partial completers who were placed in jobs or transferred to the SUS. The points associated with this measure are calculated as follows:

1. Two points for each completer placed in a full-time job earning at least $10 per hour (reduced to one point per completer beginning in 2000-01).

2. One point for each AA graduate who transferred to the SUS.

3. One point for each student (not counted as a graduate) who transferred to the SUS with 60 or more hours of college credit.

4. 0.75 point for each student (not counted as a graduate) who transferred to the SUS with 45 to 59 hours of college credit.

College Preparatory Program. Beginning in 2000-2001, these funds were distributed based upon each college's portion of the number of students in the Community College System passing the highest level college preparatory, or remedial, course in each subject area.

State Universities and Performance Budgeting

The process used to develop the universities' proposal for performance-based budgeting was long and participatory. It represented an obvious effort to win internal support for what must have seemed a controversial plan to administrators and faculty leaders. A Work Group composed of campus representatives and system staff held five meetings from November 1995 through April 1996. On May 24, 1996, the Board of Regents endorsed the proposed measures and submitted them to the governor's office for approval. Beside twelve outcome measures, they included six output, eight process, and eight input indicators, each arrayed under the three programs of Instruction, Research, and Service (Florida Board of Regents 1996).

Unlike the indicators for the community colleges, those for the SUS, where appropriate, used percentages as well as raw numbers, for example graduation rates rather than the number of degree completers. The outcome measures for instruction included annual earnings of graduates, alumni satisfaction with their education, employers' satisfaction with graduates, licensure exam scores, and degree winners continuing to graduate school. The Instruction, Research, and Service categories each had an indicator on the economic impact of SUS institutions on the community and the state. The output items for instruction ranged from the number of degrees and credit hours to graduation rates for native and transfer students. Those for research ranged from the number of patents, copyrights, and scholarly publications to the dollar volume of sponsored research.

The Office of Program Policy Analysis and Government Accountability (OPPAGA) claimed that the outcome measures for instruction provided a "good idea of what the SUS is accomplishing" and were "well established and measurable," but criticized them as "too numerous." OPPAGA suggested other measures for instruction, such as employment rates and average wages of graduates. It also proposed deleting the economic impact on the community as an indicator for instruction. If the SUS wished to continue the economic impact measure, the staff would restrict the impact to research supported by nonstate funds.

Though officials in the Executive branch did quarrel with some of the measures proposed by the SUS, the real obstacle was the ongoing disagreement between the governor's office and the Senate staff over the best approach for using performance indicators in the budgetary process. Despite their effort to respond to the mandate for performance-based program budgeting, SUS officials seemed relieved with the passage of performance incentive funding in 1996. They feared that performance budgeting might eventually extend to base budgets, although they also questioned the validity and the practicality of tying specific sums to separate outcome indicators. In the end, however, passage of the budget bill with performance incentive funding only fueled rather than finished the dispute over the form of performance funding in Florida. The Governor's Office of Planning and Budget continued to press for performance budgeting, while the staff of the Senate's Ways and Means Committee pushed for performance incentive funding.

SUS Incentive Funding

The SUS experimentation with the incentive funding component of PB^2 was short-lived, lasting from 1997-98 to 1999-2000. The initial incentive-based appropriation under PB^2 was $3.3 million, a miniscule 0.2 percent of the $1.7 billion SUS state budget (Florida Board of Regents 2001, Table 40). Proviso language accompanying the 1997-98 General Appropriations Act called for the Board of Regents (BOR) to develop a procedure for measuring performance and allocating funds among the universities on three indicators: the ratio of baccalaureate degrees to full-time equivalent enrollment; a combined graduation-retention index for first-time-in-college (FTIC) students; and the five-year change in graduation rates of FTIC and AA transfer student cohorts (Ch. 97-152, Laws of Florida, SB 2400, Specific Appropriation 172A). The BOR was to submit a draft methodology to OPPAGA, whose findings were to be incorporated into the final methodology used to allocate the performance incentive fund. Perhaps the beginning of the end for the incentive fund was signaled by the fact that the BOR staff, university representatives, and OPPAGA required the better part of a year to agree on a distribution method (Perkins 1999).

In 1999-2000, the most recent year for which the legislature provided incentive-based funds under the auspices of PB^2, the amount appropriated was $3 million. Allocation among the ten state universities was based on a combination of institutional improvement and the institution's performance in comparison with the System average (Ch. 99-226, Laws of Florida, SB 2500, Specific Appropriation 183B). It used the following indicators and standards:

- Graduation rate for first-time-in-college students, using a six-year rate (performance standard = 60 percent);

- Graduation rate for AA transfer students, using a four-year rate (69 percent);

- Percentage of students graduating with total accumulated credit hours less than or equal to 115 percent of the degree requirement (61 percent);

- Percentage of undergraduate students who enroll in graduate schools in Florida upon completion of the baccalaureate degree (16 percent); and

- Ratio of externally sponsored research and training grant funds to state research funds (BOR to determine the standard).

Rather than rely on incentive funding, the Board of Regents pursued another approach that allowed the universities control over how the funds would be spent and a greater say in how they would be held accountable for results. In FY 1999-2000, under then-Chancellor Adam Herbert, the Regents obtained state funding of $51 million for two special budget initiatives, the first called "Enhancing Undergraduate Education" and the second "Enhancing Graduate and Professional Education, Research, and Extension Service." Individual universities submitted plans to the Board detailing how they proposed to use these funds and how they would measure their own success. Bolstered by the success of this approach in 1999-2000, the 2001-02 request from the SUS again contained the same two budget issues, with funding totaling $114.6 million. By then, however, legislation had scheduled the elimination of the Board of Regents and Chancellor Herbert had resigned. The legislature did not fund the request.

Although the attempt to implement some type of incentive funding plan for the state universities has been less than successful so far, the governor and legislature remain interested in performance funding. Senate Bill 1162, the landmark governance legislation enacted in 2001 with the intent of establishing a seamless K-20 education system, also contains provisions requiring that at least 10 percent of state education funds be conditional on meeting established performance standards. The law requires that the new Florida Board of Education recommend how to implement this requirement, first for state universities, second for public schools and workforce education, and third for community colleges.

The Workforce Development Education Fund

The Workforce Development Education Fund (WDEF), established in 1997, was the decade's final piece of legislation related to postsecondary performance funding and accountability (see Table 4 in

Appendix). In the WDEF, the community colleges realized their desire for substantial performance funding that recognized the career education aspect of their mission (Chapter 97-307, Laws of Florida, SB 1688). The WDEF superseded a smaller but similar initiative, Performance Based Incentive Funding (PBIF), which had been funded by the legislature since 1994 (PEPC 2000). PBIF had been voluntary; the WDEF was not. PBIF involved the distribution of only a few million dollars annually; the WDEF involved considerably more.

In addition to focusing state resources on effective programs addressing priority labor market needs, the WDEF initiative provided a "level playing field" on which both school district-operated area technical centers and community colleges could address local workforce education needs without unfair advantage (Florida Statutes, Section 239.115). A companion initiative, the Workforce Capitalization Incentive Grant program, provided a process wherein the colleges and school districts could compete for seed money for the startup of new career education programs (Florida Statutes, Section 239.514).

Under Workforce Development Funding, institutions receive 85 percent of their prior year's workforce-related appropriation "up front." The remaining 15 percent is distributed based on completion points and placements in high-wage, high-demand fields. After two years of level funding while the incentive portion of the WDEF formula was being developed, the formula was first applied in 1999-2000. The legislature appropriated $722 million for distribution in 2001-02, with Community Colleges receiving $313 million (see Table 5 in Appendix). Taken together, the incentive funding portions of PB[2] and WDEF come to 6.5 percent of total state funding for operations, slightly more aggressive than the guidelines suggested by state financial officers who were invited to a Senate Committee roundtable in March of 1996 (cited in PEPC, October 1996, p. 6).

One consistent criticism of the WDEF has been that the dollar value of each performance point is allowed to "float" from year to year because the dollar value per point in each program — Adult General Education, Vocational certificates, Associate in Science degrees and certificates, and Continuing Workforce Education — is calculated by dividing the total performance points generated into the dollars appropriated. As a result, the institutions might generate more performance points (i.e., perform better), thus decreasing the dollar value per point. The problem is demonstrated in Table 6, which shows that while the total number of points generated by community colleges increased 21 percent between 2000-01 and 2001-02, the total dollars appropriated to community colleges remained virtually unchanged. In its recent report on *Workforce Development Funding Issues* (2000), PEPC called on the Florida Legislature to establish a fixed price per point for each of the workforce funding categories so that performance actually drives the appropriation. This recommendation is yet to be enacted into law.

The Impact of Performance Funding

The 1990s saw much legislative activity relative to accountability and performance funding for higher education in Florida. The beginning of a new decade seems an appropriate time for us to ask, "How are we doing?" For an answer to that question we look first to Florida's community colleges, in light of their more consistent track record with PB^2.

Impact on Community Colleges

The community colleges cite increases in the number of completers associated with the incentive-funded PB^2 indicators as evidence that performance funding is working. The extent to which any such increases can be attributed to the PB^2 initiative, however, is hard to determine. Table 7 contains output counts on the measures that have been in place since 1996-97, the origin of PB^2 incentive funding for community colleges. Although completers from special populations decreased 30 percent from 1996-97 to 2000-01, there were slight increases in AA degree completers and AA students who graduated within 120 percent of the semester hours required for the degree. Table 7 reveals that there was a seven percent increase (from 23,730 to 25,356) in the number of AA degree completers between the first and second years of community college incentive funding under PB^2. With the exception of a spike in 1999-2000, however, degree counts have remained relatively flat ever since. There has been anecdotal evidence that incentive funding initially led to better reporting and cutting red tape so that any student who qualified as a graduate would be reported as such. For example, an institution might now automatically initiate a "graduation check" on all students who have accumulated 60 credit hours or more, rather than requiring students to initiate the degree audit.

Even if these marginal increases are due to better institutional data or more student-friendly policies, the fact remains that, relative to the indicators in place since the advent of PB^2, community colleges have maintained or improved performance while the funding associated with those measures has decreased. In 2000-01, the funding appropriated to PB^2 incentive measures 1-3 was less than half the 1996-97 amount (see Table 3 in Appendix). Since 1996-97, community colleges' performance on the measure of AA degree completers has increased 8.4 percent while the funding associated with that measure has declined by 39 percent.

There have been other improvements since the performance funding initiative was enacted. In 2000-01, AA graduates represented 26.4 percent of full-time equivalent enrollment in Advanced and Professional courses, up from the 24.8 percent they represented in 1996-97. Further, AA degree graduates with fewer than 13 "excess hours" accounted for 34.7 percent of all AA graduates in 2000-01, up slightly from the 33.3 percent they represented in 1996-97. Are these incremental increases attributable to performance funding, better data, institutional policy modifications, or the sweeping articulation and time-to-degree legislation passed in 1995 (Florida Statutes)?

The answer is probably "all the above," but the answer one chooses perhaps does not matter. The reason is that incentive funding for Florida's community colleges still bears a much stronger relationship to enrollment than it does to performance. An examination of the relationship between community colleges' share of PB^2 incentive funds and their appropriation share under the traditional enrollment-based funding approach seems to indicate that there has not been any substantial redistribution of dollars based on performance. Prior to the onset of performance funding, community colleges' state dollars were derived primarily through the Community College Program Fund (CCPF), which was largely enrollment driven. Wright and Spencer (1997) noted that in 1996-97, the initial year of incentive funding under PB^2, a community college's percentage of the CCPF total was highly correlated (r = .93) to its share of the PB^2 incentive fund.

Our more recent analysis of performance funding percentages and institutional enrollment indicates that PB^2 allocations continue to be related more to enrollment than performance. When comparing institutions' share of 2000-01 System full-time equivalent (FTE) enrollment in Advanced and Professional courses to their share of incentive funding under performance measures 1-4 (Table 5 in Appendix), the correlation is r = .976. High correlation is also evident when one looks at the relationship between funding allocations based on remedial program performance and the institutional share of enrollment in remedial courses (r = .914).

Impact on State Universities

The state universities found it difficult to agree on the indicators, the form, and the distribution method of performance funding. These factors, combined with scant appropriations and the university system's pursuit of additional resources primarily through initiative funding — all served to minimize the impact of performance funding on the SUS. Currently, the university system submits performance data to the legislature in support of its annual state budget request. However, the tie between funding and performance remains so loose that, as one anonymous observer quipped, "The only obvious link is that the indicators and the allocations usually appear on the same page of an agency's budget" (Burke and Serban 1998a). The lack of any discernable impact on SUS performance is predictable, given the loose coupling of funding and performance in the present and the miniscule incentive dollar amounts in the past. A recent evaluation of the SUS performance-funding program shows that since 1997-98 the bachelor's degree graduation rates for cohorts of baccalaureate seeking first-time-in-college students have hovered around 60 percent (see Table 8 in Appendix) (Office of Program Policy Analysis and Government Accountability 2001). Retention rates have remained constant at approximately 70 percent. Both rates have remained relatively unchanged since 1990-91 (Florida Board of Regents 2001, Table 56).

A Lack of Leadership

Perhaps the effect of performance funding in Florida has been more cultural than demonstrable. The statewide initiatives of Performance Based Program Budgeting and Workforce Development Education Funding have been successful in changing the focus of discussions about higher education funding in the state from inputs to outputs and, in some cases, outcomes. They have been successful in turning attention from enrollment to completion, and from process alone to process only as it serves the desired result.

Further evidence of the impact of performance funding on the culture of Florida higher education is provided by the fact that 80 percent of the respondents to a Florida-specific question in the survey detailed in Chapter 10 of this volume indicated there has been action or discussion of initiating performance funding for campus units at their institution. There apparently has been more discussion than action, however. While Burke, in Chapter 11 of this volume, posits that stable performance-funding programs should serve dual purposes of external accountability and institutional improvement, PEPC (October 1996) noted that Florida's initiatives have been decidedly less successful at achieving the latter goal. Recent campus visits by OPPAGA to all the state universities, in conjunction with its legislatively mandated evaluation of the SUS performance-funding program, corroborated that only a few institutions had begun developing performance-based mechanisms for allocating funds among internal units (Office of Program Policy Analysis and Government Accountability 2001).

At the heart of the malaise surrounding performance funding in Florida has been a lack of consistent legislative leadership on this issue. In a series of interviews with legislative staff conducted in July 1999, evidence of this surfaced time and time again. One staff member noted that performance funding "has become little more than a compliance exercise." Another opined that "this was always about looking good in the shower" going on to explain that other states were developing performance-funding plans, so Florida's legislative leaders were interested in developing one too. The lack of an ongoing commitment was perceived by another staffer who observed, "I can clear a Committee meeting room in a minute by putting this issue on the agenda." Shortly after the passage of the Government Performance and Accountability Act of 1994, a leader among the community college presidents testified to PEPC that community colleges would like to see as much as 25 percent of their funding based on performance (Massey 1996). Yet, even with the addition of the workforce development initiative, performance-based dollars for community colleges amounted to 6.5 percent of state operating appropriations in 2000-01.

The Future: More Change on the Horizon

To date, performance funding in Florida has been a story of dueling interpretations of statute, add-on initiatives, and changing indicators. The concept of incentive funding gained a stronger hold in the Community College System than in the State University System. Neither system can make a strong case that performance funding has effected real change in terms of additional dollars or improved performance. Yet, despite the shortcomings and false starts, over two-thirds (68 percent) of the Florida respondents to the survey reported in Chapter 10 said that performance funding was either "likely" or "highly likely" to continue.

Indeed, landmark governance legislation, passed in the 2001 Legislative Session with the intent of establishing a seamless K-20 education system, contains yet another provision related to performance funding. Section 9 of Chapter 01-170, Laws of Florida, states that "…at least 10 percent of the state funds appropriated for the K-20 education system are conditional upon meeting or exceeding established performance standards" (Section 229.007(2), Florida Statutes). The language seems to portend incentive funding, with the release of funds predicated on the achievement of specified performance targets.

Passage of this new law leaves many questions still unanswered. Will the new legislation supersede existing initiatives? Will the new program encompass all community college programs, including workforce development? Instruction and research in the SUS have been performance funded in the past. Will the public service aspect of the university mission be performance funded in the future? Perhaps the most basic question is whether the legislature truly possesses the political will to base 10 percent of state appropriations for public higher education on performance. For community colleges, this would come to approximately $92 million of a $925 million annual state budget (Florida Community College System 2001b, Item 1). Previous attempts to introduce incentive funding into the State University System have involved only a few million dollars, but the 10 percent requirement would dictate a performance-based appropriation of some $250 million annually (Florida Board of Regents 2001, Table 41). Finally, will this latest round fired in the direction of performance funding simplify and streamline the processes currently in place, or will it become yet another point in an ever-growing scatter plot of legislative programs and policies? Higher education observers in the Sunshine State will stay tuned while remaining careful to stand out of the line of fire.

Appendix

Table 1

Operating Appropriations to Florida Community Colleges, State Universities, and Department of Education as a Percentage of State Total, 1990-91 to 1999-2000

	Dollars[1]				Agency's Percent of State Appropriations		
	State Appropriations	Community Colleges	State Universities	Total Dept. Of Education	Community Colleges	State Universities	Total Dept. Of Education
1990-1991	$27,743.5	$601.7	$1,454.4	$8,537.9	2.2%	5.2%	30.8%
1991-1992	27,965.3	550.0	1,336.4	7,576.0	2.0	4.8	27.1
1992-1993	29,809.2	540.2	1,348.7	7,749.6	1.8	4.5	26.0
1993-1994	32,496.7	561.8	1,395.1	8,135.0	1.7	4.3	25.0
1994-1995	34,536.4	576.2	1,404.6	8,378.4	1.7	4.1	24.3
1995-1996	33,910.0	581.7	1,448.4	8,590.4	1.7	4.3	25.3
1996-1997	33,561.1	610.2	1,522.1	8,973.1	1.8	4.5	26.7
1997-1998	35,836.8	398.2	1,639.7	9,284.1	1.1	4.6	25.9
1998-1999	36,832.0	419.4	1,724.5	9,648.0	1.1	4.7	26.2
1999-2000	38,511.6	435.8	1,860.7	10,110.9	1.1	4.8	26.3

NOTES: 1 In millions. Constant 1990-91 dollars. Includes general revenue, trust funds, working capital, and state infrastructure. Excludes fixed capital outlay.
SOURCE: *Florida's Final Budget Report and Ten-Year Summary of Appropriations Data 1990-91 through 1999-2000*. Executive Office of the Governor.

Table 2
Community Colleges and State Universities as a Percentage of Florida Department of Education Operating Appropriations, 1990-91 and 1999-2000

	1990-1991		1999-2000	
	Appropriations[1]	%	Appropriations[1]	%
Division of Community Colleges	$601,666,838.00	7.0%	$435,840,035.49	4.3%
Division of Universities	1,454,382,962.00	17.0	1,860,665,165.06	18.4
Community Colleges Plus Universities	2,056,049,800.00	24.1	2,296,505,200.54	22.7
Total Operations, Department of Education	8,537,948,224.00		10,110,916.737.97	

NOTES: 1 Constant 1990-91 dollars. Includes general revenue, trust funds, working capital, and state infrastructure. Excludes fixed capital outlay.
SOURCE: *Florida's Final Budget Report and Ten-Year Summary of Appropriations Data 1990-91 through 1999-2000*. Executive Office of the Governor.

Table 3
Florida Community College SystemIncentive Dollars Allocated Under Performance-Based Budgeting By Performance Measure, 1996-97 to 2000-01

Performance Measures	1996-1997	1997-1998	1998-1999	1999-2000	2000-2001
1. Completers	$5,000,000	$5,000,000	$1,920,000	$3,229,613	$3,037,270
2. Special Categories	5,000,000	5,000,000	960,000	1,614,806	1,518,635
3. Time to Degree/AA Efficiency	2,000,000	2,000,000	N/A	N/A	759,317
4. Placements, Transfers, & Partial Completers	N/A	N/A	1,920,000	3,229,613	2,277,952
5. Completed College Prep Course Sequence	N/A	N/A	N/A	N/A	725,660
Total for All Measures	12,000,000	12,000,000	4,800,000	8,074,032	8,318,834

NOTE: Current Dollars.
SOURCE: Florida Community College System, Bureau of Financial and Business Services, Legislative Funding Summaries.

Table 4

Timeline of Major Policy Developments Related to Postsecondary Education Accountability in Florida

1991	Annual accountability reporting required of public universities and community colleges.
1994	Government Performance & Accountability Act requires all state agencies to submit performance-based program budgets.
	Accountability reporting required of certain accredited, four-year independent institutions.
	Performance-based incentive funding (PBIF) initiative, optional to public community college career education programs.
1998	Community colleges may apply for competitive start-up grants for innovative workforce development programs.
1999	Performance-based incentive funding for community college and school district career education programs becomes mandatory through the Workforce Development Education Fund.

Table 5
Florida Community College System Performance Funding as a Percentage of State Funding for Operations[1]
1996-97 to 2000-01

	1996-1997	1997-1998	1998-1999	1999-2000	2000-2001
Performance Based Budgeting (PB[2]) incenting funding	$12,000,000	$12,000,000	$4,800,000	$8,074,032	$8,318,934
Community College portion of Workforce Development Education Fund (WDEF)		296,042,794	294,593,889	303,864,224	312,706,039
Community College Program Fund (CCPF) minus WDEF	679,175,853	441,064,874	473,044,549	498,777,051	527,374,086
Total	691,175,853	749,107,668	772,438,438	810,715,307	848,398,959
PB[2] as percent of Total	1.7%	1.6%	0.6%	1.0%	1.0%
WDEF as percent of Total		39.5%	38.1%	37.5%	36.9%
Performance amount as percent of Total[2]	1.7%	1.6%	0.6%	6.6%	6.5%

NOTES: 1 Current Dollars.
2 PB[2] plus the 15% of WDEF that is performance-based. The performance formula was first applied in 1999-2000.
SOURCE: Florida Community College System, Bureau of Financial and Business Services, Legislative Funding Summaries.

Table 6
Community College Performance Points Generated and Dollars Allocated
Under the Workforce Development Education Funding Formula, 2000–01 and 2001–02

Distribution Year	Performance Points				Dollars
	Vocational Certificate	Adult General Education	Associate of Science	Total Points	
2001-01[1]	317,621.25	473,914.50	172,143.00	963,678.75	$312,706,039
2001-02[2]	365,980,50	631,025.00	172,202.00	1,169,207.50	$314,826,452
Percent Change	15.2%	33.2%	0.0%	21.3%	0.7%

NOTES: 1 Performance appropriations for 2000-01 are based on 1998-99 completers and 1997-98 completers placed in 1998-99.
2 Performance appropriations for 2001-02 are based on 1999-2000 completers and 1998-99 completers placed in 1999-2000.
SOURCE: Florida Department of Education, Workforce Education and Outcome Information Services.

Table 7
Florida Community College System Performance-Based Budgeting Completers, by Measure
1996-97 to 2000-01

	1996-1997	1997-1998	1998-1999	1999-2000	2000-2001
Completers					
AA Degrees	23,730	25,357	25,357	28,368	25,720
Special Categories					
Needed Remediation	13,857	13,846.5	15,127	11,144	10,180
Economically Disadvantaged	15,024	15,662.0	17,212	10,883	9,820
Disabled	1,229	1,293.5	1,442	960	728
English as a Second Language/ English for Nonspeakers	654	883.0	921	744	790
Special Categories (Total)	30,764	31,685	34,702	23,731	21,518
Time to Degree/AA Efficiency	7,898	8,776	N/A	N/A	8,912

SOURCE: Florida Community College System, Bureau of Financial and Business Services, Legislative Funding Summaries.

Table 8
State University System Performance-Based Budgeting Measures, 1997-98 to 2000-01

Instruction Program PB[2] Measures	1997-98	1998-99	1999-2000	2000-01 Standard
Graduation Rate FTIC Students	61.1%	59.6%	N/A	61%
Retention Rate FTIC Students	71.5%	70.1%	N/A	71%
Graduation Rate AA Transfer Students	68.2%	68.6%	N/A	69%
Retention Rate AA Transfer Students	79.6%	78.6%	N/A	80%
Percentage of Students Graduating at <115% of degree requirements	60.1%	67.9%	68.6%	61%
Pass Rate on Licensure Exams	N/A[1]	N/A[1]	N/A[1]	FY 2001-02 LBR
Percentage Employed at $22,000 or More One Year After Graduation	44.9%[2]	52.4%[2]	N/A	60%
Percentage Employed at $22,000 or More Five Years After Graduation	75.7%[2]	80.1%[2]	N/A	90%
Percentage of Baccalaureate Graduates Enrolling in Graduate School	15.8%	N/A	N/A	16%

Table 8
State University System Performance-Based Budgeting Measures, 1997-98 to 2000-01 (Continued)

Instruction Program PB[2] Measures	1997-98	1998-99	1999-2000	2000-01 Standard
Of the Total Instructional Effort by Level, the Percent of Effort Provided by Faculty				
Lower Level	32.6%	31.8%	32.6%	35%
Upper Level	48.4%	47.4%	47.0%	50%
Graduate	55.5%	53.0%	51.9%	55%
Number of Degrees Granted by Level				
Baccalaureate	34,075	34,529	35,437	37,982
Masters	9,830	10,008	10,036	11,008
Professional	1,128	1,141	1,115	1,255
Doctoral	1,121	1,064	1,138	1,170
Total	46,154	46,742	47,825	51,415
Percentage of Qualified Florida Students Admitted as FTIC Students	94.0%	92.7%	95.4%	2001-02 LBR/95%
Percentage of FTICs Admitted as Alternative Admits	16.4%	17.9%	23.4%	10%

Table 8
State University System Performance-Based Budgeting Measures, 1997-98 to 2000-01 (Continued)

Research Program PB² Measures

	1997-98	1998-99	1999-2000	2000-01 Standard
Externally Generated Research and Training Grant Funds Per State Funded Ranked Faculty (Including Special Units)	$85,243	$94,100	$97,196	2001-02 LBR
Average Number of Articles in Institute for Scientific Information Publication Count Per Ranked Faculty	0.71	0.75	0.72	2001-02 LBR

Public Service Program PB² Measures

	1997-98	1998-99	1999-2000	2000-01 Standard
For Ifas Only — The Percentage of Public Service Projects Where Beneficiaries Is Satisfied With the Extension Assistance	96.7%	98.2%	N/A	98%
Output Measure				
Of Total Faculty Effort Allocated for Public Service, the Percentage Devoted to Public Schools	N/A	N/A	N/A	25%

NOTES: 1 Licensure Performance Measure: Currently licenses may be obtained through the Department of Health and the Department of Business and Professional Regulation (DBPR) for 27 different areas, including, but not limited to, medicine, dentistry, and pharmacy.
These agencies are unable to provide the licensure pass rates by type of license for consecutive years for each area.
2 For 1997-98 and 1998-99 the measure was based on an income of $25,000 per year.

SOURCE: Office of Program Policy Analysis and Government Accountability, from SUS Accountability Reports.

Chapter 8

OHIO'S CHALLENGE: A CLASH OF PERFORMANCE FUNDING AND BASE BUDGETING

Gary O. Moden
A. Michael Williford

Introduction

Pressure from state economic needs and dissatisfaction with a complex budget formula produced performance funding for public higher education in Ohio. Despite its large number of two-year colleges, branch campuses, and regional and comprehensive universities, Ohio trailed national averages in adult degree attainment. It also ranked near the top in the country on tuition and fees, especially for its two-year colleges and branch campuses. The growing appreciation of the importance of public higher education to the economic success of the state in the 1990s led to targeted budgeting that rewarded degree completion, job training, student access, and sponsored research. Underfunded at first, these performance programs became a major source of budget increases for public colleges and universities. Their success presented a problem, since they seemed to come at the cost of diminished support for the core budgets of public colleges and universities. The Ohio experience illustrates the common clash between performance funding and base budgeting.

Higher Education Governance

Until the mid 1990s, decentralization dominated the governance of higher education in Ohio. The state supports a large number of public colleges and universities, and especially branch campuses. It has 23 community and technical colleges with 28 campuses; and eight of its 13 public universities have 24 two-year branches. Each of these colleges and universities has its own Board of Trustees. Public institutions in Ohio enroll over 400,000 students. About 57 percent attend the university main campuses, 10 percent two-year branches, and a third attend two-year colleges.

The pledge of Jim Rhodes — a four-term Republican Governor — to put a campus within twenty miles of Ohio citizens produced tremendous growth in the number of institutions, especially in two-year colleges and university branches. Before Rhodes took office in 1964, Ohio had only six public universities: Ohio State, Ohio University, Bowling Green, Miami, Kent State, and Central State, a historically black institution. The first five universities also had branch campuses in approximately fifteen other communities, identified as within their service areas.

The previous governor and the state legislature created the Ohio Board of Regents (OBOR) in 1963 to coordinate higher education. The Regents develop and oversee state policies for higher education, authorize and approve new degree programs, advocate for higher education, and manage state financial aid programs. The Board of Regents also presents consolidated budget recommendations to the Legislature and allocates annual appropriations to the governing boards of the public colleges and universities.

Search for a Rational Budgeting Model

Recommending a rational budgeting model for public higher education represented a major responsibility for the new Board of Regents. It first proposed a traditional plan that determined base budgets on average costs, and made annual adjustments based on increased enrollments and inflation (Ohio Board of Regents 1992). This enrollment-driven model suited the period of student growth through the 1970s, but college and university presidents and state policy makers feared that the projected decline in students in the 1980s would produce budget cuts for many campuses. To deal with this anticipated problem, the Board of Regents created a task force to recommend changes in the enrollment driven formula (Ohio Board of Regents 1992).

The task force proposed significant changes, along with an uncommon component. It advocated formula budgeting by enrollment levels (lower division, upper division, masters, and doctorate) and by the functions of instruction, academic support, student services, library, and plant operations and maintenance. An unusual feature in the formula guaranteed past funding for each of the enrollment categories, if its number of students dropped below the 1980 level. This guarantee meant that even a university that increased overall enrollment would also receive extra protection funding if enrollments fell in one or more of the enrollment categories. Although the anticipated enrollment decline never occurred, by 1992 the unique clause for protection funding cost the state over $64 million. This anomaly, and the growing complexity of the formula, brought a return to an enrollment-driven model of budgeting, which continued till the mid 1990s (Ohio Board of Regents 1992).

By that time, Republican Governor George Voinovich and legislative leaders began questioning the performance and productivity of public colleges and universities in Ohio. The shift from the "old economy," based on manufacturing and low-skilled workers, to the "new economy," driven by technology and highly educated professionals, had left Ohio in its wake. The governor and legislators recognized that increased access and improved performance of public colleges and universities represented the source of economic success in Ohio. They complained about the failure of public higher education to meet the economic needs of the state and lamented the decline in faculty teaching loads (*Almanac* 1993).

Limited access to higher education and low degree attainment meant that the state could not compete in high-tech industries in its region and the nation. Ohio ranked below the national average in attainment of associate, bachelor's, and graduate degrees. The Board of Regents estimated that the "education gap" in Ohio fell 18 percent below the national average in undergraduate, and 22 percent in graduate and professional, degrees (OBR *Budget Review* 1996). With so many public colleges, universities, and branches, the lack of degree attainment appeared to arise not from campus and program availability but from institutional performance and budgeting practices.

Low levels of state funding and high rates of tuition and fees combined to restrict access to public colleges and universities in Ohio. In addition, depending on the indicator, taxpayer support for higher education in the state ranked near the bottom in the nation. For example, state appropriations as a percent of tax revenues in 1997-98 put Ohio in 42nd place (Halstead 1998). High tuition filled this gap in state support. Ohio ranked fourth in the country on tuition and fees as a proportion of median household income in 1996-97. These charges ran especially high in the two-year colleges, branch campuses, and the regional universities — the institutions intended to expand access. A recent State-by-State Report Card, issued by the National Center for Public Policy and Higher Education, gave Ohio a D- for affordability and a C- for participation or access (Callan 2000).

To change a flawed budget approach and respond to external complaints, the Board of Regents appointed a Higher Education Funding Commission, composed of regents, campus officers, business leaders, legislators, and officials from the executive branch. The recommendation from the Commission proposed to reward colleges and universities for improved performance in priority areas, to maximize the impact of state expenditures for higher education, and to provide greater accessibility for Ohio citizens (Ohio Board of Regents, 1996b).

Performance Funding

The Funding Commission recommended, and the Board of Regents, the governor, and the General Assembly approved a plan for increased funding tied to institutional performance, on indicators stressing access, affordability, and responsiveness to state needs (Ohio Board of Regents April 1996b). The new policy promised enhanced accountability for state priorities, improved efficiency of campus operations, and increased appropriations to higher education. The plan included the following goals:

1. Affordable access to higher education for Ohio's citizens;
2. Higher quality learning experiences;

3. Basic and applied research that contributes to general knowledge and state needs;

4. Services that help citizens, communities, regions, and the state, as well as businesses and industry, meet their goals; and

5. Effective, efficient use of limited resources and accountability for the use of public funds (OBR, *The Master Plan* 1996).

Performance and productivity became part of the budgeting process. This addition represented a significant shift for Ohio, which had relied primarily on enrollment-driven budgeting for public higher education for 30 years.

During that period, the state had experimented with incentive funding, which provides up-front allocations to encourage desired activities in colleges and universities. These programs frequently used competitive awards and often required matching grants. In the 1980s, Ohio launched a series of these initiatives: Academic Challenge, Research Challenge, Program Excellence, and Productivity Improvement. These policies sought to create centers of excellence by concentrating resources on campus strengths in special areas of instruction and research. With the exception of Research Challenge, Ohio abandoned all of these incentive programs when a recession reduced state revenues in the early 1990s (Folger and Jones 1993). Performance funding differed from these earlier efforts by allocating resources for achieved rather than promised results.

The performance funding plan in Ohio began with five separate programs (Ohio Board of Regents, 1996d). The first, *Performance Challenge* brought additional state allocations for achievements on nine service expectations. Although initially intended for all types of institutions, in practice, the program only applied to community and technical colleges and branch campuses. Although the Regents wanted to include the universities, they failed to win agreement on the service expectations for these institutions. The second initiative, *Access Challenge,* provided money to two-year colleges and three regional universities for restraining tuition and fees and increasing enrollments. The third, *Success Challenge,* had two components. It funded universities for the total number of students earning bachelors degrees in four years and additionally for the number of at-risk students who achieved that goal. The fourth, *Job Challenge*, produced funding in proportion to the amount of noncredit job training for which clients paid. The fifth, *Research Challenge,* incorporated the program started in the 1980s that allocated appropriations based on the dollars earned by sponsored research.

Ohio adopted a different strategy for performance funding than other states. Most programs established one pool of performance funds and allocated money based on institutional scores on multiple measures. Leaders in Ohio regarded this approach as another complex budget formula that only few bureaucrats would understand. Instead, they adopted five individual initiatives with separate funding pools and program goals, which simplified the relationship between campus achievements and state allocations. The goals identified state priorities that Ohio would promote with additional funding.

The plan also avoided the mistake made in South Carolina of adopting too many performance measures. Except for the Performance Challenge with nine expectations, the other four had only one or two indicators of institutional success. The Ohio plan addressed some of the practical problems often found in performance-funding programs. It offered clear goals, simple processes, and transparent results. Only the Performance Challenge with its nine, rather vague, expectations failed to follow these requirements.

As might have been anticipated, Ohio soon abandoned the Performance Challenge. Too many measures always engender too many quarrels, especially when funding is small. The other Challenges flourished after an initial period of underfunding. They benefited from focused objectives: increasing access to higher education through the two-year sector; raising graduation rates in the four-year campuses; growing sponsored research at the universities, especially in economic development; and collaborating with local businesses in training activities offered by two-year colleges and branches. These programs also avoided the mistake of imposing a monolithic plan on all public colleges and universities that mandated common indicators on campuses with diverse missions. The Ohio plan tailored its performance challenges to fit the diverse missions of different types of institutions.

Performance Challenge

Policy makers and campus leaders devoted considerable time and effort in creating the service expectations of the Performance Challenge. A statewide task force, "Managing for the Future," created by Governor

Voinovich in 1991, developed the community service expectations for Ohio's 47 two-year institutions in 1993. House Bill 152, passed in July 1993, approved the nine service expectations. In July 1995, the General Assembly provided the first funding for these nine performance measures for community and technical colleges and two-year university branches in Ohio House Bill 117. The bill allocated $1.5 million for 1995-96 and $3 million for 1996-97, based on the following service expectations:

1. An appropriate range of career/technical programs designed to prepare individuals for employment in specific careers at the technical or paraprofessional level;

2. Commitment to an effective array of developmental education services providing opportunities for academic skill enhancement;

3. Partnership with industry, business, government, and labor for the retraining of the work force and the economic development of the community;

4. Noncredit continuing education opportunities;

5. College transfer programs or the initial two years of a baccalaureate degree for students planning to transfer to institutions offering baccalaureate programs;

6. Linkages with high schools to ensure that graduates are adequately prepared for postsecondary instruction;

7. The learning environment provided to students is accessible and the college uses delivery strategies in teaching, which are of the highest quality;

8. The student fees charged by an institution are as low as possible, especially if the institution is being supported by a local levy; and

9. A high level of community involvement in the decision-making process in such critical areas as course delivery, range of services, fees and budgets, and administrative personnel.

Aside from the expectation on low tuition and fees, the other objectives proved difficult to measure.

An Advisory Committee on Service Achievement, appointed by the Regents in 1995, recommended a balanced method of awarding the funds among the nine expectations. Although the Regents accepted the recommendations of the advisory committee in principle, they made significant modifications in the actual allocation of funds. With only a small appropriation available, the Board decided to focus funding on what it considered the most important expectation. The Regents devoted two-thirds of the money for the expectation of low tuition and fees, leaving only a third of the funding for the other eight objectives. The impact of this distribution change meant most of the money went to two-year colleges with larger enrollments. The shift especially hurt regional branches, with higher tuitions and fees tied to those charged by the main campus of their universities (Williams 1996).

In July 1997, the General Assembly again allocated scant funding for Performance Challenge for the two-year sector. It increased the amounts slightly, with $3.1 million for 1997-98 and $3.2 million for 1998-1999. The emphasis continued on Expectation #8, keeping tuition and fees as low as possible. Again, the Board of Regents voted to allocate two-thirds of the funding for this expectation and one-third of the funding for the other eight objectives.

The Chancellor of the Board of Regents at the time, Elaine H. Hairston, described the goals of the Performance Challenge:

> Performance funding is intended to reward campuses for providing services and [ensuring] the quality of those services. That means Ohio's taxpayers, its two-year public colleges, and the students and communities they serve are all winners. Every campus gains a better sense of its existing strengths and the areas for improvement. Students and communities gain improved access to a range of high quality educational services. The public gains a greater accountability in the use of state revenues (OBOR 1996a).

In reality, the lion's share of the funding went to minimize tuition and fees, with little left to improve or increase the full range of services from two-year colleges or branch campuses.

Recent changes transfer funds that had been a part of Performance Challenge to the Access Challenge. With no funds available for Performance Challenge, expectation eight — keeping tuition as low as possible — is supported by the Access initiative, but the other eight service expectations no longer receive resources (Ohio Board of Regents, 1998).

Access Challenge

Access Challenge sought to increase college opportunities for Ohioans by making tuition and fees more affordable. This Challenge limited eligibility to technical colleges, community colleges, university regional campuses, and Central State University (Ohio's historically black college), Shawnee State University, and the two-year technical programs at Toledo, Youngstown State, University of Akron, and the University of Cincinnati. It required campuses to use at least half of the access allocation to restrain the growth of in-state tuition. The other half would support programs and services that raised student recruitment and retention. The Challenge sought to increase enrollments at these targeted campuses.

Jobs Challenge

Jobs Challenge funds noncredit training to improve the job skills of Ohio's workforce. Only two-year colleges participate in this program. In the first two years, the program allocated awards based on a college's share of total qualified expenditures for noncredit job-related training. Presently, the funds support three purposes: to create the needed infrastructure to better serve business and industry; to match the funding of successful campus initiatives in workforce training; and to provide resources to assist strategic industries in collaboration with the Ohio Department of Development (Ohio Board of Regents,1998).

Research Challenge

The Research Challenge incorporates a program begun in 1983, which provides state funding in proportion to the dollars won by public universities from external grants and contracts. This Challenge hoped to garner for Ohio a larger share of the dollars for university research, especially from Federal Agencies. Projects that give a competitive edge to the state's economy receive high priority. Ohio State University and the University of Cincinnati, based on their Carnegie Research I status, consistently earn most of the annual funding (Ohio Board of Regents, 1998).

Success Challenge

The Success Challenge promotes completion of bachelor's programs by degree-seeking undergraduates enrolled at Ohio's public universities. It has two components: timely degree completion for all students and degree attainment by "at-risk" students. Timely degrees meant achieving a baccalaureate within four years. The at-risk portion of the program covered students with financial need identified by receipt of an Ohio Instructional Grant. Two-thirds of the allocation goes for graduation of at-risk students and a third for timely degree completion by all students. The Regents hoped this program would encourage universities to devote more attention to program requirements, course offerings, and additional counseling for all undergraduates, and especially for "at-risk" students. Increasing the graduation rate of undergraduates and the degree attainment of adults represent the ultimate goal of the Success Challenge (Ohio Board of Regents, 1998).

Urban universities benefit most from the at-risk component, since they serve a larger proportion of low-income students receiving Ohio Instructional Grants. Conversely, residential campuses should have an advantage in the other part of the program, since they have a larger share of the "traditional" students, who are more likely to complete their degrees in four years.

The Success Challenge requires that universities submit annual plans to the Ohio Board of Regents describing their use of these funds in encouraging baccalaureate degree completion for all undergraduates and specifically at-risk students. A Board of Regent's publication, "Ensuring Student Access and Achieving Student Success," outlines the problems presented by meeting the goals of the Success Challenge (1999). The Vice Presidents for Student Affairs, whose recommendations shaped the Report, insisted: "only when the institution's administrative, academic, and service structure is transformed into an organizational model committed to student success, will there be significant improvements in student retention and graduation rates" (Ohio Board of Regents, 1999a, p. 7). They saw the Success Challenge as encouraging the universities to become student and learner centered.

The report also presented examples of implemented programs as a way of sharing best practices among the universities. These initiatives included: a one-stop center for all student services; student development centers for teaching study skills and offering counseling services;

and a testing and assessment center for math, English, reading, computer, and analytical skills, tailored to entering freshmen (Ohio Board of Regents, 1999a). The plans suggest a problem with the definition of at-risk students. One part of the Success Challenge supports only students who are financially at risk, while campus retention activities focus on students with academic deficiencies, rather than just those with financial difficulties.

Changing Leaders Bring Funding Increases

Although Chancellor Hairston and the Regents annually recommended large increases for all the Challenge programs, Governor Voinovich and the General Assembly approved only modest funding for most of these initiatives. The appointment of Roderick Chu as Chancellor of the Board of Regents in 1998, and the election of Bob Taft as Ohio's governor in 1999, brought huge increases for the four surviving Challenge Programs. As a former Commissioner of Taxation and Finance for New York State and a managing partner in government practice for Andersen Consulting, Chu had long championed management for results. As executive head of the Board of Regents, he naturally favored performance funding tied to priority results.

Chancellor Chu proposed sizeable budget increases for higher education in general, but he recommended huge increases for the Challenge programs. In 1999–2000, he and the Regents requested an additional $165 million for total state support of $2.5 billion, a 7 percent increase. In the second year of the biennium, 2000-2001, they called for another $159 million in new dollars, a 6.5 percent increase. Approximately 75 percent of the allocation would fund the "Core Funding Plus," which included the instructional subsidy, Access Challenge, Jobs Challenge, Research Challenge and Success Challenge (Ohio Board of Regents, 1998).

In his budget message to the Governor's Office, Chancellor Chu advocated performance funding. He called for a new budget "designed to create a performance-based funding system that best serves state needs" (Chu 1998).

Chancellor Chu claimed this budget would do the following:

1. Help lower tuition;
2. Improve the academic success of Ohio undergraduates;

3. Promote critically needed research in areas that are important to the state;

4. Support job training and economic development; and

5. Help support "K through Life" educational collaboration and reform (Chu 1998).

The first four purposes announced in his budget message pushed the objectives of the Challenge programs.

Governor Taft and the General Assembly clearly endorsed Chu's priority by allocating huge increases for three, and a large increase for one, of the Challenge programs (see Table 1). The budget for the biennium raised funding for Success Challenge by 1,125 percent; Jobs Challenge by 340 percent; Access Challenge by 294 percent; and Research Challenge by 47 percent. Their predecessors had pressed for the Challenge programs, but Governor Taft and the legislature put up the funding to back performance. If performance failed to improve, no one could blame the lack of funding.

Preliminary Assessment

The Challenge programs are too new to evaluate their impact on campus performance, and substantial funding came only in the last two years. The survey of campus leaders by the Higher Education Program

Table 1. State Funding Increases for Performance Challenges					
Challenge	1997-98 (millions of dollars)	1998-99 (millions of dollars)	1999-00 (millions of dollars)	2000-01 (millions of dollars)	Percent Change from 1997-98 to 2000-01
Access	$12.0	$16.0	$39.0	$63.0	425%
Jobs	$0.5	$2.5	$9.0	$11.0	2,100%
Research	$13.0	$15.0	$19.0	$22.0	69%
Success	$2.0	$4.0	$20.0	$49.0	2,350%

of the Rockefeller Institute also suggests that the existence, purposes, and results of performance funding in Ohio remains little known on campus, beyond executive officers (Burke and Lessard 2000). Department chairs, and even deans, expressed much less familiarity with performance funding than senior officers. When asked about the four Challenge Programs, university respondents expressed less familiarity with their Challenge programs of Success and Research than the two-year respondents did with their programs of Access and Jobs. Replies from the universities also revealed much less familiarity with the Success than with the Research Challenge.

As expected, in response to a question about estimated impact on performance, campus leaders from the universities claimed a moderate impact for the Research Challenge but only minimal effect from the Success Challenge. This response seems reasonable, since the former has a much longer history than the latter. Those from two-year colleges and branch campuses cite only minimal impact from their Access and Jobs Challenges. Despite this assessment, more than half of the Ohio respondents viewed performance funding as likely to continue in the next five years.

If the impact on performance remains uncertain, the effect on funding is becoming clear. The Success Challenge, especially, brought large increases to the budgets of Ohio universities. Their leaders are beginning to see funding from Success Challenge as an important and growing part of their total allocation (see Tables 2 and 3). For example, Ohio University's $5.6 million from the Success Challenge in 2000-01 represented a larger increase than it received from the enrollment-based instruction subsidy for 2000-2001. Ohio University Provost Sharon Brehm observed: "the emphasis on graduation rates is likely to increase even more in the future, making it clear that retention and graduation of our students must be a major priority of the university" (Brown 2000, p. 3). Five universities won more that $5 million each from the Success Challenge. As anticipated, institutions with more selective admissions obtained the larger allocations from the component on timely degree completion, while those with open admissions universities did better on at-risk completions. Staff members of the Board of Regents seem pleased with the Success Challenge in particular, since they see it as a breakthrough in securing new funding from the Ohio legislature. In a state such as Ohio with a stable population, performance programs replace enrollment growth as the source of budget increases for the uni-

Table 2. Success Challenge: Timely Baccalaureate Completion

Institution	Institution Type	Distribution FY 2000	Distribution FY 2001
Miami University	Selective	$992,919	$2,422,423
Bowling Green State University	Moderately Selective	$715,014	$1,744,419
University of Cincinnati		$597,054	$1,456,632
Kent State University		$ 444,378	$1,084,149
Ohio State University		$1,396,298	$3,406,549
Ohio University		$1,087,245	$2,652,552
University of Akron	Open Admissions	$272,207	$664,102
Cleveland State University		$198,535	$484,366
Central State University		$33,713	$82,249
Shawnee State University		$38,774	$94,597
University of Toledo		$389,784	$950,955
Wright State University		$313,860	$765,724
Youngstown State University		$149,588	$364,949
Statewide Total		$6,629,368	$16,173,667

Table 3. Success Challenge: At Risk Baccalaureate Completion

Institution	Institution Type	Distribution FY 2000	Distribution FY 2001
Miami University	Selective	$593,789	$1,448,666
Bowling Green State University	Moderately Selective	$1,005,930	$2,454,167
University of Cincinnati		$1,184,524	$2,889,884
Kent State University		$1,476,076	$3,601,182
Ohio State University		$2,710,973	$6,613,960
Ohio University		$1,199,789	$2,927,124
University of Akron	Open Admissions	$1,100,570	$2,685,059
Cleveland State University		$929,607	$2,267,963
Central State University		$184,700	$450,613
Shawnee State University		$146,539	$357,511
University of Toledo		$1,054,776	$2,573,337
Wright State University		$802,912	$1,958,864
Youngstown State University		$868,549	$2,119,000
Statewide Total		$13,258,735	$32,347,330

Table 4. Research Challenge

State Universities	FY 2000 (Actual)	FY 2001 (Actual)	FY 2002 (Projected)	FY 2003 (Projected)
University of Akron	$ 651,629	$ 610,387	$ 673,023	$ 741,922
Bowling Green	$ 276,555	$ 263,314	$ 290,334	$ 320,057
Central State	$ 55,865	$ 96,052	$ 105,909	$ 116,751
University Cincinnati	$3,825,661	$3,786,474	$4,175,030	$ 4,602,441
Cleveland State	$ 352,758	$ 393,442	$ 433,816	$ 478,227
Kent State	$ 712,853	$ 730,944	$ 805,951	$ 888,459
Medical College of Toledo	$ 661,827	$ 730,974	$ 805,984	$ 888,495
Miami University	$ 356,717	$ 389,361	$ 429,316	$ 473,266
Northeastern College of Medicine	$ 142,961	$ 159,992	$ 176,410	$ 194,470
Ohio State	$7,840,201	$9,289,100	$10,242,317	$11,290,856
Ohio University	$ 906,608	$ 943,419	$ 1,040,230	$ 1,146,721
Shawnee State	$ 25,862	$ 28,375	$ 31,287	$ 34,490
University of Toledo	$ 484,397	$ 509,087	$ 561,328	$ 618,793
Wright State	$ 855,945	$ 927,381	$ 1,022,546	$ 1,127,227
Youngstown State	$ 80,367	$ 58,292	$ 64,274	$ 70,854

Table 4. Research Challenge (Continued)

State Universities	FY 2000 (Actual)	FY 2001 (Actual)	FY 2002 (Projected)	FY 2003 (Projected)
Private Universities				
Case Western Reserve	$ 1,458,975	$ 1,692,690	$ 1,866,388	$ 2,057,456
University of Dayton	$ 456,663	$ 409,156	$ 451,142	$ 497,327
Subtotal	$ 1,915,638	$ 2,101,846	$ 2,317,531	$ 2,554,784
Statewide Total	$19,436,382	$21,568,440	$23,725,284	$26,097,812

versities. Most of the funding from the other initiative for the universities, Research Challenge, went to Ohio State, with lesser amounts to the University of Cincinnati.

The Access Challenge, to a lesser degree, brought additional allocation to the Community Colleges (see Table 5). The 15 community colleges won over 70 percent of this funding. Allocations to regional campuses and technical colleges grew much more slowly, while those for access universities actually declined in 2000–2001. Although the community colleges also benefited most from the Jobs Challenge, universities and their branches received a larger share of allocations than in the Access program.

Strengths and Weaknesses

Performance funding in Ohio had a weak beginning in the mid 1990s with legislative adoption of Performance Challenge for the two-year sector. It suffered from too little funding, vague objectives, and uneven implementation. These problems led to its demise. The other Challenge initiatives benefited from targeted objectives, although the Success Challenge had a problem with the definition of at-risk students. The rapid growth in funding for these four Challenges should encourage campuses to alter their activities to achieve the desired results. The total dollars devoted to the Access, Success, Jobs, and Research Challenges soared from $25 million to $145 million in just four years.

As so often happens, the strengths of public policies often represent corresponding weakness. If the limited objectives of the four performance Challenges represent strengths, their restricted goals also constitute weaknesses. By focusing on a few goals, they inevitably excluded important goals that are often targeted for performance funding in other states. Even the increased funding for the Challenge programs, while welcome, presented problems when they appeared to come at the cost of base budget for colleges and universities. So long as Ohio could afford substantial increases for both base budget and performance programs all went well. But declining state revenues and mandated school funding in 2001 forced restraint in resources for public higher education and produced a conflict between the performance programs and base budgets for colleges and universities.

Table 5: Access Challenge

Annual Increases	FY 1998	FY 1999	FY 2000	FY 2001
Universities	$ 869,868	$ 1,073,338	$ 1,508,862	$ 1,466,687
Regional Campuses	$1,305,006	$ 2,268,150	$ 3,213,190	$ 3,947,762
Community Colleges	$3,163,062	$ 5,489,430	$10,496,333	$17,523,885
Technical Colleges	$ 662,064	$ 1,169,084	$ 1,789,605	$ 2,050,314
Statewide Subtotal	$6,000,000	$10,000,001	$17,007,989	$24,988,648

Table 6: Jobs Challenge

	FY 2000 (Actual)	FY 2001 (Actual)	FY 2002 (Projected)	FY 2003 (Projected)
Universities	$1,232,518	$ 946,030	$ 954,348	$ 1,163,771
Branches	$1,569,268	$ 1,786,739	$ 1,812,733	$ 2,023,851
Community Colleges	$2,655,099	$ 3,155,867	$ 3,179,196	$ 3,957,081
Technical Colleges	$ 786,979	$ 892,364	$ 903,155	$ 1,047,904
Targeted Industries	$2,500,000	$ 4,198,694	$ 4,198,694	$ 4,198,694
Adult Workforce Ed. Centers	0	0	$ 2,500,000	$ 2,500,000
Statewide Total	$8,743,864	$10,979,694	$13,548,126	$14,891,301

Performance Reporting

The interest of Governor Taft in improving the performance of public colleges and universities led him to propose performance reporting as well as to increase support for the Challenge programs. On November 23, 1999, he wrote Chancellor Chu requesting that the Ohio Board of Regents produce an annual performance report for Ohio's public colleges and universities. He set three general goals for the report: to provide taxpayers a justification for funding higher education; to inform potential students to improve college choice; and, finally, to provide comparative information for institutions. Although the governor left the choice of the performance indicators to the Regents, in consultation with campus leaders, he stressed the importance of student success and expressed concerns about "reports showing that graduation rates for some students in our universities are significantly below those of similar institutions" (Taft 1999, 1).

The Regents issued the first performance report in December 2000 and plans to update it annually (Ohio Board of Regents 2000b). It includes the following indicators:

1. First-year student experiences: remediation; persistence; exposure to full-time faculty;

2. Numbers of degrees and certificates awarded;

3. Time and credits to degree;

4. Graduation rates;

5. Mobility and performance of transfer students;

6. Employment outcomes of graduates;

7. Research funding received by universities;

8. Workforce training; and

9. Tuition and fees.

The performance report includes a number of objectives already funded in the performance Challenges, such as degrees awarded, sponsored research, time to degrees, workforce training, and tuition and fees. Conversely, the report incorporates indicators not found in the Challenge programs, such as retention, graduation, and transfer rates. In addition, the Challenges do not address degree and certificate award for two-year colleges and regional branches. The report also departs from the Challenges by presenting common measures for two-year colleges and universities. It remains uncertain at this time whether the funded Challenges in the future will include this feature and the additional indicators. A move toward both common and more indicators in the Challenge programs would constitute dramatic changes, which would bring them closer to performance-funding programs in other states. A move in that direction would cover more of the objectives of higher education by including more indicators, but it would cause a loss of focus. A shift to more common indicators for all types of colleges and universities would also diminish the current emphasis on the different missions of two-year campuses and state universities.

A possible clue on new indicators for funding is Governor Taft's complaint about the disparity of graduation rates between Ohio's universities and their national peers. Currently, the Success Challenge funds the number of degrees but not the graduation rates. The governor also expressed deep interest in "the success of Ohio's college and university students" (Taft 1999, p. 1). Many programs of performance funding include an alumni survey as a method for assessing student success. Although the performance report does not include such a survey, work on one is already underway.

The Clash of Performance Funding and Base Budgeting

Whatever the possible changes in the Challenge components, Governor Taft's proposed budget for the next biennium (FY 2001-2002 and 2002–2003) signaled strong support for performance funding to the state legislature and to higher education (see Table 7). He recommended the following increases for the next two years for the Challenges: Access (157%), Success (31%), Jobs (159%), and Research (131%) (Ohio Governor's Office 2001).

In contrast, the governor proposed only a 4 percent increase for the two fiscal years in the State Share of Instruction, which represents the total funding for academic activities. In addition, the Executive Budget recommended a total biennial allocation for higher education of only 7.6 percent, which would barely cover inflation. These increases fall far below the recommendation for a 145 percent rise in funding for the four Challenge programs. This proposal continues the recent trend of declining increases for the "old" type of enrollment budgeting and big gains for the newer initiatives of performance funding. If the Legislature accepted Governor Taft's recommendation, performance funding would

Table 7. Executive Budget Recommendation

Challenges	FY2001	FY2002	% Change	FY 2003	% Change From 2002
Access	$ 65,268,000	$ 77,268,000	18.4%	$ 90,268,000	16.8%
Success	$ 48,741,000	$ 53,615,100	10%	$ 58,976,610	10%
Research	$ 21,568,440	$ 23,725,284	10%	$ 26,097,812	10%
Jobs	$ 10,979,694	$ 13,548,125	23.4%	$ 14,891,302	9.9%
Subtotal	$ 146,557,134	$ 168,156,509	14.7%	$ 190,233,724	13.1%
State Share of Instruction	$1,648,846,940	$1,681,450,071	2%	$1,715,288,155	2%
Total	$2,218,407,110	$2,290,436,420	3.2%	$2,391,155,839	4.4%

receive over $190 million by 2002-2003. Clearly, the performance Challenges would prosper at the expense of base budgets.

This trend concerned Chancellor Chu. He and the Regents had rec-ommended to the governor huge increases for the Challenge programs for the biennium, but they also urged 11.5 percent in additional funding for the State Share of Instruction and 29.8 percent increase in the total budget for higher education (see Table 8). Chancellor Chu lamented the shift in funding from core budgets to new initiatives.

> We appreciate the support Governor Bob Taft has given higher educa-tion in his executive budget and his recognition of the importance of a number of initiatives recommended by the Regents (The Ohio Plan, the Application New Economy Partnership, the Challenge line items).... I am concerned, however, that the current economic forecasts are forcing the Governor to issue a budget that 'robs Peter to pay Peter.' The pro-posed higher education funding does not keep up with the expected cost pressures and enrollment growth.... In real dollars, the higher educa-tion budget is being cut and resources are being taken from basic core support to fund other initiatives (Chu 2001, p. 1).

This shift from base to performance funding echoes the adage, "Be careful what you ask for, since you might get it." Ohio's performance Challenges are getting more than the Regents want, especially since its increases are coming at the expense of base budgets. Ohio's recent ex-periences illustrate a potential problem of performance funding. Educa-tional leaders sell, or at least accept, performance funding as an "add on" to base budgets, which represents their first priority, in the hope of winning increased overall funding. But governors often find perfor-mance funding more attractive than base budgets. In funding for results, they pay for what they want. In core allocations that support current op-erations, they are seldom sure what their money buys. The crunch for performance funding comes when "robbing Peter to pay Peter" means that cuts in current operations results in retrenching programs and staff that creates public opposition from students, parents, and communities, which often brings legislative opposition to these special funding pro-grams. Legislators champion performance funding, but their support wanes when budget problems force reduction in programs and staffing, which generates public opposition, especially in their home districts that often hold a public college or university.

A declining economy, restricted revenues, and the need for a huge increase in school funding to avoid an adverse court ruling led the Ohio

Table 8. Regents Recommended Budget

Challenges	FY2001	FY2002 Regents	% Change	FY 2003	% Change from 2002
Access	$ 48,741,000		54.7%	$ 138,000,000	36.6%
Success	$ 21,568,440	$ 57,812,493	18.6%	$ 66,269,523	14.6%
Research	$ 10,979,694	$ 43,136,880	100%	$ 64,705,320	50%
Jobs	$ 146,557,134	$ 27,000,000	145.9%	$ 32,800,000	21.5%
Subtotal	$1,648,846,940	$ 228,949,373	56.2%	$ 301,774,843	31.8%
State Share of Instruction	$2,218,407,110	$1,735,411,404	5.2%	$1,843,874,617	6.3 %
Total		$2,666,899,743	20.2%	$2,923,578,474	9.6 %

legislature to make tough budget choices for the biennium, 2001-02 and 2002-03. One of the difficult choices involved deciding between the State Share of Instruction, which represented the core funding for all public campuses, and the Challenge Grants. A struggle occurred between the House and the Senate. The latter wanted to shift $40 million from the Access Challenge as proposed by the House to the State Share of Instruction (Leonard 2001). In the Joint Conference Committee, the State Share of Instruction won the battle with the Challenge programs but not by much. Funding for the Challenge programs declined by 4.6% but the State Share of Instruction rose only 0.6% over the previous year. The slight increase in funding for the Share of Instruction and the decline in the Access Challenge led the legislature to remove the six percent annual cap on tuition increases. Ohio State planned for a 15 percent increase and the other universities and Community Colleges also seemed likely to approve large raises in tuition. Despite the reduction in the Challenge Grants in the coming biennium, their total funding at $139.5 million at a time of bad state budgets reflects a sizeable commitment from the General Assembly to performance funding, though less than the Governor and even the Board of Regents.

Clearly, the state of Ohio has made a significant commitment to performance funding that increasingly came at the expense of base budgets for public campuses. A slowing economy and falling revenues in Ohio will continue the crunch between core budgets and performance funding. Performance funding in Ohio faces two challenges. For the Challenge programs to succeed, they must soon show that they can improve results in student access, degree attainment, job placement, and sponsored research. They must also accomplish these challenging goals without the perception that they come at the cost of base budgets for public colleges and universities. These two requirements represent tall tasks. The history of performance funding in Ohio, and other states, also suggests that targeted funding for improved results is no substitute for insufficient state support for public higher education.

Table 9. Joint House/Senate Budget Resolution

Challenges	FY2001	FY2002	% Change	FY 2003	% Change from 2002
Access	$ 65,268,000	$ 62,268,000	-4.6%	$ 62,268,000	0%
Success	$ 48,741,000	$ 47,041,000	-3.5%	$ 47,041,000	0%
Research	$ 21,568,440	$ 20,000,000	-7.3%	$ 20,000,000	0%
Jobs	$ 10,979,694	$ 10,100,000	-8.0%	$ 10,200,000	0%
Subtotal	$ 146,557,134	$ 139,409,000	-4.9%	$ 139,509,000	1%
State Share of Instruction	$1,648,846,940	$1,659,011,727	0.6%	$1,668,611,581	0.6%

Chapter 9

PERFORMANCE FUNDING IN SOUTH CAROLINA: FROM FRINGE TO MAINSTREAM

Joseph C. Burke

Introduction

Other states used performance funding for small course corrections in budgeting. South Carolina launched a "Star Trek voyage to uncharted territory" by mandating funding based "entirely" on campus performance on a long list of 37 indicators (Musick 1995). Despite dire predictions of disaster, a reconstituted South Carolina Commission on Higher Education (CHE) at first moved toward that destination with what seemed warp speed to academics. At the controls were legislators and business leaders, who relished the prospect of South Carolina becoming the first state in the nation to fund public higher education totally on performance. A safe flight appeared to demand a plan that preserved full performance funding in theory, while somehow providing for campus budget stability in practice. It also required a strategy that kept all of the indicators in place, while reducing the number actually applied.

For several years, the Commission and its staff tried to reconcile these conflicting goals by redesigning the controls without changing the course. Finally, the CHE, in consultation with campus leaders, concluded that it had to alter the state's unique course to assure a safe landing. It abandoned funding based entirely on performance and slashed the number of indicators applied for allocations.

Background

Performance funding in South Carolina emerged in the mid 1990s amid a bitter battle between the Commission head and campus presidents. This conflict — and the shortcomings of higher education in South Carolina compared to nearby states in North Carolina and Georgia — produced a growing dissatisfaction in the legislature with the leadership of both the Commission and the campuses. Traditionally, South Carolina had one of the most decentralized systems of higher education governance in the country. Presidents dominated decision making on campus and directed policy making in the state capital, with little interference from the CHE. This imbalance of power persisted until the late 1980s, when demands largely from business leaders called for more accountability and better performance led the General Assembly to increase dramatically statewide coordination. As often happens, when higher education fights internally, the state steps in.

Eleven separate boards govern the state's three research universities, nine teaching institutions, and five two-year regional campuses. The State Board for Technical and Comprehensive Education (SBTCE) coordinates the activities of the sixteen two-year technical colleges, which also have local governing boards (McGuinness 1994; 1997). Many legislators believed that the number of public institutions far exceeded the need in a state with stable population and enrollments. Some communities had both a two-year branch of the University of South Carolina and a technical college; and several public four-year campuses competed for the same students. Constrained revenues and competing demands from welfare, corrections, and K-12 education meant that South Carolina could not supply the resources required for a nationally competitive system of higher education.

Increased Coordination and New Leadership

In the late 1980s, constrained resources and competing demands, coupled with growing complaints about performance, led to legislative mandates that diminished campus autonomy and increased statewide coordination from the CHE. The legislature took the lead in this "weak governor state." The progression of reform mandates followed a familiar national pattern. They began with outcomes assessment, moved to performance reporting, and finally turned to performance funding.

As executive head of the CHE, Fred R. Sheheen led the reform movement and made the Commission a force in the state capitol and on public campuses. A former newspaperman, aide to a U.S. senator and governor, and the brother of the powerful speaker of South Carolina's House of Representatives, Sheheen had promotional skills and powerful connections. As a member of the CHE and its former Chair, he also knew higher education and its problems. But the strengths of strong leaders are often their weaknesses. Bright, assertive, and outspoken, Sheheen courted controversy, which caused opposition (CHE Staff 2001). Campus presidents and trustees viewed the growing influence of Sheheen and CHE as an insidious intrusion on institutional autonomy.

Clark Kerr was only half right in his quip about campus attitudes toward college presidents. Campuses do want a leader who roars like a lion in the capital but squeaks like a mouse on campus. What Kerr failed to say was that governors and legislatures want no other lions roaring in their capitols. Their cries for a dynamic leader in higher education are often followed by their outcries when one appears. Sheheen roared loudly in both places, making enemies in both quarters. He suffered the frequent fate of State Higher Education Executive Officers, caught between the conflicting desires of the campuses and the demands of the capitol.

Sheheen and the Commission lost their power base in the fall elections of 1994, when Republican David Beasley won the governor's office; and his party captured control of the lower House, ousting Sheheen's brother as speaker. Faced with a CHE filled with members appointed by his Democratic predecessor, the governor appointed reform-minded Republicans when the Legislature reorganized the Commission.

A New Leader and a New Commission

If the bell tolled for Sheheen and the old CHE, it also rang for presidents and trustees, although few of them at first seemed to hear it. At its 1995 session, the General Assembly reorganized the CHE and set the stage for performance funding. The new approach to funding proved a bipartisan proposal. A Democrat, Nikki Setzler, took control of the process. As chair of the Senate Education Committee, he moved quickly to reorganize the CHE, which eventually removed Sheheen and moved to reform public higher education. Setzler achieved these goals by passing Act 137. It reorganized the membership, expanded the powers of the Commission, and authorized a Joint Legislative Committee to conduct a comprehensive review of public higher education.

Act 137 displeased campus leaders, for it gave the reconstituted CHE more, rather than less, power. If the law hit the campuses hard, it dealt a body blow to Sheheen. The law changed the title of the chief executive of the CHE from commissioner to executive director, declared the new position not subject to the state's civil service act, allowed dismissal without cause, and restricted severely the appointive power of the director.

By delaying the convening of the reconstituted CHE until July 1996, Act 137 turned the existing Commission and Sheheen into "lame ducks" for over a year, leaving policy making for higher education to Setzler and his Joint Legislative Committee. During this critical period, his Committee developed recommendations for performance funding and the future directions of higher education; and the General Assembly wrote nearly all of them into law. The Joint Legislative Committee of four senators, four members from the House of Representatives, and four business leaders, naturally chose Setzler as its chair. The Committee proposed a radical change in funding policy with little input from national experts or campus representatives (Joint Legislative Committee 1996).

The Findings in their Report issued on February 1, 1996, detailed complaints that demonstrated dissatisfaction with the performance of both the Commission and the campuses. The Committee looked to the CHE to reform and — if necessary — to restructure public higher education in South Carolina. But it was a new Commission with "strong representation by the business community" that would exercise these expanded powers. The Joint Committee recommended that the recon-

stituted CHE should submit a performance-funding plan to the General
Assembly by January 1, 1997, and fully implement the new funding formula by July 1, 1999. It suggested that no institution should receive reduced funding through this formula until its full implementation in
1999-2000.

Though the Committee Report included most of the details of the
subsequent legislation on performance funding, it omitted the most
controversial provision — funding based entirely on performance. The
Report did propose the nine "Success Factors" or general goals, in priority order and prescribed 36 of the 37 performance indicators later
adopted in legislation.

The General Assembly enacted these recommendations with little
discussion or media attention. The existing Commission, scheduled to
expire on July 1, remained neutral on the Bill. Sheheen and the Council
of Presidents publicly supported performance funding, and tried to reduce the amount to three to six percent of state appropriations to campuses. Privately, the presidents disliked the bill, but they feared that
opposition might be viewed as resistance to performance review. They
also clung to the belief that the performance funding would somehow
include support for their base budgets and hoped acceptance would
bring better budgets from the legislature (CHE Staff 2001).

Act 359 made two changes in the Joint Committee Report — one
minor, the other momentous. The former added a 37th indicator. The
latter inserted one word that gave performance funding in South
Carolina its most controversial feature. It required that the CHE develop a performance funding formula based "entirely on performance."
Adding that one word — "entirely" —made performance funding the
most contentious issue facing higher education in South Carolina and
the talk of policy makers and education leaders across the country. The
37 prescribed indicators — double the number in any other state — also
proved controversial (see Appendix).

Although unique in their range and number, the indicators represented
the traditional items found in performance reporting and funding programs across the country (Burke 1997a). The South Carolina plan arrayed the 37 indicators under nine Critical Success Factors placed in
priority order: *Mission Focus, Quality of Faculty, Instructional Quality,
Institutional Cooperation and Collaboration, Administrative Efficiency,
Entrance Requirements, Graduates' Achievements, User-Friendliness of
Institution*, and *Research Funding* (see Appendix).

Critics inside and outside South Carolina claimed correctly that the indicators were too numerous for effective implementation, especially since many of them lacked available data to judge performance. On the other hand, these critics ignored the purpose of Senator Setzler and his colleagues. They sought to reform public higher education rather than reward individual institutions for specific results on a few state priorities. The size and scope of the indicators supported their purpose of systemic reform. A shorter list would have been more efficient, but it would have left important activities unreformed. In addition, allocating all funding on performance demanded many indicators.

The Commission Takes the Challenge

The signing of the legislation in May 1996 shifted the action from the General Assembly to the newly constituted Commission on Higher Education. The Legislature had mandated performance funding and prescribed the indicators, but left to the new CHE the formidable task of developing the critical details. They included the operational definitions, indicator measures and weights, success standards, data sources, and funding mechanisms. If the task was difficult, the deadline was daunting. The law gave the new Commission little more than six months to develop the complex procedures for an unprecedented program. The tasks and the timing would have challenged an experienced Commission; and the reconstituted CHE had mostly new members. Controversy had also undermined confidence in Sheheen, who remained unpopular with the campus presidents and trustees and out of favor with legislative leaders and the new CHE members.

If the new majority of the CHE was inexperienced, their leaders were dedicated to performance funding as a lever to reform public higher education in South Carolina. Roger Whaley, a banker and the vice chair of the Joint-Legislative Committee, became vice chair of the Commission; and Austin Gilbert, the new CHE chair and a construction contractor, had also served on the Joint Committee, which proposed performance funding. Critics chided South Carolina as the only state to fund public campuses based entirely on results, but Whaley relished the prospect and the notoriety. He believed the new CHE had to dominate the development of performance funding in the beginning, or campus opposition would nibble away at its critical provisions. Both he and Austin Gilbert thought that public higher education in South Carolina needed shaking up from the top by the Commission, if it were to compete with other state universities. A "top down approach" clearly characterized the first phase of performance funding in South Carolina.

The commitment to change became apparent at the first meeting of the reconstituted CHE on July 3, 1996. Unexpectedly, the CHE member who represented the Boards of Trustees of the research universities proposed that the "new Commission" should advertise for the "new position" of "executive director." The slap at Sheheen may have pleased campus leaders. However, the next decision on the process for developing a performance-funding plan displayed a corresponding lack of confidence in campus leadership. The new CHE chair made it clear that the business community would dominate. Without consulting campus leaders or the CHE staff, Gilbert appointed a Steering Committee to oversee the process, headed by Whaley, and decided on two stages of special committees to develop the funding plan. The first stage would use three Task Forces — Academics, Administrative Management, and Planning/Institutional Effectiveness — to develop the measures, definitions, and methods of reporting for the 37 indicators. The second stage scheduled four Sector Committees, organized by institutional type, to develop indicator weights, performance standards, and the funding methodology (CHE Special Reports, No. 1 and 2, 1996).

The appointments of chairs and members of the three Task Forces demonstrated the confidence in business managers and distrust of campus leaders. The new Commissioners seemed to see the academic community as the problem, so they looked to the business community for the solution. Business leaders chaired each of the Task Forces and formed a majority of their members (CHE Special Reports, No. 1 and 2, 1996). Whaley controlled the process and the decisions.

Given the time constraints, the three Task Forces did a credible job. The real flaw was their failure to seize the opportunity for constructing performance measures that could cushion the impact of the performance indicators. The two most interesting elements in their Reports were the incorporation of "best practices" as criteria for several of the indicators and the enhancement of the CHE's authority as overseer of the funding plan and evaluator of campus performance (Task Force Academics Final Report 1996). The Steering Committee, on September 24, 1996, swiftly approved the Task Force Report, with no major changes (Steering Committee Minutes 1997).

Whaley and Gilbert, obviously pleased with the official Reports from the Task Forces, used a similar approach for setting the indicator weights, benchmark standards, and funding mechanisms, with one fateful exception. They organized the work by sectors rather than by subjects. Technical colleges, regional two-year branches of the University of South Carolina, teaching institutions, and research universities each had its own committee. If strict compliance with the law ruled the Task Forces, self-interest drove the Sector Committees.

Other difficulties plagued the Committee's work. They had to submit their Reports to the Steering Committee by December 3, 1997, leaving little more than a month for their work. The Guidelines prepared by the CHE staff also left them too much latitude, by allowing each group to propose its own sector weights for indicators, without providing a safe guard of minimums or maximums (Steering Committee Minutes 1997). In addition, Roger Whaley soon left to take a job with his bank in another state. The loss of his strong leadership undoubtedly contributed to the lack of control by the Steering Committee during the Sector phase of the process.

The final Report from the Research Sector Committee devoted 60 percent of the total weight to just four of the 37 indicators: SAT Scores, Faculty Compensation, Research Grants, and Faculty Credentials, which reflected campus interests. In contrast, many of the indicators important to legislators received weights of one percent or less, such as mission focus, faculty evaluation, and employment rates. The Committee permitted each University to select its own "aspirational" peers, with nearly all coming from the prestigious American Association of Universities (AAU). In fairness, the Report of the Joint Legislative Committee had encouraged these aspirations by insisting that these three campuses should become Research 1 Universities in the Carnegie Classification. By opting for aspirational peers with much better budgets than South Carolina's research universities, the Sector Committee hoped to win an increased share of state funding (Research Universities Sector Committee Report 1996).

The Teaching Sector Committee took the opposite tack. It spread the weights fairly evenly across the 37 indicators and emphasized student-related activities (Research Universities Sector Committee Report 1996). Making only minute distinctions between performance levels represented its flaw. For example, an institution automatically got 60 percent of full funding for the expenditure of funds to achieve the campus mission, whatever its allocations. A number of the other indicators showed small ranges in points between superior and poor performance (Research Universities Sector Committee Report 1996).

The Technical College Sector Committee not only set low weights for some indicators, it also endorsed questionable standards of performance (Minutes of Organizational Meeting of South Carolina Commission on Higher Education, July 3, 1996). For example, it weighted licensure test scores for professional programs at less than two percent and gave full funding for indicators on academic and administrative spending, so long as the allocations received a formal review and audit. But those problems paled before its recommendation of implementing only three of the 37 indicators in the first three years of performance funding (Minutes of Organizational Meeting, CHE 1996).

The recommendations from the Research and the Technical College Sectors presented the Steering committee with a dilemma. Rejecting the Sector recommendations would anger campus officials; submitting them would alienate legislative leaders. The CHE decided that half a report was better than a full report that could destroy the Commission's credibility. On January 6, 1997, it sent a report containing the measures, definitions, and methods of reporting prepared by the Task Forces and promised to submit the weights, benchmarks, and funding formula in June, using the Sector Committee reports as guiding principles (CHE, Performance Funding: A Report to the General Assembly 1997).

The submission to the Legislature proposed a phased implementation of the indicators, 14 in the first year, 26 in the second, and 37 in the third. The schedule stemmed mostly from data availability, but it also suggested a strategy of starting with the more traditional and least controversial indicators.

Phase Two: Campus Consultation and Covert Changes

The "top down phase" of performance funding ended with the submission to the General Assembly. Now a "bottom up" phase began. The Report to the General Assembly promised to consult broadly in developing the full plan. From mid-January 1997 through mid-March 1998, the CHE and its staff held an estimated 200 meetings, largely with campus representatives to resolve the political and practical problems of implementing performance funding (CHE Staff 2001). The political strategy became clear. The concept of "100 percent funding" and the integrity of 37 indicators remained untouchable, but everything else became negotiable. The job of developing an acceptable performance-funding plan fell to the CHE staff and the Planning and Assessment Committee, now led by a new vice chair of the Commission (Commission on Higher Education, Performance Funding Time Line 1997).

The change in chairs of the committee directing performance funding symbolized the shift in strategy. Dalton B. Floyd, a lawyer accustomed to negotiation and accommodation, replaced Roger Whaley, who had pushed performance funding with the fervor of a founding father. Whaley looked and acted like a banker, impressive in presence and aloof in manner. He focused on results and became impatient with process. His actions showed a single-minded devotion to enforcing Act 359, which he had helped author as vice chair of the Joint Legislative Committee. Floyd had the tweedy look of a professor and the skills of a negotiator. Warm, personable, and talkative, he communicated well in consultations with campus leaders. His recent appointment to the CHE also proved advantageous, since he had not been embroiled in the controversies surrounding the reorganization of the Commission and the ouster of Fred Sheheen, who was replaced in June 1997. The new executive director of the CHE, Rayburn Barton, also helped to dampen the contentiousness of performance funding by assuming a supportive but less assertive role than his predecessor.

The search for solutions to the problems of performance funding followed two separate tracks. The first sought a funding formula for campus allocations; the second, a rating system for scoring institutional performance. The funding model developed an institutional funding requirement based on the budgets of regional or national peers (Steering Committee, March 27, 1997). The model generated higher resource requirements than the current budgets in the Palmetto State, since national and even southern state averages of expenditures by sectors exceeded those in the South Carolina. By incorporating sector differences into the resource requirement, this plan negated the need for different sector weights on each of the indicators. It seemed to satisfy both campus desire for budget stability and the legislative insistence on funding based "entirely" on performance (Steering Committee Agenda Attachments, March 27, 1997).

In parallel with the work on a funding formula, the CHE staff consulted on a performance rating system with institutional representatives. Its final form gave each institution a performance score for each indicator based on a five-point scale: 1. Noncompliance; 2. Needs Improvement; 3. Satisfactory Progress; 4. Meets Goal; and 5. Exceeds Goals. The scale later added a sixth score for "Exemplary Performance" and included a zero for noncompliance, after a probationary period. The rating plan called for institutions to report their current level of performance and to propose their annual benchmarks for performance on each indicator. The CHE would develop sector benchmarks and approve institutional benchmarks. At the end of the assessment period, institutions would report their performance on each indicator; and the CHE would rate their effort from one to six. This approach appeared to give something to all parties. It allowed campuses to propose their own benchmarks, which could protect institutional diversity. It also transformed the sector benchmarks from the minimalist goals proposed by the Sector Committees into the aspirational or directional goals for each institutional type.

The CHE senior staff combined the two elements of the funding formula and the rating system into a Resource Allocation Plan (RAP). It first determined sector-funding requirements, using the average cost per student of national or regional peers by institutional type. Then it divided the state appropriation into sector pools. Institutions competed for funds within, but not across, sectors. Although the possibility for large reductions or increases in funding remained possible in theory, under this plan, they appeared unlikely in practice.

Floyd presented the preliminary plan at the Steering Committee Meeting on March 11, 1997 (Steering Committee Minutes 1997). The Minutes claimed: "It was the consensus of the group that the RAP as presented is a workable one with some room for modification." An account of the meeting in *The Chronicle of Higher Education* presented a different picture (Schmidt 1997). That article described a contentious meeting filled with constant complaints from institutional representatives. In response, the usually mild-mannered Austin Gilbert, the CHE Chair delivered a blunt warning to the presidents. If they wanted more money from the Legislature, they had better agree to a credible performance-funding plan.

Though the campus presidents from the beginning had carefully avoided taking a public position against performance funding, the *Chronicle* article brought their opposition into the open. The chair of the Council of Presidents claimed the campuses were at the mercy of legislators who knew little or nothing about higher education "and do not appreciate how difficult it is to define, much less measure, what a 'good' public college does." A Technical College president believed Act 359 appeared "with too much haste, with too little research, and with an effort to measure far too many indicators." The president of the University of South Carolina questioned whether the state could validly measure performance of faculty members at the three public research universities. These presidential comments displeased Senator Setzler. The senator told the *Chronicle* reporter why he had set such a short deadline in Act 359 for the development of the funding plan. "He wanted to carry out the major reforms in higher education and management before higher education could resist the changes with the old refrain about not being able to measure the performance of colleges and universities" (Schmidt 1997).

Despite presidential complaints, the Commission approved the plan and sent it to the General Assembly on May 1 in the final weeks of its 1997 session. With the time for adjournment approaching, the Senate decided to include the performance funding as a proviso in the appropriations bill rather than propose separate legislation. The proviso approach meant that the performance funding would have effect only during that fiscal year, unless renewed the following year. The real advantage of a proviso rather than separate legislation became apparent only later. A separate act would have frozen most of the performance-funding plan in legislation. The proviso left the CHE free to revise the measures, benchmarks, and the Resource Requirement Plan.

Most of the parties should have been relieved, if not pleased, with the results. Senator Setzler had protected the fundamentals of his law on performance funding, while consenting to changes that could soften the impact on institutions. The CHE had shown courage in rejecting the Sector Reports that would have undermined the credibility of the Commission, while creating a resource requirement and rating system that responded to at least some of the campus concerns. Presidents recognized the efforts to mitigate the impact of Act 359, while worrying that institutional and sector benchmarks would bring big budget cuts for some campuses and budget instability for all public colleges and universities. The proviso method allowed the CHE and its staff to respond to these campus concerns.

Phase Three: Adjusting the Controls

The CHE staff consulted frequently with institutional groups to devise acceptable sector benchmarks on the 14 performance indicators for the first year. Staff accepted most of the institutional benchmarks as proposed by the campuses, even though many set performance levels that the institutions had already met or exceeded (Steering Committee, Minutes of Meetings. Performance Funding 1997). The performance scores for the first year (1997-98) showed the effects of these efforts to cushion the impact of performance funding (Commission on Higher Education, Score Card, 1997-98). Most institutions earned a four, five, or six on nearly all of the indicators. Unfortunately, the Technical Colleges scored much lower than the other sectors. The high raw scores of the institutions in the Research, Teaching, and Regional sectors led the CHE to reduce their ratings to an average of 85 percent for an adjusted score, while retaining the raw scores of the Technical Colleges.

The first scoring in August of 1997 confirmed the worst fears of huge swings in state funding among sectors and campuses. Although only a trial run, since no campus could lose funding for three years, it foreshadowed unacceptable results. Twenty-one points separated the top score of the Lancaster branch campus from bottom rating of Williamsburgh Technical College. The low scores of nearly all of the Technical Colleges proved especially alarming. Moreover, the first round of scores came on only 14 indicators; and the more difficult items started in 1998 and 1999. Worse still, the experts felt that the high rating of Lancaster appeared to have little relation to the quality of its performance (Trombley 1996).

If the first score cards rang alarm bells within the CHE and the higher education community, the reverberations also reached the General Assembly. Although the Joint Legislative Committee had openly spoken of performance funding as a way of closing campuses, and Act 359 had seemed to endorse this intent, few observers believed that legislators would allow campus closures (Trombley 1996). Rumors circulated that the ratings disturbed John Drummond, the president pro tempore of the Senate and chair of its Finance Committee. This senator had Lander University in his home district; and leaders of that campus feared performance funding might hurt their institution. Although the General Assembly had passed Act 359, it would not be the first time that a legislature had approved a reform in theory and then rejected it in practice when it hurt their home district. During the first phase of performance funding, the CHE had to resist changes to Act 359 to avoid legislative ire. It could use legislative insistence to win campus acquiescence. Now it had to find further ways of modifying the mandate's impact to mollify both campus presidents and legislative leaders.

The first year's scoring had revealed huge gaps between the high- and low-performing campuses, despite lenient benchmarking and generous ratings. As the Steering Committee prepared for years two and three, it adjusted the impact of the indicators by revising the measures that determined their achievement. Many of the changes stemmed from absence of available data, but they also reduced the rigorous requirements of a number of the measures adopted by the Task Forces.

The CHE Chair, Austin Gilbert, described this strategy of leaving the funding and indicators unchanged while altering the measures. "…It's like the knob on your radio," he said. "If it's not right, you adjust it but you don't remove it…" (Trombley 1996). While officially complying with the law in practice, the changes made performance funding in South Carolina much more flexible than Act 359 appeared to mandate, and certainly more than campus leaders or national experts perceived.

Performance Funding had from the beginning reflected a conservative approach by proposing just 25 percent of the additional monies in 1997-98 to performance and 75 percent of the new money in 1998-99. Governor Beasley undercut this cautious approach with his budget proposal for 1998-99, Year Two of performance funding. He recommended no increases for public colleges and universities and proposed devoting $250 million of their state appropriations to performance funding. The General Assembly passed this proposed budget. The budget had less fiscal impact than it seemed, since Act 359 stipulated that no college or university could receive less funding based on performance until 1999-2000. The real impact was psychological. Rumors circulated that public higher education would receive no increases until the advent of full performance funding in 1999-2000 (CHE Staff 2001). This possibility disheartened campus leaders, who had at least hoped that performance funding would increase state appropriations. It also highlighted the performance ratings of 1997 as a trial run for full performance funding.

The CHE and its staff again tried to respond without challenging "100 percent funding" or changing indicators. They attempted to prevent the wide variations in scoring by accepting lower institutional benchmarks for many of the Technical Colleges for scoring in Year Two. This strategy corrected the variations in the first year of scoring, but it undermined the integrity of the benchmarking process. Many campus leaders believed that the scores in the second round owed more to "benchmark bargaining" by campus negotiators than to institutional performance (Commission on Higher Education, Score Card, 1998-1999). This time, 15 of the

16 technical colleges increased their scores, more than half of them by ten or more points.

Although the funding shifts involved only small sums, because of the guarantee against campus losses until the following year, the results were frightening. The second year scoring showed a gap of 21 points between the highest and the lowest scoring campus. Under full funding, the latter would have lost from 10 to 15 percent of its state support. The results of the Year Two scoring revealed problems of budget stability and campus equity.

Phase Four: Radical Revisions

Again, the Steering Committee and the CHE staff consulted sector and campus representatives for solutions. In the fall of 1998, the Commission members and staff held seven sector meetings and individual sessions with 16 campuses. The meetings exposed serious concerns about measures, benchmarking, scoring, and the funding model, now called the Mission Resource Requirement (MRR). Most campus leaders claimed that performance funding could not work without additional state money. Many complained that some measures duplicated goals, while others had contradictory purposes. The problem of benchmark gaming — or setting easy to achieve targets — received wide criticism. The six-point scale of scoring, said some participants, widened rather than narrowed the swings in campus funding. Several participants believed the MRR had become the problem rather than the solution, since without new money it merely reallocated inadequate funding based largely on enrollment. Clearly, campus leaders believed that merely "adjusting the knobs" could not solve the problems of performance funding.

When the Commission members and its staff got the same message from Colloquium of Commission and campus representatives, they abandoned the strategy of incremental changes for real reform in March 1999. The new plan shifted from "100 percent funding" to a limited "Performance Incentive Pool." The Pool included:

1. One-half of the new funds beyond the appropriations for the current year;

2. 1.75% of the current allocation plus one-half of the new year appropriation distributed by the MRR; and

3.   Funds derived from institutions within the sector that scored below the achieved category.

Institutions would receive 1 percent of their allocations for "Achieving," 3 percent for "Exceeding" and 5 percent for "Substantially Exceeding" their institutional benchmarks. They would lose 3 percent of their allocations for "Not achieving" and 5 percent for "Substantially Not Achieving" the standards.

With the revisions to the funding formula, the CHE once again had to consider the legislative reaction first and the campus response second. CHE staff felt that they had the funding side where they wanted, although they privately conceded that the number of indicators remained a problem (CHE Staff 2001). For the first time in the long road of implementing performance funding, the changes had altered a major tenet rather than a minor nuance of the law.

The proof of whether they achieved the appropriate balance would depend more on the campus scoring than on campus performance. The results of the third round of scoring on all 37 indicators in April 1999 suggested the changes had worked. No campus failed to achieve and none substantially exceeded its goals. Fifteen achieved and 18 exceed their standards.

Nearly every action by the CHE on performance funding kept one eye on the reaction of Senator Setzler. Shortly after the adoption of the limited funding pool, the senator got the General Assembly to authorize an Ad Hoc Committee — which he chaired — to review "the implementation of performance funding...to determine if the intent of the Legislature is being met based on the methodology adopted by the Commission on Higher Education" (Appropriation Bill 4775, 2000-01). The composition of the Ad Hoc Committee was similar to the Joint Legislative Commission that proposed performance funding — two members from each House and two business and/or citizen representatives. Concern about the reaction of Setzler and the Ad Hoc Committee diminished when the group failed to issue a preliminary report in December. Any anxiety ended when Setzler lost his chairmanship of the Education Committee when a party switch of a Democrat member gave the Republicans the control of the Senate.

As worries about Setzler's reaction began to subside, the CHE moved to reduce the 37 indicators, although campus leaders had long advocated and the Business Advisory Council had previously recommended reductions. The CHE had already diminished the burden of the indicators in several ways short of cutting their total number. It first addressed the problem of so many indicators by assessing only for compliance a number of measures once scored and benchmarked. It also combined several indicators, which reflected similar goals. Finally, the CHE assessed many of the indicators, not annually but on a two- or three-year cycle.

The Commission and staff consulted with campuses by asking each sector to recommend their preferences for indicator cuts; and the CHE staff recommendations responded to the general concerns about the indicators from all sectors. They proposed eleven common indicators for all sectors, but allowed one unique sector indicator and one selected by each campus from its strategic plan (CHE Staff 2000).

The revision addressed many of problems of the performance indicators. Aside from reducing their unworkable number, it eliminated duplicate and hard-to-evaluate indicators and those used for compliance rather than scoring. Other changes provided welcome flexibility with more institutional choice and emphasis on sector and institutional missions. The Research Sector would focus on Research, the Teaching institutions on teacher education, the Regional Campuses on student transfers, and the Technical Colleges on job training.

If the proposal increased campus autonomy, it also diminished external accountability. The revised indicators looked more like those from a Not Mandated than a Mandated and Prescribed plan of performance funding. The changes clearly reflected the concerns of administrators and faculty members rather than the interests of legislators and business leaders, and seemed more faculty than student friendly. They ended funding for the indicators on faculty performance and posttenure reviews, faculty teaching loads, faculty community and public service activities, continuing education programs, availability of faculty to students outside of the classroom, and transferability of credits among institutions. The proposal also dropped the indicators on the use of best management practices and the elimination of unjustified duplication and waste in administrative and academic programs. It kept job placement and employer feedback only for Technical Colleges and applied student transfers only to the Regional Colleges, which seem to absolve the research universities and teaching institutions of responsibility for jobs for their graduates and for admitting transfer students. The plan also applied the indicators relating to teacher training only to the Teaching Sector and not to the Research Universities that had teacher education programs.

With active campus support and without obvious legislative opposition, the CHE approved the indicator Changes on February 1, 2000. This act removed the last unique feature of performance funding in South Carolina and moved its program from the fringe to the mainstream. The new plan called for the CHE to continue monitoring performance on the abandoned indicators, with the possibility of reinstating them should campus performance not meet acceptable standards.

In June 2001, at the request of the General Assembly, the Legislative Audit Committee reviewed the process and the results of performance funding in South Carolina (Legislative Audit Counsel 2001). Its Report reached the following conclusions.

1. Although the law required the CHE to allocate all funds based on performance beginning in FY 1999-00, the amount affected reached only three percent annually in the last two years.

2. The legislature should change the provision for funding based entirely on performance, since a simulation of its effect by the Council showed that allocations for campuses could vary as much as 30 to 40 percent annually.

3. The current performance-funding measures do not provide a comprehensive assessment of institutional quality.

4. The state should not use the current performance-funding system as the sole determinant of institutional funding, because of "changes and volatility of the system, problems in measurement, the narrow focus of the indicators, and the use of some indicators that may be inappropriate for some institutions."

5. Act 359 envisaged "the reduction, expansion, consolidation, or closure of an institution as a result of institutional performance, but the possibility of this occurrence is remote."

6. Inadequate state funding of higher education had hindered the effort to implement performance funding and to improve institutional performance.

The officials of the CHE issued a short statement saying they "substantially agreed" with the Report. In effect, the Report said what the Commission and staff could not say. It validated the efforts of the CHE to alter an unworkable mandate to a realistic approach to performance funding. State lawmakers did not comment on the Report, but at the time of its issuance, they were hurrying to complete a budget that would cut funding for higher education up to eight percent.

Impact of Performance Funding on Sector Results

It is still premature to judge the impact of the program. A funding policy not yet five years old could hardly change performance of colleges and universities, especially since no campus could lose state support for three years. CHE staff believes performance funding has sharpened sector and campus missions and the survey results confirm that conclusion (CHE Staff 2001). CHE staff also contends that, without the indicator on Post-Tenure Review, few if any campuses would have developed and implemented this controversial policy. These results represent challenging changes, since they run counter to campus preferences (see Appendix B for statistical trends in performance).

On the other hand, some of the greatest improvements in performance came on indicators long favored by faculty. The Research Sector now has 100 percent of its academic programs accredited or on track for accreditation, and the other sectors are moving rapidly toward that goal. The Research and Teaching sectors raised the SAT and ACT scores of incoming students and all sectors increased average faculty salaries, although they vary little from legislatively appropriated cost-of-living increases. The percent of administrative expenses also declined in the Research, Teaching, and Technical Sectors and increased only in the Regional Group. Sponsored research soared at the Research Universities and produced a large percentage increase on a small base in the Teaching sector. Student/faculty ratios dropped as intended in the Teaching and Technical Colleges, but rose in the Research universities and Regional campuses.

The results on the least desirable indicators on campus often revealed less success. For example, teaching loads declined, except for a slight increase in the Technical Colleges. Despite an indicator to cut class size at the lower division, the Research and Teaching universities exhibited small increases. Graduation rates declined slightly or remained stable in all but the Research Universities, which showed a substantial increase. The unpopular indicator of time-to-degree proved the exception. The Research and Teaching group reduced the credit hours acquired by graduates.

The Teaching and Research Sectors responded well to the indicators related to teacher training and school reform. Their pass rates on the professional part of the national teachers exams improved and they produced large increases in graduates entering critical teaching fields and in financial support for reforms in teacher education. The Research and Technical groups expanded considerably the credits granted in continuing education courses to meet local needs. But pass rates on professional licensure exams fell in the Technical, while remaining stable in the Research and Teaching sectors.

Of course, performance funding can neither claim full credit for improved performance, nor should it accept the entire blame for declining results. Outside influences, such as economic and budget conditions, obviously had an impact. During its first four years, performance funding remained a work in progress, with phased implementation of indicators and changes in performance measures, benchmarks, scoring scales, and funding formula. The true test will come in the next few years, when the funding pool and the revised indicators have time to take effect. The past record suggests that results on the indicators retained for funding are the ones more likely to improve. Only time will tell whether those results will meet the educational needs of South Carolina and its citizens.

Conclusion

Coordinating boards of higher education are caught continuously in the middle between the conflicting demands from capitols and campuses. They have a foot in each camp. They are public representatives appointed to protect the public interests and campus advocates obligated to voice academic concerns. Performance funding, like all policy questions in public higher education, demands a delicate balancing of external societal interests with internal professional concerns. After an initial moment of unquestioning enthusiasm that insisted on strict compliance, the CHE began to play the traditional role as an honest broker for a balanced program of performance funding. Such a program had to spur improved performance for all public campuses, while safeguarding campus diversity and budget stability. In four years, South Carolina moved from the fringe to the mainstream of performance funding. This effort is not complete, for performance funding in South Carolina remains a work in progress, with its precise provisions in doubt.

Whatever the changes to come, South Carolina has aborted its Star Trek voyage into the uncharted territory of 100 percent funding. It tried to complete the fantastic voyage safely by constantly readjusting the controls without altering course. Two rounds of campus scoring showed that full funding would produce unacceptable shifts in funding among campuses. These virtual voyages persuaded the CHE to adopt a less adventuresome flight plan.

Appendix

1. Mission Focus

- 1A, Expenditure of Funds to Achieve Mission (combined with scored indicator 5A)

- 1B, Curriculum Offered to Achieve Mission (scored)

- 1C, Approval of Mission Statement (scored)

- 1D, Adoption of Strategic Plan (combined with scored indicator 1E)

- 1E, Attainment of Goals of Strategic Plan (scored)

2. Quality of Faculty

- 2A, Academic and Other Credentials of Professors and Instructors (scored)

- 2B, Performance Review System for Faculty (assessed for compliance with standards)

- 2C, Post Tenure Review of Tenured Faculty (assessed for compliance with   standards)

- 2D, Compensation of Faculty (scored)

- 2E, Availability of Faculty to Students (combined with indicator 2B, which is assessed for compliance with standards)

- 2F, Community and Public Services Activities of Faculty (combined with indicator 2B, which is assessed for compliance with standards)

3. Classroom Quality

- 3A, Class Size and Student/Teacher Ratios (assessed for compliance with standards)

- 3B, Number of Credit Hours Taught by Faculty (assessed for compliance with   standards)

- 3C, Ratio of Full-time Faculty to Other Full-time Employees (assessed for compliance with standards)

- 3D, Accreditation of Degree-Granting Programs (scored)

- 3E, Institutional Emphasis on Quality of Teacher Education (scored)

4. **Institutional Cooperation and Collaboration**

- 4A, Sharing and Use of Technology, Programs, Equipment, Supplies and Source Matter Experts within the Institution, with Other Institutions, and with the Business Community (scored)

- 4B, Cooperation and Collaboration with Private Industry (combined with scored indicator 4A)

5. **Administrative Efficiency**

- 5A, Administrative Costs as Compared to Academic (scored)

- 5B, Use of Best Management Practices (assessed for compliance with standards)

- 5C, Elimination of Unjustified Duplication (combined with indicator 5B, which is assessed for compliance with standards)

- 5D, Amount of General Overhead Costs (combined with scored indicator 5A)

6. **Entrance Requirements**

- 6A, SAT and ACT Scores (combined with scored indicator 6B)

- 6B, High School Standing, GPA, Activities (combined with indicator 6A into a single scored indicator)

- 6C, Post-Secondary Non-Academic Achievement (assessed for compliance with standards)

- 6D, Priority on Enrolling In-state Students (assessed for compliance with standards)

7.   Graduates' Achievement

- 7A, Graduation Rate (scored)

- 7B, Employment Rate (scored)

- 7C, Employer Feedback (scored)

- 7D, Scores on Examinations (scored)

- 7E, Graduates Who Continue Education (scored)

- 7F, Credit Hours Earned of Graduates (assessed for compliance with standards)

8.   User-Friendliness of the Institution

- 8A, Transferability of Credits (assessed for compliance with standards)

- 8B, Continuing Education Programs (assessed for compliance with standards)

- 8C, Accessibility to the Institution (scored)

9.   Research Funding

- 9A, Financial Support for Reform in Teacher Education (scored)

- 9B, Public and Private Sector Grants (scored)

Summary

23   Indicators scored singly or in combination on an annual basis

14   Indicators assessed for compliance with standards singly or in combination

---

37   Total indicators

Chapter 10

PERFORMANCE FUNDING: EASIER TO START THAN SUSTAIN

Joseph C. Burke

Four states with performance funding programs in 1996 had abandoned them by 1999. The experiences of Arkansas, Colorado, Kentucky, and Minnesota illustrate both the attractiveness of performance funding in theory and its difficulty in practice. Although each has a different history, collectively they highlight the problems of performance funding — changing government leaders and state priorities, poor design and hurried implementation, and state prescription and campus opposition.

Arkansas: A Collaborative Process Produces a Surprising Product

The Department of Higher Education in Arkansas wanted to avert a threatened mandate of performance funding. "We saw what was coming," said a Department Officer. "We did it to ourselves before they could do it to us" (Arkansas Department of Higher Education 1996).

Agency officials also wanted to avoid the Texas failure, where campus opposition had helped scuttle performance funding. These dual demands appeared a "mission impossible." They required a method of getting skeptical campus leaders to approve a tough program acceptable to the governor and the Legislature that improved quality and increased productivity. The strategy selected let presidents and chancellors dominate the Committee that developed the funding plan. This improbable process produced an unlikely product. Instead of proposing a plan that protected campus self-interest, the Committee astonished government leaders by preparing a program that addressed their major concerns.

Governance

Higher education in Arkansas in the late 1980s and early 1990s exhibited the common conflict between campus prerogatives and state coordination. Declining state revenues and competing demands for funding, and dissatisfaction with the productivity and performance of public higher education led to increased state mandates and expanded coordination. Legislation in 1989 had strengthened the authority of the Department of Higher Education (DHE) and the State Board of Higher Education (SBHE) over the policies and programs of public colleges and universities (McGuinness 1994). In practice, their statutory powers clashed with the constitutional authority of the six university governing boards. The Boards governed both multiple and single campuses. University of Arkansas had five campuses and Arkansas State University and Southern Arkansas University each had two units. Arkansas Tech University, University of Central Arkansas, and Henderson State University had their own boards. The ten community and ten technical colleges also had local boards of trustees (McGuinness 1994).

Between 1989 and 1993, the Legislature passed, and the governors approved, a drumbeat of mandates, including outcomes assessment, performance reporting, and productivity standards (Acts 1989 No. 98, 244, 267; 1991 No. 856; 1993 No. 376, 874, 1141). Hope for additional money, as well as fear of state mandate, explains the participation of campus leaders in proposing performance funding. Governor Jim Guy Tucker and the Legislature provided no increase for higher education in 1993-94 and only a 2.6 rise in 1994-95 (Hines 1994, 1995).

In 1992, the president of a council of campus heads and the director of the DHE appointed an Institutional Productivity Committee, dominated by presidents and chancellors to develop a performance-funding plan. The Committee Report astonished legislators and state officials, who could not believe that a group of presidents and chancellors would develop a document that stressed "institutional accountability and educational quality" and "centered on improving the state's investment in higher education and campus commitment and service to its constituencies" (Arkansas State Board of Higher Education 1997).

The proposed indicators were tough, especially in comparison with Missouri and Tennessee, which also had Not Mandated Programs (see Table 1). Nearly all of the indicators reflected the external concerns of state officials more than the internal concerns of the academic community (Burke 1998b; Chapter 4). The Report applied the same indicators to both two- and four-year institutions and allowed no campuses choice of indicators.

Although efficiency indicators obtain the highest total weights, quality won some attention. The success standards for nearly all of the indicators involved either meeting statewide goals or significant levels of institutional improvement. Contrary to the usual complaints about setting the bar too low, the levels required for significant improvement seemed quite a stretch, although the statewide goals appeared easier to achieve. Scores on licensure and exit exams used national rather than state averages.

Most programs in other states avoided campus competition for performance money by returning unearned funds to the state treasurer or by using them for programs that benefited all public higher education. Arkansas took the opposite task, because the DHE wanted to retain all of the allocated money for performance funding. Funds not earned by campuses went to others with high performance, which pitted colleges and universities against each other.

The Report recognized the impossibility of implementing immediately all of the indicators. For the first biennium, it recommended funding to campuses for development of an alumni/employer survey, a phase-in of the program review process, and limited licensure exams for four-year institutions to nursing and teacher education. It also proposed a central fund for development of rising junior exams in general education as recommended by campus academic officers. The proposal to delay graduation rates for baccalaureate campuses till 1998-99, but to start them for two-year colleges in 1995-96, seems strange since leaders

Table 1. Arkansas: Performance Funding Indicators and Weights	
Indicator	*Weight*
Retention (39.0%)	
Overall	24.375%
Minority	4.875%
Developmental	4.875%
Transfer Two-Year to Four-Year	4.875%
Quality (29.625%)	
Rising Junior Exam	15.000%
Licensure/Exit Exams by Discipline	4.875%
Academic Program Excellence (Program Review)	4.875%
Alumni/Employer Surveys	4.875%
Efficiencies (17.25%)	
Program Productivity	7.500%
Administrative Costs	4.875%
Teaching Load	4.875%
Workforce Development (6.75%)	
Noncredit Business & Industry Training	4.500%
Credit Business & Industry Training	2.250%
Diversity of Faculty/Staff (4.875%)	
Graduation Rates (2.5%)	
Overall	2.000%
Minority	0.500%

of two-year colleges considered such rates unfair measure for their institutions.

Productivity Funding in the 1995-97 Biennium

Delighted with the Report, the governor and Legislature approved $10 million in 1996-97 for performance funding and an additional 15 million in 1997-98. In April 1995, Governor Tucker signed Act 1029 creating a Productivity Fund, which constituted an endorsement of the program by the governor and Legislature, although not a mandate.

It is always easier to get campus presidents to support a proposal for increased funding than to retain their backing after the actual allocations. In FY 1995-96, the universities received 70 percent of the productivity fund, while the two-year colleges obtained 25 percent (five percent went to the development of the alumni/employer survey). Although this distribution reflected the division in enrollment, it disappointed the leaders of two-year colleges who had long complained of underfunding. The flagship campus at Fayetteville obtained 29 percent of the funding. (As the only campus with a rising junior exam in place, it received most of the first year funding for that indicator.) In contrast, the University at Little Rock got only 7 percent of the performance money. Its chancellor complained to the governor that the formula slighted part-time students and the special mission of urban campuses. Arkansas State University, which received less than the average performance funding for the system, appealed to the powerful speaker of the House, who appeared before the SBHE to appeal for a change in its budget allocation for performance. Despite these pressures, the Board backed the staff on the budget allocations. Efforts to include a component for graduate studies and research also failed due to disagreements between the Flagship at Fayetteville and the other universities (Arkansas Department of Higher Education Staff 1996).

In spite of these controversies, the DHE staff believed that even the start of performance funding changed the approach of the presidents and chancellor to the budget hearings. Formerly the presidents and chancellors talked mostly about campus funding and the budget formula. Now they spoke of plans to serve students and to improve retention. The DHE staff obviously hoped that, in time, performance funding would change attitudes and activities on campus.

A New Governor and New Priorities

When the Whitewater scandal drove Governor Tucker from office in July 1996, the lieutenant governor, Mike Huckabee, succeeded him. At first proponents of performance funding thought he would support the program. As a Republican, he considered increased productivity appealing, but found tax cuts irresistible. The new governor's proposal for a large tax rebate naturally shifted the concern of the academic community from protecting performance funding to defending the base budgets of public colleges and universities. Governor Huckabee failed to get his tax rebate, but this failure did not alter the fate of performance funding.

The Demise of Performance Funding

No single development killed performance funding in Arkansas. It suffered from an accumulation of antagonisms against the Department of Higher Education and the State Board. The expansion of authority of the Department and the Board had long disturbed campus leaders and their governing boards. Legislators soon repeated the complaints that the Department was overstaffed, intrusive, arrogant, and controlled rather than coordinated campus activities. These themes echoed the attacks on state boards of higher education across the country (Hollander 1994; Lively 1993).

These conflicts brought down the director of the Department of Higher Education and helped scuttle performance funding (Schmidt 1997). The architect of the attack was Nick Wilson, a powerful state senator, long time critic of the Department, and a vocal champion of the community and technical colleges. The presence of Black River Technical College in his district undoubtedly colored his attitude and his actions. Wilson expressed disdain for the Department and the Board and described the staff in unprintable language. He drove Diane Gilleland, long considered his nemesis, from the office of director of the Department of Higher Education. Governor Huckabee replaced her with Lu Hardin, chair of the Senate Education Committee.

Pushed by Wilson, in February 1997, legislation cut the Department's budget by 30 percent and its staff by 20 percent (Arkansas Code 1987). It also abolished the old State Higher Education Board and replaced it with a Higher Education Coordinating Board. The law required the new Board to include three trustees from two-year colleges, three from four-year universities, and six nominated by business and industry. The requirement of equal representation for two-year colleges responded to the repeated complaint that the old Board had underfunded and not understood these institutions.

The new law also brought down performance funding. It required the new Coordinating Board to cease further allocation of funds based on performance and to develop a new formula for funding public colleges and universities. The legislature, again led by Senator Wilson, also responded to the complaints from two-year colleges by distributing the existing performance funds equally between two- and four-year institutions. Performance funding was more of a victim than the culprit in its demise. The unpopularity of the Department, its director, and of the State Board caused the legislative backlash.

Campus presidents and chancellors had become Wilson's accomplices in dismantling the Department and the Board and discarding performance funding (Schmidt 1997). The payoff for their support came with increased appropriations. The 1997 legislative session raised the funding of colleges and universities by about 15 percent for biennium (*Almanac* 1997). The chancellors and presidents had never been proponents of performance funding. They abandoned the project when support from the new governor seemed lukewarm and the legislature declared war on the Board and the department.

Inherent flaws in the productivity program contributed to the failure of performance funding. Devising a plan that protected and reflected the diversity of colleges and universities constitutes a major difficulty of performance funding in all the states that adopted the program (Burke and Serban 1997b). Instead of addressing this problem, the Arkansas plan presented a monolithic model that covered all institutions, whatever their differences in sector or mission. Neglecting campus differences deepened the divisions between two- and four-year campuses, urban and rural institutions, and research and comprehensive universities.

Conclusion

If Productivity Plan was not the cause of its demise, neither was it an innocent victim without culpability. Its origin, motivation, and content undoubtedly contributed to its fall, for it was flawed from the start. Conceived as a reaction to external pressure, it lacked the internal commitment that could sustain it once the pressure was removed. A preemptive strike can succeed, but only when the program adopted appears appreciably better to internal groups than the one threatened by outsiders. The Arkansas program failed this test. Its indicators resembled those of Mandated/Prescribed rather than Not-Mandated programs (Burke 1998b; Chapter 3). The added allocation generated by the program became lost in the squabble over its distribution among campuses. A unique provision that forced campuses to compete for performance funds contributed to the divisions among campuses.

Campus leaders will support programs that may produce more money, but their enthusiasm wanes when the funding falls below expectations and when the actual allocations shows losers as well as winners. Legislators welcome programs that promise increased productivity and performance, but become less supportive when the results appear to penalize their home campuses. Governors are natural champions of performance funding, which promises increased efficiency and improved performance of public colleges and universities. But governors change; and their successors seldom make a name for themselves by continuing their predecessor's programs. All of the above factors plagued performance funding in Arkansas, and sooner than expected. On the other hand, the legislature at its 2001 session revived performance funding with a pilot program for a two- and four-year institutions. Apparently, policy makers have learned their lesson. This time the approach is more cautious and more flexible.

Colorado: Up, Down, and Around Again

Legislative frustrations with the costs, performance, and productivity of state colleges and universities led to performance funding in Colorado. Tensions between the state legislature and public higher education rose in the late 1980s and early 1990s as funding increases stalled and student enrollments grew. A projected increase of 20 to 30 percent in new students in the next decade and a constitutional limitation on spending fueled these tensions. Divided governance hampered a coordinated response of public higher education to state needs and public accountability. Six boards governed the operations of 15 community colleges and 13 baccalaureate and graduate institutions, under the coordinating authority of the Colorado Commission on Higher Education (CCHE) (McGuinness 1994).

Despite campus opposition, in the closing minutes of the 1993 Regular Session, the Legislature passed SB 196 (1993), which mandated performance funding. It required that the governor, legislative leaders, and CCHE officials adopt each year up to five Policy Areas in higher education. These areas represented the only budget items that would receive additional monies beyond the allocations driven chiefly by enrollment formulas. The CCHE would allocate performance funds among the six governing boards based on its assessment of institutional performance in the five Policy Areas. The collaborative process for setting state priorities constituted its real innovation.

Funding Priority Areas

The governor, lawmakers, and CCHE members specified five Policy Areas in late 1994 (HB 1110): K-12/College Coordination (grant program), Increased Productivity, Workforce Training, Increased Enrollment, and Increased Student Financial Aid. In 1995, they substituted Use of Technology for Financial Aid and in 1996 added Quality and Efficient Undergraduate Education, apparently to replace Increased Enrollment. These changes confirmed campus fears that state priorities would constantly change.

Funding began in FY 1994-95 and continued through FY 1996-97. Some phase out monies also came in 1997-98 (HB 1196 and 1088; CCHE Spreadsheet). The funding provided the following:

1st year	2nd year	3rd year	4th year
$14.5m	$5.3m	$6.2m	($4.6m not new dollars)

Most of the money in the first year paid for unfunded past enrollment. In latter years, the grant program in technology received the lion's share of the allocation.

Legislation prescribed indicators for most of the Policy Areas. The CCHE proposed indicators for those Areas without prescribed measures (CCHE Meetings, March 1996). The program required good or improved performance on indicators such as the following:

Graduation Rates	Faculty Teaching Load	Licensure Test Scores
Student Transfers	Use of Technology	Credits on Graduation
Time-to-Degree	Job Placement	Noninstructional Costs
Workforce Training	Faculty Evaluation	K-12 Linkage
Student Access	Course Availability	Space Utilization
	Student Advising	

The Colorado approach to performance funding presented practical problems. The different schedules of the consultative and the budget processes meant that collaboration on the Policy Areas had little impact on the budget deliberations. Scheduling also gave the CCHE too little time to determine the performance allocations among the governing boards. In addition, the participation of the institutional finance officers meant that allocations reinforced the status quo rather than redirecting resources to reinforce state priorities. The annual determination of the Policy Areas also generated uncertainties about continuing state priorities (McGuinness 1995).

Performance Reporting

In 1996, the Legislature altered its approach to accountability and suspended performance funding (HB 1219). This Act required each governing board with the approval of the CCHE to select a set of quality indicators for reporting by institutions in five areas — now called statewide goals and expectations — by the Fall Semester 1999. These indicators, plus statewide measures, would form the basis for a new reporting and funding system, as well as a consumers guide for prospective students and parents. The indicators proposed by the institutions differed widely in number and substance. The CCHE Measures emphasized better advising, reduction of time-to-degree, use of technology to lower cost, more emphasis on teaching by faculty members, and greater awareness of what students know and can do upon graduation (CCHE Meeting, June 1997).

Although the legislation spoke of the possibility of providing additional state funding for performance in the future, it merely required the CCHE and the six governing boards to consider the performance of the public systems and their institutions in their allocation of regular state appropriations. The Law required reports on how the funds were spent and authorized the CCHE to recommend to the General Assembly whether any performance funds would be included in institutional base budgets. In 1997, the Legislature eliminated the policy areas (HB 1352).

A New Performance Funding System

The election of a new Republican governor, Bill Owens, who replaced the long-term Democrat Roy Romer, renewed interest in performance funding. Previously, the CCHE had played a buffering role between state government and higher education, much to the consternation of some legislative leaders. Governor Owens appointed a new majority of the CCHE and named Tim Foster, a long time critic of the Commission and former chair of the Joint Legislative Budget Committee, as its Executive Director (Ewell 2000). Foster pushed hard to create a new performance-funding system.

The General Assembly allocated $12.6m in FY 2000-01 for a performance funding system based on nine indicators. The CCHE requested $16.8m for FY2001-02 based on the following ten indicators (Colorado Commission 2000):

- Graduation Rates

- Freshmen Retention

- Minority Retention and Graduation Rates

- Faculty Workload

- Licensure Test Scores (4 Year)

- Job Placement or Baccalaureate Enrollment (2 Year)

- Institutional Support Cost

- Required Course Availability

- Number of Courses Required for Degrees

- Two Instruction Specific Indicators Chosen by the Campuses

Conclusion

Unlike the suspended effort, the Coordinating Board in consultation with the governing board and campus leaders developed the indicators. Despite this consultation, the indicators reflected legislative rather than campus concerns. The CCHE is now moving to use standardized tests to access student undergraduate learning and may include test scores in their funding indicators. With the push from Foster, the governor, and the Legislature, Colorado — which once abandoned performance funding — now seems likely to continue it, at least for the foreseeable future (Burke et al. 2000; Burke 2001).

Kentucky: A Tale of Two Governors

Performance funding in Kentucky is largely a tale of two Democratic governors, with similar goals but different plans. Brereton Jones started the program with his Higher Educational Review Commission in 1993. Paul Patton stopped it with his Task Force on Postsecondary Education in 1997. Governor Jones offered a blunt bargain to university presidents: support his reforms, including performance funding; and he would save higher education from a statewide budget cut. The resulting legislation mandated performance funding but left the details to the Council on Higher Education (CHE) in collaboration with the university presidents.

The ensuing controversy exhibited the classic conflict between a coordinating agency pushing public accountability and university presidents protecting campus autonomy. In the end, the conflict undercut the credibility of both the Council and the campuses. The new Governor, Paul Patton, brought a new agenda that promised nationally competitive universities, restructured higher education governance, and replaced performance funding with incentive funding. The Kentucky story poses the question: Can performance funding proposed by one governor survive under a successor — even one from the same party?

Government and Governance

The structure of state government and academic governance in Kentucky hampered reform (McGuinness 1994). The state weakened executive authority by limiting governors to one term, leaving campus presidents and local boards of trustees with greater influence on educational policy. The eight public universities and fourteen community colleges gave campuses considerable clout in the General Assembly. In addition, the governance of higher education in Kentucky had a decentralized tradition (Musik 1996). Separate boards of influential trustees governed the universities, along with the community colleges, which were part of the powerful University of Kentucky System. The CHE had the legal powers of a strong coordinating body. In practice, the tradition of decentralization made the exercise of the CHE powers depend on the agreement — or at least the acquiesce — of the university presidents, especially the head of the University of Kentucky. A constitutional amendment in 1992 shifted the balance of power to the Executive Branch by allowing the next governor, elected in December of 1995, to run for a second term.

By the early 1990s, business and political leaders in Kentucky recognized the increasing importance of a high-quality system of higher education to the states' economy. In 1992, the Accountability Act mandated annual reporting from public colleges and universities on their results on fourteen indicators, which later shaped the measures for performance funding. Unlike other performance-funding states, Kentucky had no established tradition in outcomes assessment.

The Jones Commission

Governor Jones chose the classic mechanism of a statewide commission to launch his "remaking of higher education." In September 1993, he appointed the Higher Education Review Commission (HERC Report, Vol. 1, 1993). The university presidents and governing board chairs, who constituted nearly three-quarters of the Commission membership, could not have been pleased with the governor's proposal for a strong CHE and performance funding. But governors promising money usually get what they want. The presidents decided to accept the money and performance funding, probably with the hope of diminishing the negative elements as they developed the details.

The Higher Education Reform Commission delivered its Report in December 1993. The staff of the HERC, drawn from the governor's office and the CHE, learned that balancing state and campus interests constitutes the critical issue in designing and implementing performance funding. Conflict between these interests arose during the deliberations of the governor's Commission and would reappear repeatedly during the two-year struggle to develop a permanent performance funding plan for Kentucky. The Commission grappled with two threshold questions in performance funding. First, should the performance indicators cover all institutions or be largely discretionary for individual campuses? Second, should individual institutions have a wide or restricted choice in setting indicator weights? The Report compromised by adopting com-

Table 2. Kentucky: Performance Areas and Measures (1993)

Persistence of Students

1. Persistence of first-time degree-seeking freshmen

2. Persistence of Black first-time full-time freshmen

3. Percentage (later changed to number) of degree-seeking students sent by community colleges to universities or received by universities from community colleges

4. First to second year retention rate (later added "of degree-seeking first-time freshmen")

5. First to second year retention rate of Black students

Student Outcomes

6. Graduation rates

7. Graduation rates of Black students

8. Success rates of students enrolled in remedial Math and English courses, exiting remedial courses, and successfully completing entry-level curriculum courses (community colleges only)

9. Satisfaction of graduating students

10. Satisfaction of alumni

11. Satisfaction of employers

Table 2. Kentucky: Performance Areas and Measures (1993) (Continued)

Periodic Comprehensive Student Assessment

12. Quality of instructional programs

13. Evidence of elimination of programs

14. Percentage of hours allocated to instruction by faculty (including course preparation and non-instructional student contact)

15. Quality of incoming class by ACT score

16. Success rates on licensure exams

Quality of Research/Service Programs

17. External research support per full-time faculty

18. Evidence of school improvement activities

19. Evidence of faculty involvement in service mission

20. National ranking among U.S. research universities (UKUS only)

Campus Management

21. Percentage of Black employees in selected EEO categories

22. Percent of funds expended for institutional support

23. Adoption of strategic plans and program priorities setting

24. Evidence of periodically updated campus facilities maintenance plan

25. Evidence of comprehensive staff development

26. Classroom and lab utilization rates for degree credit activity

mon indicators, but let campuses choose indicator weights. The HERC Commission approved a comprehensive array of 26 specific and quantifiable indicators (see Table 2).

Accountability Versus Autonomy

The HERC Report had determined the areas, measures, and weights for performance funding but left the standard for judging institutional success to the CHE and the Conference of Presidents, which included the heads of all the universities (CHE Chair May 1, 1994). Gary Cox, the executive director of the CHE, proposed that a committee of his staff and institutional representatives prepare the criteria and that campuses recommend their own standards to the Council staff by February 1995. As Cox might have anticipated, most campuses proposed low standards, some below current levels of performance. In response, Cox suggested an alternative approach based on higher standards. Although the university representatives acquiesced, with $18 million for performance funding at stake, many presidents believed Cox reneged on a prior agreement that institutions should select their own success standards. The Budget Act for FY 1995-96 allocated the performance moneys based on the transitional plan for that year only and directed the CHE and the Conference of Presidents to develop a permanent plan for the 1997-98 biennium.

A working group, dominated by campus representatives, developed the *Kentucky Higher Education Funding Model*, and the CHE approved in May 1994 for the 1997-98 biennium (CHE Meeting 1994). The Model stressed base budgets, with two-thirds of any additional state appropriation going to current activities and services. The remainder would go 60 percent for equity and just 40 percent for performance. The plan also proposed postponing performance funding in years with budget cuts. It included common indicators for all institutions as well as unique items to reflect their diverse missions. Each campus retained the right to propose its own success standards for the indicators, subject to final approval by the CHE. The Model showed a shift to campus autonomy from the accountability concerns apparent in the HERC Report. The end of Governor Jones' term and the election of a successor who might not champion performance funding undoubtedly influenced this shift.

The plan, adopted by the CHE in November 1995, allocated 12 performance objectives among five goals (CHE Meeting 1995). The document designated five objectives as of "high value" for the State. Three of these were common for all institutions: Educational Outcomes, Attainment through Access, and Equal Opportunities Commitment. The eight baccalaureate universities had an additional high-value objective — Support of K-12 Education. The community colleges had the special objective of Educated Workforce Development. Each campus could choose among the other objectives to reflect its special mission and propose indicators for all of the objectives, so long as the total number did not exceed twelve. The model also permitted each campus or the community college system to assign a minimum of 5 to a maximum of 35 points to all objectives. Funding the first year went solely for preparing a campus plan and that in the second year merely for implementing it. Only year three required real evidence of improved results.

The universities proposed 91 different indicators for the 12 performance objectives. Campus leaders also played it safe by spreading the weights across a large number of the indicator objectives rather than emphasizing selected areas. By the time Cox received the campus proposals in early February 1996, the new governor, Paul Patton had proposed reform of higher education as his top priority. Cox again rejected the campus recommendations and proposed a plan that featured more standardized indicators, greater weights for high-value measures, minimum expectations of progress, and a common schedule for implementation and improvement.

Cox's response again caused a chorus of complaints from university presidents and charges of bad faith. Only fear that the governor and legislators would view complaints as resistance to accountability prevented open opposition from presidents. They had reason to worry. In March 1996, the Senate sent to the House of Representatives a concurrent resolution to create the Task Force On Postsecondary Education, proposed by Governor Patton (General Assembly 1996). The resolution declared, "efforts to implement a meaningful system of performance funding have been ineffective, and efforts to improve the formula for funding higher education have not resulted in meaningful change" (General Assembly 1996).

The presidents did get some changes in Cox's plan (CHE Meeting, July 1996) (see Table 3). All institutions had four common indicators, which they could weigh from 10 to 30 points each, so long as these priority measures attained at least 50 percent of the total weights. The final plan also contained eight voluntary and up to two "institution specific indicators."

Table 3. Kentucky: Performance Funding Indicators (1996)

	Common (Mandatory) Indicators
1. Quality of Educational Outcomes	All academic degree programs and general education programs using student outcomes assessment results for program improvement
2. Student Advancement	Student progress through the higher education system, as measured by: a) persistence rates; b) graduation rates; or c) both
3. Use of Technology in Student Learning	Number of uses of technology in student learning faculty
4. Preparation of P-12 Teachers	Revised certification programs resulting in scores of Kentucky teachers on the multiple choice component of all Praxis II subject area assessments as compared to teachers nationally
5. Educated Workforce Development	Development of an educated workforce that can adapt to state-of-the-art technologies, learn new skills on the job, and find new solutions as problems emerge in a changing and highly competitive workplace
	Institution-Specific (Including Mission-Specific) Indicators
6. Effective Use of Resources	Improvement of administrative and academic management effectiveness and efficiency through the use of innovative management practices
7. Global Perspective in Academic Programs	Incorporation of global/international perspective into academic degree programs
8. Review of Gender Issues	Address gender issues on campus

Table 3. Kentucky: Performance Funding Indicators (1996) (Continued)

9. Cooperative Academic Degree Programs	Cooperative academic degree programs or agreement, i.e., joint or cooperative programs, articulated programs, transfer agreements, and reciprocity agreements with other public or independent postsecondary education institutions, consistent with institutional missions and CHE policies
10. Alternative Educational Delivery	Number of courses or degree programs using alternative delivery systems, as measured by: a) course sections using interactive TV; b) course sections using nontraditional time blocks (evening and weekends); or c) degree programs with required practice-based/service learning (co-op, internship, practice, and community service) component
11. Level of Gifts, Grants, and Contracts Funding	Amount of funding received from federal and private grants, and contracts and private gifts revenues
12. EEO Plan Implementation	Achievement of equal opportunity goals as established by the CHE

The consultative process had altered dramatically the proposal for performance funding in the HERC Report of December 1993. The indicators had changed from the standardized, statewide, prescriptive measures in the HERC Report to the diverse, campus specific, and flexible items in the July 1996 document. The CHE approved the revised plan in July 1996, but it was already too late. Legislators must have wondered why there was a fuss with so little money involved, $3.3 million for FY 1996-97 and $2.6 million for FY1997-98.

On March 26, Governor Patton issued his plan for reforming postsecondary education in Kentucky. He proposed a new and powerful Council on Postsecondary Education (CPE), headed by a President, with a salary higher than that of any public university president in the state, which diminished authority of the state's universities, especially the University of Kentucky. It removed the community colleges from UK's control by combining them with the state's technical colleges in a separate system. Those were the sticks to compel the new order on higher education. The carrots came with the promise of generous increases in funding. The Report recommended incentive in place of performance funding. Additional allocations would go for promised rather than achieved results. After a bitter battle with the President of the University of Kentucky over the removal of the community colleges from UK control, the legislator finally approved the governor's plan.

Conclusion

The tale of performance funding in Kentucky offers a classic case of the conflict between statewide coordination and campus autonomy and between the priorities of different governors. Campus resistance to linking resources to results undermined the credibility of the program and a new governor chose incentive over performance funding.

Performance Funding in Minnesota: Hardly a Milestone

Minnesota has long led the states in performance management with its Minnesota Milestones. Launched by Governor Carlson in 1991, this plan set the directions for the state and anticipated that all public organizations would adopt performance goals to support that vision. Although postsecondary education produced the graduates and research that helped make a bright future possible for Minnesota, both the governor and the Legislature felt that their public colleges and universities fell short of achieving that promise.

Rising costs and poor coordination of postsecondary education in Minnesota meant that its financial needs far exceeded available state resources. National recession and competing demands from health care and public schools severely strained state resources in the first half of the 1990s. As state support declined, the perception grew that educational quality had eroded (Minnesota Planning 1992). The Higher Education Coordinating Board had statutory authority for supervising postsecondary education, but the real power lay with the governing boards of no less than four systems. The Board of Regents of the University of Minnesota had constitutional authority over three senior universities and one technical college. The State Board for Community Colleges had responsibility for 18 colleges and three centers. A State Board of Technical Colleges governed 18 colleges with 34 campuses. Finally, a separate Board governed seven regional universities (McGuinness 1994).

A 1991 law merged the state universities, community colleges, and technical colleges into a single system in 1995 (Minnesota Laws 1991, Chapter 365, Article 9, Section 9). It also directed the Coordinating Board to make recommendations on linking appropriations to achieving student learning outcomes and accomplishing other goals (Article 3, Sec. 15). In addition, the law established a Task Force on Future Funding to develop "an alternative funding formula" that created incentives for quality to replace the traditional approach based on current costs and student enrollment (Article 2, Sec. 3). A 1992 report from a Governor's Commission also urged linking resources to quality indicators, such as student learning, graduation rates, retention of minority students, and job placements.

The response of the Higher Education Coordinating Board in January 1993 seemed both slow and cautious. Its Report discussed in detail the problems of performance funding and outlined the guidelines that should shape such a funding policy (Minnesota Planning 1992). The report hardly represented a ringing endorsement of performance funding. The guidelines called for decentralization, campus consultation, additional funding, and a gradual and incremental approach to performance funding. The Coordinating Board presented it to the 1993 Legislature and promised to introduce a specific plan for the 1995 budgeting cycle for implementation in Fiscal Year 1996-97.

The Legislature refused to wait. In 1994, it passed a new funding policy that included up to a one percent increase in the noninstructional budgets of systems that met the performance indicators and standards established by their governing boards (Minnesota Laws 1994, Chap 532 Art 3 Sec 3 and 4). Instead of implementing this provision, the Legislature in the following year imposed its own program with prescribed indicators.

The 1995 legislative session produced dramatic changes for higher education. A single act abolished the Higher Education Coordinating Board; implemented the merger of the state universities, community colleges, and technical colleges into a single system, and imposed performance funding with prescribed indicators on the new System (MMSCU) and the University of Minnesota (Minnesota Laws 1995 Chap 212 Art 1 Sec 3 and 4, Art 3, Sec 58), The legislation prescribed a separate set of indicators for each System and required the release of $1 million when one of them demonstrated the achievement of one of the performance measures. The common indicators included increasing the following for both Systems:

- Academic versus administrative budgets
- Credits through telecommunications
- Freshmen retention
- Graduation rates
- MNSCU
- Placement rates for two-year colleges
- University of Minnesota
- Freshmen in top 25 percent of high school class
- Minority freshmen
- Minority and woman faculty

The law also required both Systems to establish a set of Accountability measures for themselves and their campuses and to report on their results as part of the budget process and for use in System allocations to their campuses. As the economy improved and the appropriations to higher education increased, the interest in performance funding declined. A state planning report in August of that year merely notes that the legislature experimented with performance funding for only one year and replaced it with performance reporting. A 1999 survey of State Higher Education Finance Officers suggests that Minnesota is unlikely to readopt performance funding (Burke et al. 2000). Rising appropriations and system and campus resistance, especially from the University of Minnesota, seemed to stop performance funding in Minnesota.

Conclusion

The causes for closure of performance funding in the four states demonstrate differences, but also identify common problems that plague the program. A change in governor had a major impact in Kentucky and an important influence in Arkansas. Hurried implementation in Colorado and Minnesota created opposition in those states. Campus resistance undermined performance funding in all four states. Colorado and Minnesota had a mandated/prescribed program, where the lack of consultation is unlikely to win campus cooperation. Kentucky's mandated program allowed consultation, but the squabble between coordinating officers and campus presidents over indicators and weights destroyed the credibility of both groups and the performance program. The higher education community in Arkansas adopted performance funding with full consultation and without legislation. But the process produced a program to please a sitting governor, who was soon removed from office. The history of the programs in these four states surely shows that performance funding is easier to start than sustain. The re-adoption in Arkansas and Colorado suggest that the program may have more than one life.

Chapter 11

PERFORMANCE FUNDING: ASSESSING PROGRAM STABILITY

Joseph C. Burke

Introduction

If performance funding experienced rising popularity, it also exhibited increasing volatility. Practical difficulties in design and implementation matched its abstract appeal for encouraging external accountability and institutional improvement. Although 17 states had performance funding by mid-2000, no fewer than five states had abandoned their initiatives (Burke and Modarresi 2000a). These results raise intriguing questions. Why did some states keep while others quit performance funding; and what characteristics distinguished stable from unstable programs?

This chapter examines the results from a 1996-97 survey of state and campus policy makers in nine states for signals that supply answers to these questions (Serban 1997). It identifies the characteristics of stable programs by comparing the replies from Tennessee and Missouri, which the literature suggests show stability, to those from four states that later abandoned their initiatives: Arkansas, Colorado, Kentucky, and Minnesota (Burke and Modarresi 2000a). The survey responses from the continuing programs in Florida, Ohio, and South Carolina are then compared to these characteristics to assess their stability (Burke and Modarresi 2000b).

Tentative Assumptions

Previous studies of performance funding suggest some tentative assumptions about the characteristics that distinguish stable from unstable programs (Albright 1998; Burke 1997; Burke and Serban 1998a; Morrison 1995; and Stein 1996).

1. *Collaboration* between governors and legislators, state coordinating and university system officials, and campus leaders and trustees. Stable programs require initial and continuing collaboration among all of these stakeholders. Governors and legislators provide the state funding; coordinating and system officials supply the policy support; and campus leaders and trustees set the institutional priorities required for success in performance funding.

2. *Goals* of institutional improvement, external accountability, and increased state funding. Despite inherent tensions between institutional improvement and external accountability, state-funded programs for public colleges and universities cannot survive for long without satisfying both goals. Campus leaders often prefer institutional improvement and complain of the restraints of external accountability. Governors and legislators naturally demand evidence that performance funding increases accountability, but they also desire improvement in programs and services. The prospect of increased state funding offers an obvious incentive for campus cooperation.

3. *Policy values* stressing quality more than efficiency. Quality is the hallmark of higher education. All public programs should incorporate both quality and efficiency, but the fundamental purpose of pursuing quality in educational institutions makes it the top priority. Even state policy makers acknowledge that efficiency, while desirable on its own, is diminished unless coupled with quality programs and services.

4. Sufficient time for *planning* and *implementation*. Complex-
    ity of program design, controversy over program compo-
    nents, consultation with multiple stakeholders, collection of
    required data, and complications of program execution de-
    mand considerable time for planning and implementation.

5. Neither too few nor too many *performance indicators*. Too
    few indicators ignore too many of the multiple objectives of
    colleges and universities. Too many indicators trivialize ma-
    jor priorities by tying trifling sums to important objectives.

6. *Success standards* emphasizing institutional improvement
    supplemented by peer comparisons. The diverse types and
    multiple missions of public campuses make institutional eq-
    uity an essential element of stable programs of performance
    funding. Given this diversity, the fairest standard of success
    looks first at the improvement of individual institutions and
    then at their performance in comparison with similar col-
    leges or universities. The first consideration supports cam-
    pus differences; the second ensures fair standards. Stable
    programs avoid competition among institutions.

7. Restricted but substantial and discretionary *funding*. Re-
    stricted funding prevents budget instability on campuses.
    Substantial funding recognizes the priority and difficulty of
    improving results in higher education. Performance funding
    works best at the margin of a campus budget, but the amount
    of funding must match the importance of its goals and the
    difficulty of its tasks. Institutional discretion over even
    small sums is valuable when mandatory expenditures ab-
    sorb nearly all of campus budgets.

8. Additional rather than reallocated resources as the *funding
    source*. Additional allocation makes performance funding a
    desirable project on campus. It becomes a special initiative
    with its own funding rather than another activity competing
    for limited resources.

9. Resolution of the *major difficulties* of choosing perfor-
    mance indicators, assessing higher education results, pro-
    tecting mission diversity, and safeguarding campus
    autonomy. The multiplicity of goals in higher education
    makes choosing a limited number of the indicators a per-
    plexing problem. The ambiguity of these goals and the lack

of agreement on how to measure their achievement compli-
cate the task of assessing results in higher education. Designing a funding program that not only covers but also fits a
wide diversity of campus missions presents another difficulty. Finally, performance funding must specify and support
statewide priorities without diminishing the campus autonomy required for institutional diversity and faculty creativity.

10. *Stability* of state priorities and program requirements.
Achieving results in higher education takes time. State priorities and program requirements must continue long
enough to allow campuses to produce the desired and demanding results.

11. *Prospects* of a favorable long-term future. The effort required by campus professionals to raise performance and
produce results demands that they perceive a long-term future for performance funding. Long-term results are unlikely in programs with uncertain prospects.

Method

Population

To test the validity of these assumptions, this chapter uses the returns
from a 1996-97 survey of state and campus policy makers in nine study
states (see Chapter 4). State officials included governors, their education aide, chief budget officers, and the legislative chairs of higher education and fiscal committees. Campus leaders comprised presidents,
vice presidents, deans, and chairs of faculty senates in public two- and
four-year colleges and universities. Two mailings went to nearly 2,000
state and campus leaders and achieved an overall return of slightly more
than 50 percent. The main limitation of the survey is the disproportion-
ate number of campus leaders as opposed to state officials in both the
population and the responses.

Design

Responses from the four states that later dropped performance funding
form the unstable group (Arkansas, Colorado, Kentucky, and Minne-

sota). Of the five states in the survey that retained performance funding, this study uses Missouri and Tennessee for the stable group. Performance funding in these two states seem to incorporate the characteristics projected in the assumptions about stable and successful programs. Both initiatives benefited from careful design, gradual implementation, and considerable continuity. Their efforts exhibited close collaboration between coordinating officials and senior campus officers, a limited but sufficient number of indicators, and restricted but substantial funding. Their goals stressed institutional improvement, without ignoring external accountability; and their policy values emphasized quality over efficiency (Banta 1996; Bogue and Brown 1982; Burke and Serban 1998b; Ewell 1994; Morrison 1995; Stein and Fajen 1995; and Stein 1996). In contrast, the continuing programs in Florida and Ohio seem too uncertain, and the one in South Carolina too controversial, to represent stable and successful examples of performance funding (see Chapters 6, 7, and 8; Burke and Serban 1998b; Trombley 1998; and Williams 1996).

The average response rates for both groups of states were nearly identical. The stable group achieved an average of 51 percent, ranging from 49 percent in Missouri to 52 percent in Tennessee. The response rate for the unstable group averaged 51 percent, running from 42 percent in Kentucky to 63 percent in Arkansas. Colorado's rate reached 48 percent and Minnesota's 50 percent. The stable group had 177 respondents; the unstable group 351.

The Survey questions fall naturally into seven categories: stakeholders' input, future prospects, goal achievement, main difficulties, current and desired policy values, suggested improvements, and the appropriateness of indicators frequently used in performance funding. These questions form the major issues for testing the stability of performance-funding programs.

Data Analysis

This study uses discriminant analysis to identify and rank the variables, based on their comparative contribution to differentiating the responses from stable and unstable programs. The two groups constitute the dependent variable. Responses to the relevant questions represent the independent variables. The discriminant procedure of the SPSS system with linear classification rules and prior probabilities proportional to the sample size was used for the analysis.

Results

This study identifies the variables that explained significantly ($p<0.01$) the total variation in responses between stable and unstable programs. The correlation of 0.55 indicated a moderate degree of association between the responses and group membership. The negative group means (-0.85) represent the replies from Missouri and Tennessee; the positive means (0.42) are those from the group that dropped performance funding. These mean scores suggest significant differences between the two groups. A correct classification of 50 percent represents no better than chance. Our model classified correctly 79 percent of the respondents into stable or unstable groups.

The two groups differed most sharply on the achievement of program goals, the importance of stakeholder inputs, the appropriateness of performance indicators, and the prospects of the program's future (see Table 1, Appendix). The stable group composed of Missouri and Tennessee appeared much more positive about achieving all of the program goals than the unstable group consisting of Arkansas, Colorado, Kentucky, and Minnesota. Improving higher education constituted the top variable in discriminating between the two groups. Two additional program goals — demonstrating accountability and increasing state funding — also produced substantial differences. Clearly, respondents from Missouri and Tennessee felt their programs had a better chance of achieving these goals than did the group that stopped performance funding. Perhaps for this reason, they foresaw a favorable future for their programs, while the unstable group predicted uncertain prospects for their efforts.

The relative inputs of various stakeholders in the design and development of performance funding also divided the two groups. The replies from the unstable group rated the input from external groups —business leaders, legislators, community leaders, and governors — as more important than did the responses from the stable group. Conversely, Missouri and Tennessee considered the input from coordinating boards and coordinating officers as more significant than those from the four states that ended performance funding.

Attitudes toward the appropriateness of particular indicators also separated the two groups. The unstable group strongly preferred the efficiency indicators of administrative size and faculty workload. The stable group showed more preference for quality indicators of external peer reviews, alumni survey results, standardized test results, and licensure exam scores. Fewer indicators represented the only recommendation for improving performance funding that differentiated the stable from the unstable group.

The policy value of quality also separated stable from unstable programs. Respondents from Missouri and Tennessee indicated that their current program stressed quality more than replies from the unstable group. The difficulties that characterized the replies from the unstable group read like a litany of the complaints about performance funding. They included implementation costs, changing state priorities, erosion of campus autonomy, measuring the results of higher education, budget instability, and insufficient time for implementation.

Findings and Assumptions

The findings confirm most but not all of our tentative assumptions. They suggest that stable programs of performance funding exhibit the following characteristics more than unstable programs:

- Important input by state coordinating boards and their officers;

- A sense of achieving the goals of improving higher education, demonstrating accountability, and increasing state funding;

- Policy values stressing quality more than efficiency;

- Sufficient time for planning and implementation;

- A limited number of indicators;

- Restricted but substantial funding;

- Prediction of a long-term future;

- Stable state priorities;

- Protection against budget instability; and

- Curbed costs of implementation.

Agreements, as well as differences, also deserve attention when identifying the characteristics of successful efforts of performance funding. Responses on the variables show that the group that kept and the one that ended performance funding agreed on the following desirable characteristics:

- Careful choice of performance indicators;

- Recognition of the difficulty of measuring results in higher education; and

- Preservation of institutional diversity.

The combined findings of differences and agreements form the tentative characteristics of stable and successful programs of performance funding. Case studies of the programs in Tennessee (Ewell 1994; Morrison 1995) and Missouri (Stein 1996) suggest some of the same reasons for their success.

Unstable programs showed significantly more input from those outside of higher education, such as legislators, governors, business leaders, and community representatives. Stable programs exhibited more input from boards and officers of coordinating agencies for higher education. The differences in stakeholder input probably stem from the two methods of initiating performance funding. Coordinating boards in Missouri and Tennessee voluntarily adopted performance funding, while governors and legislators mandated it in three of the four states that later abandoned the program. In the fourth state, Arkansas, the coordinating board acted only after the governor threatened to impose performance funding (Burke 1997, Chapter 10). Although analysis identifies significant differences in stakeholder inputs, the mean scores of the responses show that both groups stressed the importance of collaboration among leaders from state government, coordinating agencies, and university systems.

The relatively low mean score for Missouri and Tennessee on input from campus leaders is surprising. The coordinating officials in these states actively engaged campus representatives in the design, implementation, and revision of their programs (Morrison 1995; Stein 1995). In contrast, three of the four unstable programs had only slight input from campus leaders. The coordinating agency in the fourth, Arkansas, used a committee dominated by campus officers to design performance funding, but that group developed a program to please the governor and avoid a state mandate (see Chapter 9; Burke and Serban 1998b).

All three of the listed goals of performance funding — improved higher education, demonstrated accountability, and increased state funding — proved most useful in predicting the groups of stable and unstable programs. The preponderance of campus leaders in the survey sample undoubtedly contributed to the finding that improved higher education constituted the most significant variable. It may also explain the importance attributed to increased state funding. However, the significance assigned to increased accountability — hardly a preferred goal on campus — recognized that performance funding must pursue external accountability as well as institutional improvement. The literature supports the perception that performance funding in Missouri and Tennessee has improved performance, demonstrated accountability, and increased state funding (Banta 1996; Stein 1996). The questionnaire in this study failed to include meeting state needs, which might have changed the relative ratings of the other goals.

The perception of favorable future prospects of performance funding is critical to stability. A sense of an uncertain future characterized responses from the states that later dropped the program. Conversely, a belief in the long-term prospects of performance funding marked a majority of the replies from Missouri and Tennessee. For a controversial program that challenges campuses to change, success depends on the sense of a long-term commitment to ensure the cooperation of colleges and universities. Concern about changing state priorities and program requirements in the replies from the unstable group underscores the importance of this continuing commitment.

It is not surprising that the returns from the states that stopped performance funding showed more concern about major difficulties than did those from the stable programs. The former expressed greater anxiety about protecting campus autonomy, avoiding budget instability, rushing program implementation, changing state priorities, shifting program requirements, and incurring implementation costs. These ratings reflected the belief that their programs had not dealt well with some of the major problems of performance funding. On the other hand, both groups agreed on the top difficulties of choosing performance indicators, protecting institutional diversity, and measuring higher education results.

The results on policy values suggest that stable programs of performance funding favor quality more than unstable programs, although both groups viewed quality as the most desirable policy value. A previous study of performance indicators supports these results. It concluded that the indicators used in Missouri and Tennessee clearly stressed quality, while the indicators in the four states that ended performance funding emphasized efficiency (Burke 1997).

The two groups of respondents show a preference for the indicators in their existing programs. For example, the efficiency indicators of administrative cost and faculty workload appear as top factors in separating unstable from stable programs. Neither Missouri nor Tennessee included these measures. However, Arkansas and Colorado had administrative costs and teaching loads, and Minnesota used an indicator reflecting administrative costs (Burke 1997). Although the last plan in Kentucky omitted administrative cost and faculty workload because of campus resistance, an earlier version had included both items (see Chapter 10).

The performance programs in Missouri and Tennessee stressed quality indicators on teaching and learning — such as program reviews and standardized tests in general education and academic majors. Three of the four unstable programs did not use program reviews or standardized tests. Arkansas included both measures, but its range of indicators emphasized efficiency more than quality (Burke 1997).

The survey data on the desirable number of indicators seem confusing. The responses from Tennessee and Missouri recommend both more and fewer indicators, which differs significantly from the replies of the unstable group. Although this result sends a mixed message, it does emphasize the importance of adopting enough but not too many indicators. Analysis revealed that fewer indicators represent a more significant variable than more measures in distinguishing the stable from the unstable group. This result seems surprising, since Missouri and Tennessee had fewer indicators than three of the four states that ended their programs (Burke 1997). Perhaps respondents from the stable group worried more about spreading limited funding over too many objectives than they did about slighting priority areas by omitting their indicators.

Assessing the Stability of Continuing Programs

What do these findings on the characteristics of stable programs suggest about the continuity of the programs in Florida, Ohio, and South Carolina? To seek answers, discriminant analysis is again used to compare the combined responses from Missouri and Tennessee with the replies from each of the three other study states that retain performance funding. The goal is to examine the extent to which the initiatives in Florida, Ohio, and South Carolina incorporate the characteristics that seem to distinguish the stable from unstable programs (Burke and Modaressi 2000b).

The stable group combining Missouri and Tennessee produced 177 responses. Florida provided 115 replies; Ohio, 160; and South Carolina, 113. The response rate for the stable group reached 49 percent in Missouri and 52 percent in Tennessee. The rate for the other three states ran from 48 percent in Florida, to 50 percent in Ohio, and 59 percent in South Carolina.

Analysis explained ($p<0.01$) the total variation in responses between the stable group and for each of the three states. Table 3 gives group means on the variables for the stable group of Missouri and Tennessee and for each of the study states. The negative sign represents the responses from Missouri and Tennessee; the positive sign, those from Florida, Ohio, or South Carolina. The results reveal huge differences between responses from the stable group and those from South Carolina and significant differences from Florida and Ohio replies. The analysis classifies correctly 92 percent of the responses from South Carolina and the stable group, 83 percent from Florida, and 78 percent from Ohio.

South Carolina

Sixteen variables produced significant differences between the responses from South Carolina and the stable group composed of Missouri and Tennessee (see Table 2, Appendix). Input from leaders outside higher education characterized South Carolina's replies on program development. The contribution from business leaders represented by far the most powerful variable in distinguishing South Carolina from the stable group. The influence of community leaders and legislators also received strong support. The difficulties of performance funding dominated the discriminating variables for South Carolina. They included insufficient time for implementation, data costs, and budget instability. Respondents from that state questioned the ability of their program to achieve any of the goals of performance funding. In contrast, those from Missouri and Tennessee believed their programs could demonstrate accountability, improve higher education, and increase state funding. The South Carolina respondents predicted an uncertain future for their program, while the stable group forecasted favorable long-term prospects.

These two groups also divided on the number and choice of performance indicators. Not surprisingly, South Carolinians preferred fewer indicators, since their program then had 37. A preference for the efficiency indicators of administrative size and faculty workload also distinguished South Carolina's replies from the stable group. Most of the variables on policy values failed to differentiate South Carolina's responses from those from Missouri and Tennessee. The former did think their current program afforded greater choice than did the latter.

Ohio

Fifteen variables contributed significantly to separating the Ohio respondents from the stable group (see Table 3, Appendix). Stakeholders from Ohio had less confidence than did those from Missouri and Tennessee about achieving the goals of performance funding. Increased accountability and improved higher education constituted the top variables in discriminating between the two groups. In addition, the stable group also had more faith that their program had increased state funding. The Ohio respondents also expressed more concern about the difficulties of eroding institutional autonomy and too little funding.

Ohio's recommendation of more indicators and preference for the indicators of faculty workload and K-12 linkage also distinguished their responses from Missouri and Tennessee. The latter group preferred standardized tests and professional licensure exams. The stable group perceived more input than did the Ohio respondents from governing boards, university system officers, and state coordinating officers. The stable group also thought their program stressed quality, while the replies from Ohio suggested less emphasis on this policy value.

Florida

Only thirteen variables proved significant in discriminating between the responses from Florida and from the stable group of Missouri and Tennessee (see Table 4, Appendix). The differences on significant variables were somewhat smaller than those recorded for Ohio and far below those from South Carolina. The difficulty of changing state priorities exhibited the highest discriminating power. Other problems, such as insufficient time for implementation and frequent changes in program requirements, also distinguished the Florida responses. Once again, Missouri and Tennessee cited more input from coordinating officers, coordinating boards, and university system officers. The Florida group seemed somewhat less confident than did the stable group about achieving the goals of performance funding. However, unlike South Carolina and Ohio, only improvement of higher education showed a negative correlation. Consistent with its positive response to program goals, the stable group showed more confidence in the long-term future of performance funding. Only external peer reviews distinguished that group from the Florida replies on appropriate indicators. The Missouri and Tennessee group believed their current program stressed quality as a policy value, while Florida respondents believed their effort emphasized efficiency.

Discussion

South Carolina

Clearly, the South Carolina effort conflicted with most of the model characteristics proposed for stable programs of performance funding. Legislative and business leaders from outside higher education, and not the coordinating board and officers, designed and initiated performance funding in that state. Legislation mandated state funding based entirely on performance and prescribed a long list of 37 indicators. Once the legislation had passed, the coordinating board and its staff have tried to moderate the impact on campuses of these unique features in the South Carolina program. The short deadline for submitting to the legislature a plan of execution left insufficient time for planning and implementation, although South Carolina did phase in full funding and the performance indicators over three years (see Chapter 10). The difficulties of performance funding plagued the program in South Carolina. They included the high costs of data collection and the obvious fear of budget instability.

The mandates and prescriptions in the legislation caused dissent on campuses in South Carolina. Campus leaders contended that funding based only on performance would create budget instability and complained about the ambiguity, duplication, and conflicting purposes of a number of the indicators. This division probably contributed to the predictions of an uncertain future and the doubts about achieving program goals. The preference for the efficiency indicators of administrative size and faculty workload differs from the accent on the quality measures of peer review and test scores in Missouri and Tennessee. Outside input, hurried planning and implementation, too much funding, too many indicators, and doubts about goal achievement contributed to the perception of an uncertain future for performance funding in the Palmetto State.

Ohio

The governor and legislators pushed for performance funding in Ohio primarily to coordinate the activities and increase the accountability of its many campuses and multiple governing boards. The survey results showed a negative correlation with the inputs of university system and coordinating board officers. Under pressure, the coordinating board and officers did develop a comprehensive plan to improve performance, increase access, enhance job training, and expand sponsored research. Failure to develop the required service expectations for universities meant that performance funding applied mostly to two-year colleges. Despite their advocacy, the governor and the legislature rejected the recommendations of the coordinating board for a comprehensive program and substantial funding (see Chapter 8). Inadequate allocations in the early years of the program undoubtedly prompted the complaint of the survey respondents about too little funding.

The limited scope of campus coverage and lack of sufficient funding at the time of the Survey probably fueled the doubts in Ohio about achieving the goals of accountability, improvement, and increased state support. Clearly, the respondents thought the plan stressed efficiency more than quality. The Ohio program suffered from its limited coverage, inadequate funding, uncertain future, and unachieved goals.

Florida

The Florida responses reflected uncertainty about the approach to performance funding. Pressed by the governor, Florida first adopted a comprehensive program mandating performance-based budgeting for all state agencies, including public colleges and universities. The college and university systems rushed to develop comprehensive plans to meet that mandate. However, the Legislature, after a lengthy quarrel between the two houses over the purpose and scope of performance funding, adopted a minimal program with only a few indicators and relatively little funding. Later, the Legislature adopted a huge program for community colleges that tied most of their funding to degree completions and job placements (see Chapter 6). Small wonder that the survey responses from Florida cited the contribution of legislators and business leaders, and complained about the difficulties of shifting state priorities and program requirements and insufficient time for implementation. Respondents also believed performance funding in their state stressed efficiency over quality and expressed doubts about its long-term future and its ability to improve higher education. In contrast to the stable group, Florida's program suffered from unclear directions and changing priorities and program requirements.

Summary: All Three States

Survey results show that outsiders, not leaders of coordinating agencies, directed performance funding in South Carolina, Ohio, and Florida. Respondents from all three of these states rated the possibility of achieving the goals of performance funding considerably lower than Missouri and Tennessee. Although replies from all five states called quality the most desirable policy value, those from the three states thought their existing programs slighted quality. Respondents from Missouri and Tennessee believed their current program reflected quality as their primary policy value. Unlike Missouri and Tennessee, none of the three study states allowed sufficient time for planning and implementation. The funding program in the three states also conflicted with the characteristic of a reasonable number of performance indicators. South Carolina had too many and Florida too few. Ohio respondents expressed a rather weak preference for fewer indicators. The group also divided on the level of funding, with too much in South Carolina and too little in Florida and Ohio. Despite these differences, all three lacked the restricted but substantial funding provided in Tennessee and Missouri.

The respondents from Missouri and Tennessee foresaw a long-term future for performance funding, while those from Florida, Ohio, and South Carolina seemed less certain. The replies from South Carolina expressed anxiety about changing state priorities and budget instability. Changing state priorities topped the list of the discriminating variables for the Florida group, which also gave a high mean score to budget instability. Respondents from Ohio seemed relatively unconcerned about changing state priorities and budget instability. The cost of data collection raised strong concerns in the South Carolina group and lesser reactions from Ohio and Florida.

Comparing the survey results with the model characteristics seemed to spell trouble for performance funding in Florida, Ohio, and, especially, South Carolina. However, the newness of their programs makes predictions premature. All of these states have now entered the stage of policy reformulation. Missouri and Tennessee built reformulation into their initial programs. They provided for periodic review and possible revision of their performance indicators and funding levels. In South Carolina, the coordinating board early in 1999 moved from funding based entirely on performance to a limited pool for incentives and disincentives and has substantially reduced its number of indicators used for funding. The Ohio Board of Regents has changed some goals and indicators; and the state has greatly increased the funding. Florida's program is far from fixed. Performance funding for the universities remains a marginal program with few indicators and little funding. As a result, the state has scuttled the program for the universities. On the other hand, the Sunshine State has initiated a huge funding program for two-year colleges based on job training and degree completion. New legislation also calls for 10 percent of state funding based on performance. These changes in the three study states since the 1996-97 Survey may well affect the attitudes of stakeholders toward performance funding and could reduce some of the characteristics that suggest program instability.

Conclusion

The findings of this study demonstrate the dilemma of performance funding — its desirability versus its difficulty. The replies from Missouri and Tennessee centered on the desirable objectives of performance funding, while those from the unstable group and the three continuing programs concentrated on its inherent difficulties. The former suggested its possibilities; the later stressed its problems. Taken together, the differences and agreements of these two groups of stakeholders offer signals of the characteristics of stable and successful programs in performance funding. Incorporating these characteristics will not ensure the stability of performance funding in any state, but success is unlikely without considering them.

Every discussion of public policy must also recognize that each state is different, with different needs and diverse resources. This dictum holds especially true in higher education, where the range of campus types, the forms of governance, and the histories of public support differ dramatically. Given these differences, no state can build a stable and successful program in performance funding by copying the plan and approach of another state. The programs in Missouri and Tennessee are neither perfect nor applicable in every state. Changing state priorities and governors and legislators could undermine their stability. Despite these dangers, they have lasted much longer than other programs; and their longevity and stakeholder support suggests that they have addressed adequately many of the problems posed by performance funding.

The model characteristics of stable programs are too tentative and imprecise to predict with certainty whether a particular program will persist. They do point to potential problems and pose possible solutions that could improve a program's prospects. They represent a reasonable check for potential stability rather than an infallible prescription for success. Policy makers in each state will have to decide whether to keep or start performance funding. They will have to balance its attractive goals against its definite difficulties. Whatever the ultimate choice, they can benefit from the signals sent by stakeholders from the groups that kept and those that left this attractive but volatile program.

Appendix

Table 1. Canonical Structure Ranked by Correlation Coefficient for Stable and Unstable Groups

Variable Ranked by Function	Function	
	Stable Group	Unstable Group
1. Improvement of Higher Education	-.045	0.39
2. Administrative Size		0.39
3. Faculty Workload		0.36
4. Input from Business Leaders		0.34
5. Input from Legislators		0.32
6. Increased Accountability	-0.32	
7. Uncertain Future		0.28
8. Input from Community Leaders		0.23
9. Increased State Funding	-0.23	
10. Input from Governor		0.22
11. Favorable Long-term Future (4-7 Years)	-0.21	
12. Input from State Higher Education Coordinating Boards	-0.21	
13. Improvement by Fewer Indicators	-0.20	
14. External Peer Reviews	-0.15	

Table 1. Canonical Structure Ranked by Correlation Coefficient for Stable and Unstable Groups

Variable Ranked by Function	Function	
	Stable Group	Unstable Group
15. Input from State Higher Education Coordinating Officers	-0.14	
16. Choice, Should Be Value		0.14
17. Retention/Graduation Rates	-0.14	
18. Alumni Satisfaction Survey	-0.13	
19. Implementation Costs		0.13
20. Changing State Priorities		0.12
21. Erosion of Campus Autonomy		0.12
22. Quality, Is Value	-0.12	
23. Improved Public Perception	-0.11	
24. Student Satisfaction Survey	-0.11	
25. Standardized Tests	-0.11	
26. Measuring Results		0.11
27. Professional Licensure Exams	-0.11	
28. Budget Instability		0.10
29. Job Placement	-0.09	
30. Choice, Is Value		0.08
31. Insufficient Time for Implementation		0.08

Table 2. Canonical Structure Ranked by Correlation Coefficient for South Carolina by Stable and Unstable Groups

Variable Ranked by Function	Function	
	Stable Group	Unstable Group
1. Input from Business Leaders		0.56
2. Insufficient Time for Implementation		0.39
3. Increased Accountability	-0.30	
4. Improvement by Fewer Indicators		0.29
5. Input from Community Leaders		0.28
6. Uncertain Future		0.28
7. Administrative Size		0.27
8. Improvement of Higher Education	-0.24	
9. Favorable Long-term Future (4-7 Years)	-0.22	
10. Implementation Costs		0.22
11. Input from Legislators		0.20
12. Improvement by More Indicators	-0.18	
13. Choice, Is Value		0.17
14. Budget Instability		0.16
15. Faculty Workload		0.15
16. Increased State Funding	-0.15	

Table 3. Canonical Structure Ranked by Correlation Coefficient for Ohio by Stable and Unstable Groups

Variable Ranked by Function	Function	
	Stable Group	Unstable Group
1. Increased Accountability	-0.40	
2. Improvement of Higher Education	-.034	
3. Standardized Tests	-0.31	
4. Erosion of Campus Autonomy		0.30
5. Improvement by More Indicators	-0.28	
6. Faculty Workload		0.27
7. K-12 Linkage		0.24
8. Input from Higher Education Governing Boards	-0.21	
9. Improved Public Perception	-0.20	
10. Quality, Is Value	-0.19	
11. Professional Licensure Exams	-0.19	
12. Input from Higher Education System Officers	-0.15	

Table 4. Canonical Structure Ranked by Correlation Coefficient for Florida by Stable and Unstable Groups

Variable Ranked by Function	Function	
	Stable Group	Unstable Group
1. Changing State Priorities		0.31
2. Improvement of Higher Education	-0.30	
3. External Peer Reviews	-0.30	
4. Quality, Is Value	-0.29	
5. Insufficient Time for Implementation		0.29
6. Input from State Higher Education Coordinating Officers	-0.26	
7. Input from Legislators		0.25
8. Input from State Higher Education Coordinating Boards	-0.24	
9. Favorable Long-term Future (4-7 Years)	-0.23	
10. Efficiency, Is Value		0.20
11. Input from Business Leaders		0.19
12. Input from Higher Education System Officers	-0.19	
13. Frequent Change of Goals/Indicators/Criteria of Success		0.15
14. Too Little Funding		0.15
15. Increased State Funding	-0.15	
16. Input From Higher Education Coordinating Officers	-0.15	

Chapter 12

ARGUMENTS ABOUT PERFORMANCE FUNDING: RHETORIC AND REALITY

Joseph C. Burke

Introduction

Arguments about performance funding have generated more heat than light. Governors, legislators, and business leaders generally champion its possibilities. Presidents, vice presidents, and faculty leaders usually criticize its problems (Ashworth 1994; Burke and Serban 1998b; Caruthers and Layzell 1996; Education Commission of the States 1998; Serban 1997). Arguments for and against performance funding focus on different points in the process. Advocates applaud its ends and goals, while adversaries attack its means and implementation. Champions commend the potential benefits, while slighting the practical problems. Critics concentrate on the problems, while dismissing the possible benefits.

Proponents of performance funding have the best of the media sound bites. They merely assert why the program should be done, without defending how it can be done. Opponents have the negative position

— prized by debaters — of attacking a proposal without offering an alternative. Advocates follow the common fallacy in state government of adopting a new program and neglecting its execution. Adversaries exhibit the common fault on campus of condemning new proposals without examining the flaws in current practices.

As is often the case in such controversies, performance funding is neither as good as its champions contend nor as bad as its critics complain. Both sides are partly right and partly wrong. The goals proposed by proponents are worthy, but the problems posed by opponents are weighty. Considered together, the arguments could help build programs that achieve the possibilities of performance funding, while addressing its problems. These arguments deserve careful consideration by state and campus policy makers when they consider initiating or revising programs for performance funding.

Arguments For and Against Performance Funding

The arguments are assembled from an analysis of programs in 11 states (Burke and Serban 1998b), an opinion survey of state and campus policy makers in nine states (Serban 1997), and a study of funding indicators in eight states (Burke 1997). They are also collected from articles in the *Chronicle of Higher Education* and from the literature on performance funding, which is mostly limited to particular programs in a few states. It is instructive to note that only three of the nine arguments offered for each side even deal with the same subject.

Arguments For Performance Funding

1.   *Adds performance as a factor in state funding.*

State funding of public campuses traditionally considers current cost, student enrollment, inflationary increases, and special initiatives (Burke and Serban 1998a; McKeown 1996). These input factors say nothing about the quality or quantity of student learning or the services provided to states and society. Providing some funding for institutional results would encourage colleges and universities to become more effective and efficient in their use of resources and more responsive to the needs of their students and their states. If improved performance is a good goal for effective organizations, surely it is good enough to fund for public campuses. Money gives meaning as well as support to programs and priorities. Performance funding tilts the budget question somewhat from what states should do for their campuses toward what campuses do for their states and their students.

This rhetoric about budgeting for results exaggerates the reality of performance funding. In many programs, process measures far exceed output and outcome indicators that directly reflect institutional results (Burke 1997, Chapter 3). Moreover, the funding for performance remains minimal, running from less than one to about six percent of state operating support for campuses. South Carolina began its program with the intent of basing funding entirely on performance, but in 1999 the coordinating board limited the potential amount to around five percent of campus base budgets. Workload factors of current budgets, student enrollments, and inflationary increases still determine nearly all of the funding. Performance funding really represents more of a conceptual than a funding shift. Whatever the weight of workload, it is difficult to deny the proposition that performance should count for something in state funding for public colleges and universities.

2. *Links planning and budgeting.*

Funding for inputs disconnects budgets from planning; and plans unconnected to budgets stay on the shelf. Plans propose the organizational objectives and the actions required to produce those results. Budgets supply the funds to support those actions. Linking planning, budgeting, and performance constitute an explicit or implicit goal in nearly all of the performance-funding programs (Albright 1998; Burke and Serban 1998b). Setting goals, determining actions, and funding priorities form the trinity of effective planning. Although funding cannot ensure successful plans, few succeed without resources.

Two factors limit the potential for linking performance funding to campus planning. The small amounts allocated for the program diminish its actual impact on planning. The second factor is the lack of visibility of performance funding on campuses below the senior administration. Deans and faculty leaders are much less familiar with performance funding than presidents or vice presidents. Performance funding assesses the achievements of institutions and not the accomplishments of their colleges, schools, and departments. Consequently, the program has no obvious impact on campus units below their central administrations. A funding program with no link to campus divisions and departments is unlikely to influence institutional planning or performance. One suggestion is to provide additional funding to institutions that include results on relevant statewide indicators in their internal allocations to campus units (Burke and Serban 1998b). Such a provision would supply a missing link in planning, budgeting, and performance.

3.   *Pushes state officials to identify their priorities and encourages dialogue with campus leaders.*

Traditionally, educational leaders have had to surmise state priorities from budget documents or random comments from state officials. The absence of indicated state goals for higher education leaves governors and legislators free to shift their priorities for higher education to satisfy political exigencies and constituent complaints. Performance-funding forces governors and legislators to set or accept some priorities for public colleges and universities (Folger and Jones 1993). Campus leaders quarrel with some of the priorities in the performance-funding plans. But these programs do require governors and legislatures to state their priorities and, at least by implication, to limit their demands on public higher education. State leaders can always change their minds and their demands, but it becomes more difficult when education leaders can point to the priorities and goals in the performance-funding plans.

Most states lack regular forums for dialogue between state and campus leaders on higher education issues. This absence leaves such discussions mostly to the charged atmosphere of budget battles or the episodic commissions created to deal with particular problems. Although performance funding offers an opportunity for dialogue, its programs seldom require it in practice. The initial plan in Colorado did mandate such discussions. It required annual meetings of a committee composed of the governor and legislative leaders and coordinating board and campus representatives to set the policy areas of performance funding. Unfortunately, the requirement for annual meetings encouraged frequent and sudden shifts in state priorities (Burke and Serban 1998b).

Performance-funding programs should build such dialogues into their plans. Discussion between state and campus policy makers should begin with the design and initiation phase and persist with periodic reviews of the program's content. A provision for regular reviews, every four or five years, of priorities and plans of performance funding by state and campus leaders could ensure dialogue on educational issues and permit sufficient time to produce and evaluate results. The program in Tennessee provides for review and possible revision in five-year cycles (Burke and Serban 1998b). Scheduled reviews would allow input from the governor and legislators on priorities, encourage dialogue with educators, and ensure program continuity. Periodic reviews for possible revisions would also give both state and campus officials a sense of ownership of performance funding.

4.   *Fosters both external accountability and institutional improvement.*

All of the performances-funding programs claim to pursue the critical purposes of both external accountability and institutional improvement (Burke and Serban 1998b). In practice, the choices of performance indicators usually stress one purpose over the other (Burke 1997). The origin of the program obviously influences this relative emphasis. Many states mandate performance funding in legislation; and some even prescribe the performance indicators. In some states, coordinating boards in collaboration with campus leaders adopt the program without legislation. Not surprisingly, the Not Mandated programs in Missouri and Tennessee stress institutional improvement. In contrast, mandated or legislated programs exhibit more interest in external accountability.

Despite this emphasis in indicators, the choice of success standards for most programs demonstrates the concern with institutional improvement. Nearly all of the initiatives use institutional improvement as their success criteria (Burke and Serban 1998b). In the nine-state survey, a high percentage of both campus and state leaders cite both increased accountability (55%) and the potential to improve higher education (63%) as two of the advantages of performance funding (Serban 1997). On the other hand, most campus leaders in five states believe the program achieved the purpose of external accountability but not institutional improvement (see Chapter 4).

5.   *Presses campuses to become more client — and less provider — centered.*

Performance funding can help transform public campuses from provider-centered enterprises driven by the aspirations of administrators and faculty into client-centered organizations focused on the needs of students, states, and society. The funding indicators reveal relatively few items that reflect the resource and reputation model of institutional excellence, based on the best students, the biggest budgets, and the best reputation (Astin 1991). This model represents a provider-driven ideal tailored to academic rather than external interests (Burke 1997). Not surprisingly, the programs of Missouri and Tennessee, developed in consultation with campus leaders, show much more interest in this model than the mandated efforts. However, over half of the indicators used in 11 states imply a combination of cost/benefit and client-centered models of institutional excellence (Burke and Serban 1998b, Chapter 3). This mixed model stresses the quantity, quality, and costs of programs and the services for students, states, and citizens. Critics attack this customer focus as better suited to business organizations than academic institutions. Despite this charge, service organizations should respond more to the needs of the clients than to the desires of the providers.

6.   *Centers attention on undergraduate education.*

Responding to external complaints, the objectives and indicators of performance-funding programs center almost exclusively on undergraduate education. State officials and business leaders complained about the quality and quantity of faculty teaching and student learning, the preoccupation with graduate studies and research, and the neglect of undergraduate education. Campus leaders quarreled with the particulars of this indictment, but most accepted the need for renewed attention to undergraduate education. The bill of particulars clearly influenced the list of funding indicators (Chapter 3).

7.   *Rewards good — and penalizes poor — campus performance.*

All of the programs purport to reward good and penalize poor performance of state colleges and universities. In spite of this announced intention, the success standards and scoring scales in practice limit the funding shifts among campuses. The compromises and concessions necessary to gain consensus — or at least to diminish dissent — tend to prevent large swings in funding. The comparatively low levels of performance standards and benchmarks — often adopted for colleges and universities — seem set to encourage, if not ensure, success. The scoring scales and institutional benchmarks tend to narrow the differences in scores among institutions. Contrary to the rhetoric in state capitals, legislators do not favor large budget losses for colleges or universities based on poor performance, since most have a campus in their home districts. Consequently, the rewards or reductions often fail to fit the performance. The motto of performance funding might well read: "reward or penalize, but not too much."

8.   *Decentralizes authority without loss of accountability.*

States traditionally ensured accountability by controlling campus operations and activities through rules and regulations. Performance funding trades operational flexibility for increased attention to achieved results. It focuses on the objectives assigned to public colleges and universities and leaves the means of achieving these ends to the individual institutions (Gaither et al. 1994). Performance funding — by setting priorities and assessing achievements — transforms the concept of accountability from controlling means to funding results. Critics welcome the increased flexibility for campuses, but fear that performance funding may become a more forceful and insidious form of control. The precedent of federal funding for faculty research demonstrated the power of funding to determine priorities without the approval of campus officers or governing boards.

Critics also complain that, despite the rhetoric of concentrating on results, performance funding often attempts to control means. Many programs include indicators on teaching loads, administrative size, and the distribution of campus budgets among the major organizational functions (Burke and Serban 1998b). Mandated programs with prescribed indicators most often include those measures. Apparently, governors and legislators concerned about swelling bureaucracies and declining teaching loads could not resist reverting to form by including indicators that attempted to control these practices. Some critics see performance funding as extending the old accountability to include control of means as well as ends.

9.   *Stimulates concern with institutional as opposed to individual performance.*

Performance funding, which focuses on institutional performance, should stimulate increased interest in institutional achievements as opposed to individual activities of professors and professionals. Faculty autonomy and administrative decentralization encourages individual creativity, but diminished collective responsibility for institutional results. In theory, performance funding, by focusing on institutional results, addresses this defect. In practice, as noted before, these programs apparently have little impact below the levels of presidents and vice presidents. This lack of visibility and the absence of financial consequences for internal units diminish the potential for emphasizing collective responsibility for institutional performance.

Missouri addresses this problem with a separate program that funds each institution for campus-based projects, often at the departmental level (Burke and Serban 1998b, Chapter Six; Stein 1996). This campus component — only loosely tied to the statewide indicators — does not close completely the gap between individual and institutional performance. Campuses currently fund their internal units in much the same manner as states fund their colleges and universities. Current costs, enrollment levels, and salary increases largely determine internal allocations to divisions and departments.

Performance-funding programs could achieve the advantage of encouraging internal concern with institutional performance by adding an indicator on internal campus allocations. This proposal would fund colleges or universities based on their use of appropriate statewide indicators in their internal budgeting of colleges, schools, and departments. It would leverage state funding with institutional allocations. More important, this provision would engage directly the departments and the professionals most responsible for performance in meeting the institutional goals set in performance funding programs.

Some of the most common performance indicators in state programs seem suited for inclusion in departmental allocations. After all, the actions of academic departments are most responsible for the results on the common indicators of retention, graduation, and transfer rates; licensure test scores; and the satisfaction levels of students and alumni. Such a proposal would certainly make performance funding more visible on campus. It would also clarify the link between planning, budgeting, and performance and the connection between institutional and individual performance.

Arguments Against Performance Funding

1.   *Fails from the difficulty of assessing results in higher education.*

More than two-thirds of all the campus respondents from both two- and four-year institutions in our nine-state survey cite the difficulty of measuring the results of higher education as a major disadvantage of performance funding (Serban 1997). Surprisingly, replies from governors' offices share this view, although legislators, coordinating staff, and system officers seem much less concerned about this problem. Most commentators on higher education concede the difficulty of measuring the results of undergraduate education (Ashworth 1994; Gaither 1995). They cite as causes, the ambiguity, subjectivity, and diversity of the objectives of undergraduate education and point to the lack of appropriate measures and the absence of agreement among academics about learning outcomes.

Performance funding clearly struggles with this difficulty. Few of the funding programs even try to evaluate directly the knowledge and skills possessed by graduates, probably because academics dispute the validity of standardized tests. Only three of the 11 states in one study include an indicator of test scores on standardized exams for general education or academic majors (Burke and Serban 1998b). More of them use licensure exams, which seemed more acceptable to academics because they are limited to professional fields, where external authorities require passage for practice.

Despite this opposition to standardized tests as valid measures of learning outcomes, both administrators and faculty complain that few of the indicators in performance-funding programs assess quality. Many outsiders believe that standardized tests can measure the learning outcomes of undergraduate education as they do for public schools. Campus critics complain that tests can never assess the complex outcomes or capture the elusive character of quality in higher education.

The Working Group on Student Outcomes of the National Postsecondary Education Cooperative (NPEC) has begun to address the question of undergraduate outcomes from a policy perspective. Their reports identify a number of quality outcomes relevant to governmental policy, but they suggest that much more work is required to develop the methods of measuring their achievement (Erwin 1998; Terenzini 1997). The absence of acceptable direct measures of student learning outcomes explains in part the heavy emphasis on process indicators as surrogates for educational quality. Many programs also use student and alumni surveys to access perceptions of quality in undergraduate education (Burke 1997, Chapter 3).

2.   *Diminishes campus diversity.*

In the 1996-97 survey, over 70 percent of the presidents and vice presidents — from both two- and four-year institutions — list preserving campus diversity as a major problem in designing and implementing performance funding (Serban 1997). Over half of the system officers, academic deans, and faculty leaders from both types of campuses also cite this difficulty. Critics claim that no single program could reflect —much less encourage — campus differences in type and mission (Schmidt 1999). This problem obviously concerned the designers of performance funding, which in many cases included representatives from a range of campuses. They selected success standards and scoring systems to protect institutional diversity. Most of the programs use institutional improvement as their standards for success and set targets by comparisons with campuses in the same sectors (Burke and Serban 1998b). Several programs allow campuses to choose an indicator or two that emphasizes some aspect of their diverse missions (Burke 1997).

Seven of the 11 states in one study also use the performance indicators to reflect the different missions of two- and four-year institutions. Florida and Washington (which later dropped the program) have separate indicators, while five states have at least one alternate indicator for these campus types. South Carolina's original initiative waives several items for its technical colleges; and its revised plan has an alternate indicator for its four types of institutions.

These precautions have not silenced the complaints that performance funding disadvantages small campuses with low enrollments and two-year colleges that emphasize career rather than transfer programs (Schmidt 1999). Many graduate and research universities also contend correctly that the indicators slight the importance of their graduate and research missions.

Some critics carry the diversity argument to its extreme conclusion. They contend that every campus is unique and requires its own set of indicators. They drive the differences among institutions to a point where commonalties disappear. In contrast, outsiders assume that institutions granting the same degrees should share some indicators of success, although not necessarily the same success standards.

3.   *Produces budget instability.*

According to one survey, over 40 percent of the senior campus officers consider budget instability as a major disadvantage of performance funding (Serban 1997). Aside from the initial plan in South Carolina, the small sums allocated for the program tend in practice to prevent budget stability. Although the funding levels in most programs change annually, the actual amounts have averaged from less than one to six percent of state support for the operating expenses for public campuses

(Burke and Serban 1998b). In addition, the setting of weights, standards, and scoring reduce the possible swings in budgets. As noted above, the coordinating commission and staff even in South Carolina have altered the original plan to avoid large losses for its colleges and universities. The fear of budget instability really represents more anxiety than reality.

4.   *Punishes the poorest institutions.*

This argument reflects the reality that the amount of resources often affects the level of performance. Performance and funding are not synonymous, but they are related. Using institutional improvement as success standards and peer comparisons as institutional benchmarks reduce the possibility of penalizing campuses with the least resources. Performance-funding programs should include further protections against this possibility. They should add an indicator commonly found in performance reporting, that shows state support per student in comparison with state and national peers. Adding such an indicator to performance-funding programs could provide additional monies for campuses that are underfunded in comparison with peer institutions.

Critics also charge correctly that removing resources from institutions with poor performance may make improvement more difficult, if not impossible. Rather than taking resources from these campuses, the unearned funds should go into an escrow account held by coordinating agencies. Release of these funds to the colleges and universities would come on receipt of acceptable plans to address campus deficiencies. Loss of funds would come only after repeated failure to improve performance (Burke and Serban 1998b). Such a provision would also reinforce the requirement in most programs that campuses compete against their own past performance and not against other institutions.

5.   *Combines the incompatible purposes of external accountability and institutional improvement.*

The claim of incompatibility comes from champions of student outcomes assessment, who became convinced that a single program could not achieve both accountability and improvement (Ewell 1994). The evidence needed for external accountability, they contend, differs from the information required for institutional improvement. External accountability focuses on results, while institutional improvement flows from activities. The former presents campus results. The latter indicates the changes in activities and programs required to improve performance. These critics would separate the two purposes, since few indicators that assess the levels of performance required for accountability can also supply the suggestions for improvement. Simple output indicators, they say, should provide evidence of performance for external authorities, while process measures (largely drawn from the research on good practices in undergraduate education) should supply suggestions on how to improve performance.

Although the initial goals of external accountability and institutional improvement are different, the two purposes are complementary and inseparable. Despite their differences, the first step in both external accountability and institutional improvement is the same — identification of problems with particular results. In the next step of developing a plan for improvement, the two purposes do diverge. External accountability concentrates on the identification of problems and institutional improvement focuses on the processes that can improve performance. Despite this divergence, they converge in the end, for both purposes share the ultimate goal of improved performance. Evidence of anything less than good or improved performance can never satisfy external accountability. Governors and legislators naturally demand evidence that performance funding increases accountability, but they also desire improvement in programs and services.

Treating external accountability and institutional improvement as two trains on separate tracks could damage both purposes. It could encourage the trend toward privatization of public higher education and reduce further the states' share of the costs of public colleges and universities. If state accountability has different goals than institutional improvement, then perhaps state governments should pay mostly for their priorities, such as job training, economic development, and improved efficiency. Such a decision would leave qualitative outcomes such as student and faculty development largely to the support of income generated by institutions, mainly tuition. It would encourage the notion that higher education is mostly a private benefit for graduates rather than a public benefit for states. Severing the connection with external accountability would also cut off a major impetus for institutional improvement. Along with most institutions, colleges and universities have a poor record of reforming themselves without external pressure.

Separation of the two purposes would also allow administrators and professors without external input to determine the definition and goals of institutional excellence. Most public universities and many colleges would continue to follow the resource and reputation model that defines institutional success in terms of the best students, the richest resources, and the best reputations. This model would not further the goals of developing the talents of the students admitted and of using the available resources in the most effective and efficient manner. External accountability and institutional improvement are inseparable, not incompatible. They are actually two sides of the same coin.

6.   *Creates excessive costs for data collection and analysis.*

A constant complaint is the high cost of data collection for assessment, performance reporting and funding, federal requirements, and accreditation purposes (Ashworth 1994, Chapter 3; Gaither 1994, Gaither et al. 1995; Schmidt 1999) No current analysis of the costs of these activities appears available. Most of the efforts are outdated and relate to assessment, although Freeman (1995) does briefly discuss the issue in a study of performance reporting for the State University of New York. The cost estimates vary considerably, depending on assumptions about what to include in the expenditures. Astin (1985) notes that the out-of-pocket costs are easy to calculate. The real problem is estimating faculty and staff time. Complaints about the high cost of data collection for the performance funding in South Carolina led to a survey of campuses on the expense of these activities. Responses from institutions varied so widely that the staff could reach no consistent conclusions about the costs of data collection and analysis (Commission on Higher Education 1997). A report from a NPEC Group in 1997 notes campus concerns about the increased costs of data collection on institutions reporting to state and federal governments, accreditation agencies, and college guides (Gray 1997). On the other hand, this group perceives the concerns as confined primarily to the initial development phase. Banta and her colleagues (1996) conclude that in Tennessee's funding program "the reward is several times as large as the amount spent on assessment and reporting..."(p. 42).

It is difficult to assess complaints about the cost of data collection, given the lack of a comprehensive study of the expense involved and the use of the information for a variety of purposes. Many states already require performance reports on many of the same or similar indicators as performance funding. The best response to the complaint is to examine carefully whether the information derived from each indicator is worth the cost of data collection; and whether with some revision the data could satisfy several purposes (Freeman 1995). State and institutional policy makers should also review the requirements of data collection to ensure that the process is both efficient and effective. They should stop the collection of data that are seldom used.

Given the current opposition to unfunded mandates, it seems reasonable that states should pay for the costs of data collection that would impose unreasonable burdens on campuses, university systems, and coordinating agencies. It also appears reasonable that campuses should not complain about collecting and analyzing information that indicates their effectiveness and efficiency in achieving their mission and goals.

7.   *Stresses efficiency over quality.*

Critics charge that the performance-funding programs stress efficiency over quality. Analysis of the indicators used for both two- and four-year institutions seems to support this claim (Burke 1997). Indicators implying efficiency do constitute 45 percent of the total in the eight programs studied, while those suggesting quality reach only 16 percent. However, 22 percent of the indicators combine the policy values of both efficiency and quality. This last statistic suggests that state policy makers have not abandoned their interest in educational quality, but they do consider quality and efficiency as complementary, not conflicting, values. The five-state survey shows even more interest in indicators of quality and those that reflect both quality and efficiency (Chapter 3).

The choice of indicators fails to support a related charge — that the performance-funding indicators slight teaching and learning in favor of job training and economic development. A study of the subject areas of funding indicators shows that 64 percent relate to issues of undergraduate education and only 10 percent to economic and workforce development (Serban and Burke 1998b).

8.   *Subjects higher education to shifting state priorities.*

Critics charge that politics, in an age of term limits and changing issues, shifts state priorities too frequently for use in performance funding (Ashworth 1994). Improved performance in higher education does require a sustained effort, at least over several years. Although performance funding is largely a phenomenon of the nineties, its history supports this complaint. Arkansas, Colorado, Kentucky, and Minnesota have already dropped the program because of political shifts and changing priorities (Burke and Serban 1998b, Chapter 10). Performance funding clearly requires a patience and persistence rarely found in state budgeting and policy making.

Performance funding offers two advantages that help to avoid sudden shifts in state priorities for public higher education. Governors and legislators have officially set the priorities in performance-funding programs or endorsed them in budgets. These actions give these priorities an official status that makes them more difficult to change. The second is more meaningful. The priorities expressed in performance-funding programs are not new, for they have already persisted for over a decade and a half. Governors and legislators have repeatedly challenged public colleges and universities to become more efficient and effective in meeting the needs of their students and their states. Their concerns have also continued about retention and graduation rates; job placements; transfers between two- and four-year institutions; growth of administrative positions; decline of faculty teaching loads; and the satisfaction of students, alumni, and employers. States have taken a series of steps to address these concerns since the mid-1980s, first by mandating outcomes assessment, next by requiring performance reporting, and now by adopting performance funding. These mandates prove the persistence of state priorities.

9.   *Favors traditional over nontraditional campuses.*

The provisions in performance-funding programs are often unfair to two-year colleges and baccalaureate campuses with nontraditional programs and students. Many of the indicators seem set for traditional baccalaureate campuses with full-time enrollments rather than the nontraditional part-time students of community and technical colleges and urban universities. For example, measures, such as retention and graduation rates, use only full-time students. This definition is undoubtedly intended to avoid penalizing two-year colleges for their high proportion of part-time students who are less likely, and who may not intend, to continue and graduate. The dearth of data on part-time students also explains their exclusion. Community colleges and urban universities contend that this emphasis on full-time enrollments penalizes them for meeting the diverse needs of nontraditional students.

Policy makers could address this problem by including an additional indicator on course completions. This measure would provide an indicator for the progress of part-time students and would give campuses credit for serving students who take a course or two for career or personnel development. In addition, several programs count for graduation rates only students who have completed at least a semester of full-time enrollment. This device applies graduation rates to students who are more likely to desire degrees. Performance programs should also take care to count certificates as well as associate degrees. An indicator on contracts with local businesses and industries for short-term training would emphasize another of the critical purposes of two-year colleges. On the other hand, performance indicators should include measures that capture the common goals of both two- and four-year campuses, since community colleges are increasingly the entry points through transfer to baccalaureate education.

Some Suggestions

Unfortunately, the arguments for and against performance funding have done little to improve the programs or inform policy makers. Despite their biases and flaws, performance funding could benefit by learning from the arguments of both champions and critics. The following suggestions could help those programs capture the benefits, while minimizing the problems, presented in both arguments.

1. States should continue funding public campuses largely on the traditional workload measures but should consider devoting three to six percent of their operating support to institutional performance, especially if additional new money is provided.

2. Performance funding should include process indicators of good educational practices and satisfaction surveys of students and alumni, while the academic community works to develop better direct measures of learning outcomes.

3. Program priorities should remain in place four or five years, followed by reviews and possible revisions by state and campus leaders.

4. Funding programs should provide special support to campuses that link internal allocations to institutional plans and statewide priorities.

5. State officials should cut the costs of data collection and analysis by confining the reporting requirements to a limited number of critical indicators.

6. Unearned funds of campuses with poor performances should be held and released when they submit an acceptable plan for addressing their deficiencies.

7. Performance-funding programs should seek external accountability and institutional improvement as complementary, not conflicting, purposes.

8. Performance funding should encourage decentralization by concentrating on institutional results rather than on controlling the means to achieve them.

Conclusion

The arguments about performance funding have done little to improve these programs. For this result to occur, both sides must reduce their rhetoric and look for the reality in their opponents' position. State supporters will have to grapple with the realistic problems of design, implementation, and continuation posed by the critics. Campus critics must concede that funding resource inputs and ignoring performance results is becoming unacceptable to state officials and taxpayers. It should become unacceptable to an academic community, which has always avowed its devotion to quality performance.

Performance funding is the latest in a series of attempts to resolve several of the fundamental dilemmas of public higher education. These dilemmas pose the critical questions of balancing external accountability with institutional improvement, statewide concerns with campus diversity, and societal expectations with academic aspirations. Whatever the fate of performance funding, both state and campus policy makers must forge programs that determine these delicate balances between state needs and campus concerns. In searching for this balance, state and campus leaders should listen to and learn from the arguments for and against performance funding.

Conclusion

LINKING FUNDING TO PERFORMANCE: A TREND NOT A FAD

Joseph C. Burke

Performance funding is the latest in a series of policies designed to hold public colleges and universities accountable for their performance. From the mid-1980s through the 1990s, states progressively tightened the screws of accountability through a progression of policy initiatives — from outcomes assessment, to performance reporting, and finally to performance funding. All of them attempted to achieve external accountability by setting statewide purposes and goals, while protecting institutional autonomy by leaving the means and methods to campus choice. All of these efforts tried to balance the external needs of states and society with the professional concerns of faculty and administrators. Each policy corrected the faults of its predecessor at the price of introducing new problems.

Assessment accented undergraduate outcomes by stressing student growth in knowledge and skills, from admission to graduation. The movement floundered from the reluctance of the academic community to assess student learning and its own performance. It also failed the accountability test, because legislation let colleges and universities develop unique programs that prevented campus comparisons, which governors and legislators wanted to evaluate institutional performance. To correct this defect, legislation mandated public reporting of institutional results, which allowed comparisons of institutional results on statewide indicators. Although the first publication of the reports often created concern in the public media, state capitals, and public campuses, they soon became routine exercises that attracted diminishing attention. State officials and campus leaders tended to ignore the reports, since their results lacked fiscal consequences. To remedy this omission, an increasing number of states initiated performance funding, or coordinating boards adopted the program to avoid legislative mandates.

The three policies pursued similar purposes. To the goals of external accountability and institutional improvement of outcomes assessment, performance reporting often added — and performance funding continued — meeting state needs. Each had the tacit goal — for coordinating boards and campus leaders — of winning increased state funding by demonstrating public accountability. All three used performance indicators as signs of institutional accomplishments, and incorporated success standards that accented institutional improvement. Although each introduced a new element, all of these initiatives depended on the ability and willingness of the academy to develop an acceptable means of assessing the performance of colleges and universities, especially in student learning.

Assessing the results of undergraduate education represented the Achilles heel of these initiatives. For all of the talk about quality, the academy has never identified the elements of educational excellence, nor developed acceptable methods for evaluating their achievement. Instead, the academic community relied on the resource and reputation model, based on inputs of the brightest students, biggest budgets, and best research reputations.

Although all of the initiatives suffered from the difficulty of assessing the results of higher education, particular problems plagued performance funding. The early programs often presented rigid mandates and prescribed indicators, with little or no campus consultation. They frequently suffered from hurried implementation, leaving too little time for planning and design. Early efforts also provided too little funding in states such as Ohio and Florida, and too much funding in South Carolina. Lacking acceptable indicators of institutional results, they relied more on process rather than on output and outcome measures. Changing state leaders and shifting public priorities, along with a penchant for instant results, also undermined the stability of many of these first efforts at performance funding.

Campus reactions to the program, and its phases of development, often resemble the Stages of Death and Dying of Kubler-Ross (1997). In *Stage I — Disbelief and Denial*, campus leaders often greeted proposals for performance funding with the disbelief of innocent victims and denied the need for the program. In *Stage II — Anger and Antagonism,* passage of performance funding produced angry reactions from campus leaders, and provoked first passive and then active resistance. Campus resistance helped kill the programs in Kentucky, Minnesota, and Washington, and seriously undermined the initiative in Colorado and Arkansas. In *Stage III — Acceptance and Adaptation*, acquiescence, if not acceptance, led campus leaders to adapt performance funding to meet many of their concerns. Four of the five states in our case studies (Missouri, Ohio, South Carolina, and Tennessee) now appear to have entered Stage III. Unfortunately, adaptation at times takes the form of gaming the indicators by setting low benchmarks to improve campus scores rather than institutional performance.

None of the current programs of performance funding have yet moved to *Stage IV — Challenge and Competition*. This creative stage would have campus leaders accepting the challenge of improving performance and competing to produce the highest levels of achievement. Few leaders of colleges and universities brag as much about their graduation rates, job placements, and alumni satisfaction, as they do about their national rankings, based largely on the test scores of admitted students, the high level of expenditures, and the faculty reputation for scholarly research. Entrance to Stage IV requires nothing less than a radical change in academic culture and a new notion of institutional excellence based on service to students and states rather than on resources and reputation.

The reaction of state officials often reverses the Four Stages. Stage I is *Challenge and Competition,* where they expect public colleges and universities to accept the challenge of performance funding and to compete to produce the highest levels of performance. In response to campus resistance, legislators and governors move reluctantly to *Acceptance and Adaptation* as Stage II, by accepting revisions to win acquiescence. Stage III for them is *Anger and Antagonism*, when campus resistance persists despite these changes. Their final Stage is *Disbelief and Denial*, characterized by disbelief of campus complaints, and denial of campus interest in demonstrating accountability. Performance funding represents a classic case of the chasm between state expectations and academic aspirations.

New efforts of performance funding and recent revisions of old initiatives have not transformed public campuses, but they exhibit some — though not all — of the characteristics of stable programs. They show more collaboration with campus representatives and more initiation by coordinating and system boards rather than by legislative mandates. New and revised programs limit the number of indicators, provide limited but substantial funding, and some offer multiyear commitments to increased state funding as the price of improved institutional performance. More programs encourage diversity by allowing campus choice of one or two indicators emphasizing institutional missions. Perhaps the most hopeful sign in this second stage of performance funding is the growing perception by campus leaders of program persistence.

Despite these changes, campus leaders still see serious problems with performance funding. Most of them believe the program has achieved the least preferred purpose of external accountability but not the most prized goal of institutional improvement. Their greatest disappointment comes on their hope that the program would increase overall state funding. Apparently, performance funding receives no credit for funding increases, but gets the blame when state allocations fall below campus expectations. As a result, the prospect of winning campus approval of performance funding — as opposed to acquiescence —remains largely unfulfilled, even in states with stable programs, such as Missouri and Tennessee.

Of course, the bottom line for any accountability policy is its impact on institutional performance. Unfortunately, the most desirable question is always the most difficult to answer. Assessment of the impact of performance funding must consider several factors, such as program longevity, indicator continuity, and funding levels.

It is still too soon to give a fair assessment for Florida, Ohio, and South Carolina, since their programs have only been fully implemented for five years or less. Only the programs in Missouri and Tennessee meet the tests of longevity, continuity, and funding. Although these two programs remain remarkably stable, still some indicator changes makes even assessing their achievements difficult.

Survey responses from campus leaders give a critical assessment of the use of performance results and of the impact of the funding program on institutional performance. Overall, respondents, including those from Missouri and Tennessee, claim that their campuses made only moderate use of performance results for decisions in most campus areas usually targeted in performance funding plans. Moreover, they conclude that performance funding had only a considerable impact on *campus planning* and *administrative efficiency*. Not surprising, senior administrators tend to see more use in decision making and more impact on performance than did academic deans and department chairs. Performance funding appears to have more use and impact in areas controlled by senior administrators than those influenced by deans and chairs.

Although state policy makers would probably applaud the impact on campus planning and administrative efficiency, they would undoubtedly look for more than a minimal effect on faculty performance, faculty-student interaction, job placements, cooperation among campuses, and especially the quantity and quality of student learning. They could take some solace from the more favorable assessment of the State Higher Education Officers of the impact of performance funding in all of the study states except Florida.

The authors of the case study give a mixed review of the use of performance results in campus decision making and of the program impact on campus performance. Not surprising, they see the most success on the performance indicators prized by the resource and reputation model of academic excellence ingrained in the national ratings of colleges and universities. For example, performance funding has pushed campuses to attain national accreditation for nearly all of their eligible academic programs. The dollar volume for sponsored research has also increased. In addition, the indicator of administrative versus academic costs has encouraged campuses to cut administrative positions, reversing the rampant growth in the 1980s.

The inclusion of both increased student access and raised admission standards in some plans of performance funding has encouraged the trend toward mission differentiation, with most baccalaureate institutions being pushed to raise admission standards and two–year colleges being used to provide student access. Although nearly all performance-funding initiatives include indicators on retention and graduation, in general, these rates have not improved. For opposite reasons, institutions with lower and those with higher standards find it difficult to raise graduation rates. Two- to four-year transfers, once considered an odd way of entry to a baccalaureate education, represent an increasing proportion of new students at many four-year colleges and universities. The common measure on time-to-degree — though the least desired indicator — has produced an increased concern with the issue on campus as well as in state capitals. Although the indicator on teaching loads may have helped prevent further reductions in teaching loads, it probably has not increased them.

Standardized tests of student learning have not shown the expected increases in Missouri or Tennessee. Opposition to standardized testing has encouraged alumni surveys as a surrogate for assessing student learning in performance-funding programs. These surveys usually show relatively high levels of satisfaction with their alma maters, even on course availability, faculty accessibility, and student learning. Job placements show improvement, but this success may owe more to the booming economy of the late 1990s than to performance funding.

If performance funding should not take full credit for these improvements, neither should it get full blame for obvious shortcoming. Performance funding can never alone achieve the desired changes in campus performance. No policy is people proof. Policies set directions, but they rely on professionals for implementation. Funding consciously kept at the margin can only influence, not determine, campus performance. Both the successes and the shortcomings of performance funding suggest that this policy, like most accountability initiatives in higher education, can only steer a better course but not shift dramatically the direction desired by the academic community.

Even marginal change is unlikely without correction of a glaring weakness of performance funding. Performance funding is a powerful lever, but it currently is not long enough to reach the right place — the schools and departments largely responsible for performance. A swift way to raise the visibility, use, and impact of performance funding is to include a special indicator that provides substantial funding for colleges and universities that use performance results on relevant indicators in their internal allocations to schools and departments.

The short history of performance funding suggests that its faults flow mostly from detailed prescriptions, inadequate consultation, poor design, inappropriate indicators, hurried implementation, and too little or too much funding. Recent developments suggest creative ways to address those problems. But the fatal flaws are the reluctance of state officers to adopt and maintain long-term priorities for higher education and the resistance of the academic community to identify and assess the learning outcomes of college graduates.

The future of performance funding remains cloudy, despite the growing interest in the program in state capitals. Declining economies and revenues in some states have presented serious challenges to the continuance of performance funding, even in states where it had strong support. Base budgets are usually protected at the expense of special initiatives such as performance funding. Bad budgets in Missouri have led the Coordinating Board reluctantly to suspend allocations for its Funding Results program and the Ohio legislature has eliminated or reduced funding for its Performance Challenges. On the other hand, the popularity of performance funding persists in state capitols and the record suggests that performance funding may fare better in bad than good times. Even states that abandoned performance funding have reinstated or reconsidering the program. Colorado has readopted it, Arkansas has launched a pilot program, and Kentucky is planning to start a new initiative.

It is still to soon to assess the impact of performance funding. But it is time to take the question mark off of linking state resources to campus results. That movement is looking more like a trend than a fad, although the form of linkage remains in doubt. Public higher education is too important and too costly to states and their citizens to fund only inputs and ignore results. Taxpayers are unlikely to accept forever the proposition that performance should count in all endeavors except state funding of higher education. Academics are too good at criticizing the performance of outside organizations to plead the impossibility of assessing their own performance. We may be able to persuade state officials that only academics can assess the quality of undergraduate education, but they will never accept the answer that it cannot be done.

Donald Langenberg (1992), chancellor of the University of Maryland System, eloquently voiced the difficulty, the necessity, and the inevitability of assessing the results of undergraduate education.

Like many university systems nowadays, mine is trying to develop mechanisms for assessing students' learning. This is extraordinarily difficult if you really try to measure learning rather than some easily measurable but irrelevant surrogate, such as course-credit units. Nevertheless, I refuse to believe that people who can detect and measure minute ripples in the fabric of the universe as it existed billions of years ago cannot also determine the quality and quantity of their own product.... Such a project may be a major research challenge in itself, but surely not an impossible one. Controversial, political, and unpalatable, perhaps, but not impossible.... Moreover, there is plenty of evidence that if we do not do this ourselves, others will do it for us and we probably won't like the results (Langenberg 1992, p. A49).

Results will eventually count in the funding of public colleges and universities. The real questions are how to reconcile the external needs of society with the professional concerns of educators, how to assess campus results, and whether academics will lead or leave the action to outsiders. Recent developments suggest creative ways to use performance in budgeting. Only time will tell whether state and campus policy makers will have the will to use them. Given the importance of colleges and universities to the success of states and their citizens and the series of efforts to reconcile accountability and autonomy, neither campus nor state leaders can allow performance funding to become just another accountability fad that failed.

REFERENCES

Act 1029, An Act for The Department of Finance and Administration, State of Arkansas, 80 General Assembly, Regular Session, 1995.

Act 137 of 1999. South Carolina Session 113 (1999-00) H. 5144.

Act 359 of 1996. South Carolina Code of Laws. Critical Success Factors. [59-103-30,SC Code of Laws].

Alabama Commission on Higher Education. *High Lights of the FY 2000-2001 Education Trust Fund (ETF) Budget Bill.* Montgomery, AL, 2000.

Albright, Brenda N. *The Transition From Business As Usual to Funding for Results: State Efforts to Integrate Performance Measures in the Higher Education Budgetary Process.* State Higher Education Executive Officers. Denver, CO: SHEEO, 1998.

Albright, B.N.; and D. Jones. *External Review of Missouri's Funding for Results Program.* Unpublished internal report, October 1996.

Almanac. Washington, DC: The Chronicle of Higher Education, September 1, 2000: 67-68.

Almanac. Washington, DC: The Chronicle of Higher Education, August 25, 1993.

Almanac. Washington, DC: The Chronicle of Higher Education, 1997.

Anonymous, interview by author, phone interview, Florida, 1996.

Arkansas Acts 1989, No. 98, 244, 267; Acts 1991, No 856; Acts 1993, No. 376, 874,1141.

Arkansas Code of 1987 Annotated. Prepared under the direction and supervision of the Arkansas Code Revision Commission. Charlottesville, AR: Michie Company, 1987.

Arkansas Department of Higher Education Staff, Conversations, 1996.

Arkansas State Board of Higher Education, Meetings. Little Rock; State Board of Higher Education, 1992-1997. Little Rock, AR: State Board of Higher Education, 1997.

Arkansas. Two Year College Leaders, Personal Conversations, 1996.

Ashcroft, Governor John, Speech to the 1989 Governor's Conference on Higher Education, Sponsored by the Missouri Coordinating Board for Higher Education (copy provided to sponsoring agency), 1989.

Ashcroft, Governor John, *Redefining the Possible: Achieving the National Education Goals.* Chairman's Initiative Leadership Group Readiness Action Team, National Governors Association, 1991.

Ashcroft, Governor John, *Executive Budget, Fiscal Year 1993*, State of Missouri 1993.

Ashworth, K. H. "Performance-Based Funding in Higher Education: The Texas Case Study," *Change: The Magazine of Higher Education* 26, 6 (November/December 1994): 8-15.

Association of American Colleges. *Integrity in the College Curriculum: A Report to the Academic Community. Redefining the Meaning and Purpose of Baccalaureate Degrees.* Washington, DC: Association of American Colleges, 1985.

Astin, Alexander W. *Achieving Educational Excellence: A Critical Assessment of Priorities and Practices in Higher Education.* San Francisco, CA: Jossey-Bass, 1985.

Astin, Alexander W. *Assessment For Excellence: The Philosophy and Practice of Assessment and Evaluation in Higher Education.* New York, NY: Maxwell Macmillan International, 1991.

Banta, T. W.; L. B. Rudolph; J. Van Dyke; and H. S. Fisher. "Performance funding comes of age in Tennessee," *Journal of Higher Education*, 67, 1 (1996): 23-45.

Bennett, William. *To Reclaim a Legacy: A Report on the Humanities in Higher Education.* Washington, DC: National Endowment for Humanities in Higher Education, 1986.

Birnbaum, Robert. *Management Fads in Higher Education: Where They Come From, What They Do, Why They Fail.* San Francisco, CA: Jossey-Bass, 2000.

Bloom, Allan. *The Closing of the American Mind.* New York, NY: Simon and Schuster, 1987.

Blumenstyk, Goldie. "Florida Bill Offers Campuses Fiscal Autonomy in Return for Accountability," *The Chronicle of Higher Education* 37, no. 32 (April 24, 1991): A-22-23.

Board of Governors, Incentive Funding Report, Phase 1. Chapel Hill, NC. The University of North Carolina: General Administration, 1997.

Bogue, E. G. and W. Brown. "Performance incentives for state colleges," *Harvard Business Review* 60 (1982): 23-128.

Bogue, E. G.; J. Creech; and J. Folger. *Assessing Quality in Higher Education: Policy Actions in the SREB States.* Atlanta, GA: Southern Regional Education Board, 1993.

Bogue, E. G. and R. L. Saunders. *The Evidence For Quality: Strengthening the Tests of Academic and Administrative Effectiveness.* San Francisco, CA: Jossey-Bass, 1992.

Bogue, E. and W. Troutt. *Allocation of State Funds on a Performance Criterion.* Nashville, TN: Tennessee Higher Education Commission, 1980.

Boot, Max. "Redefining Higher Education," *Christian Science Monitor,* November 16, 1992.

Borden, V. and T. Banta, eds. *Using Performance Indicators to Guide Strategic Decision Making.* San Francisco, CA: Jossey-Bass, 1994.

Boyer, Carol. *Assessment and Outcomes Measurement — A View from the States: Highlights of a New ECS Survey and Individual State Profiles.* Education Commission of the States. Boulder, CO: ECS, 1987.

Brown, L. "Trustees Consider University Budget," *Outlook.* Athens OH: Ohio University, April 2000: 3.

Burke, Joseph C. *Performance-Funding Indicators: Concerns, Values, and Models for Two- and Four-Year Colleges and Universities.* New York, NY: Rockefeller Institute of Government, 1997.

Burke, Joseph C. *Managing Campus Budgets in Trying Times: Did Practices Follow Principles?* Albany, NY: Rockefeller Institute of Government, 1998.

Burke, Joseph C. "The Assessment Anomaly: If Everyone's Doing It, Why Isn't More Getting Done," *Assessment Update* 11, 3 (July-August 1999): 3, 14-15.

Burke, J.C. Phone survey of the State Higher Education Finance Officers. Albany, NY: The Rockefeller Institute of Government, 2001.

Burke, J. C. and T. Lessard. *Survey of Campus Leaders in Florida, Missouri, Ohio, South Carolina and Tennessee,* 2000.

Burke, J.C. and H.P. Minassians. *Linking State Resources to Campus Results From Fad to Trend: Fifth Annual Survey.* Albany, NY: Rockefeller Institute of Government, 2001.

Burke, J. C. and S. Modarresi. *Performance Funding and Budgeting: Popularity and Volatility – The Third Annual Survey.* Albany, NY: Rockefeller Institute of Government, 1999.

Burke, J. C. and S. Modarresi. "To keep or not to keep performance funding: Signals from stakeholders," *The Journal of Higher Education* 71, 4 (July/August 2000a): 432-453.

Burke, J. C. and S. Modarresi. "Performance Funding Programs: Assessing Their Stability," *Research in Higher Education* 71, 4 (2000b): 432-453.

Burke, J. C.; J. A. Rosen; H. P. Minassians; and T. A. Lessard. *Performance Funding and Budgeting: An Emerging Merger? The Fourth Annual Survey.* Albany, NY: Rockefeller Institute of Government, 2000.

Burke, J. C. and A. M. Serban. *Performance Funding and Budgeting For Public Higher Education: Current Status and Future Prospects.* Albany, NY: Rockefeller Institute of Government, 1997a.

Burke, J. C. and A. M. Serban. *Funding For Results: Results Should Count.* Albany, NY: Rockefeller Institute of Government, 1997b.

Burke, J. C. and A. M. Serban. *Current Status and Future Prospects of Performance Funding and Performance Budgeting for Public Higher Education: The Second Survey.* Albany, NY: Rockefeller Institute of Government, 1998a.

Burke, J. C. and A. M. Serban. "Performance Funding for Public Higher Education: Fad or Trend?" *New Directions for Institutional Research*, Number 97. San Francisco, CA: Jossey-Bass, Spring 1998b.

Burke, J.C., and A.M. Serban. "State Synopses of Performance Funding Programs." In *Performance Funding for Public Higher Education: Fad or Trend?* (Volume 97), edited by J.C. Burke and A.M. Serban. San Francisco, CA: Jossey-Bass Publishers, 1998c.

Callan, P. Measuring up 2000: *The State-by-State Report Card on Higher Education, 2000* (http://measuringup2000.highereducation.org/stateglance.cfm).

Carnahan, Governor Mel. *Moving Missouri Forward — The Missouri Budget 1994.* Missouri State Printing Center, 1994.

Carnahan, Governor Mel, *Missouri on the Move — The Missouri Budget, Fiscal Year 1995.* Missouri State Printing Center, 1995.

Carnahan, Governor Mel, *Missouri — Moving Forward — The Missouri Budget 1998.* Missouri State Printing Center, 1998.

Caruthers J. K. and D. T. Layzell. "Performance Funding at the State Level: Trends and Prospects." Paper presented at the annual meeting of The Association for the Study of Higher Education. Orlando, FL: ASHE, 1996.

Caruthers, J. K. and J. L. Marks. *Funding Methods for Public Higher Education in the SREB States.* Atlanta, GA: Southern Regional Education Board, 1994.

CHE Chair to University Trustees, February 10, 1994, Agenda. CHE meeting of May 1, 1994.

CHE Staff. Notes from campus and sector meetings on performance funding. Unpublished, 1996.

CHE Staff. Preliminary staff recommendations for proposed changes to the performance funding system. Unpublished, November 8, 2000

CHE Staff. Anonymous conversations with CHE staff members 2001.

Cheney, Lynne. *Humanities in America: A Report to the President, the Congress, and the American People.* Washington, DC: National Endowment for the Humanities, 1988.

Christal, Melodie E. *State Survey on Performance Measures: 1996-97.* Denver, CO: State Higher Education Officers, 1998.

Chu, R. G. W. Conversation with the Chancellor of the Board of Regents. Ohio, December 7, 1998.

Chu, R. G. W. Conversation with the Chancellor of the Board of Regents. Ohio, January 29, 2001.

Colorado Commission on Higher Education, meeting agenda, November 1995

Colorado Commission on Higher Education, meeting agenda, March 7, 1996

Colorado Commission on Higher Education, meeting agenda, March 14, 1996

Colorado Commission on Higher Education, meeting agenda, July 1996

Colorado Commission on Higher Education, meeting agenda, June 5, 1997

Colorado Commission on Higher Education. *Ten Indicators Used in FY 2001-02.* Denver, CO: Commission on Higher Education, 2000.

Colorado SB 196 (1993). In A.C. McGuinness, Jr. *Linking State Policy for Higher Education to Financing: The Colorado Experience.* Boulder, CO: NCHEMS, 1995.

Commission on Higher Education. Higher Education Performance Indicators Report Card — 1997-98. South Carolina: CHE Unpublished, 1997-98

Commission on Higher Education. "Performance Funding: A Report Of The Commission On Higher Education To The General Assembly." Columbia, SC: Commission On Higher Education, January 1, 1997.

Commission on Higher Education. "Performance Funding Time Line: Key Commission Meetings and Deadlines." South Carolina: Commission On Higher Education, Spring, 1997.

Commission on Higher Education. "Performance Funding. Special Reports No. 1 and 2." Columbia, SC: Commission on Higher Education, September 3, 1996.

Commission on Higher Education. "Performance Funding: A Report of the Commission on Higher Education to the General Assembly. Special Reports No. 4: Performance Funding." Columbia, SC: Commission on Higher Education, January 14, 1997.

Commission on Higher Education. Discussions with the staff of the South Carolina Commission on Higher Education. South Carolina, 1997.

Commission on Higher Education. "Score Card for 1997-98." South Carolina: Commission on Higher Education Unpublished, 1997-98.

Commission on Higher Education. "Score Card 1998-99." South Carolina: Commission on Higher Education, unpublished, 1998-99.

Coordinating Board on Higher Education (CBHE) Board Book. *Recommendations for Four-year Institutions' Operating Appropriations — FY 1993.* Missouri, October 1991.

Coordinating Board on Higher Education Board Book. *Progress Report of Task Force on Critical Choices for Higher Education.* Missouri, April 1992.

Coordinating Board on Higher Education Board Book. *Recommendations for Four-year Institutions' Operating Appropriations — FY 1994.* Missouri, October 1992.

Coordinating Board on Higher Education Board Book. *Implementation of the Report of the Task Force on Critical Choices for Higher Education — Proposed Clarifying Comments and Definitions for Goal Statements.* Missouri, December 1992.

Coordinating Board on Higher Education Board Book. *CBHE Internal Budget Appropriations Request, FY 1995, Community College Operating Requests.* Missouri, October 14, 1993.

Coordinating Board on Higher Education Board Book. *Internal Budget Appropriations Request FY — 1995.* Missouri, 1995.

Coordinating Board on Higher Education Board Book. *Discussion of FY 2000 Funding for Results Elements.* Missouri, February 1998.

Coordinating Board on Higher Education Board Book. *Coordinated Plan for Missouri Higher Education.* Missouri, February 2001.

DePalma, Anthony. "Universities Grope for Lost Image," *New York Times*, (April 5, 1992): EDUC 32.

Education Commission of the States. "Transforming Postsecondary Education for the 21 Century — Views of the Governors." Denver, CO: Education Commission of the States, June 11, 1998.

El-Khawas, Elaine. *Campus Trends Survey.* Washington, DC: American Council on Education, June 1995: 67.

Erwin, T. D. *Definitions and Assessment Methods for Critical Thinking, Problem Solving, and Writing: National Postsecondary Education Cooperative Student Outcomes Pilot — Cognitive Working Group.* Washington, DC: NPEC, 1998.

Ewell, Peter. *Information on Student Outcomes: How to Get It and How to Use It.* Boulder, CO: National Center for Higher Education Management Systems, 1983.

Ewell, P. T. "Tennessee Charting higher education accountability: A source book on state-level performance indicators." In Ruppert, S. S. (ed.),

Charting Higher Education Accountability: A Source Book On State-Level Performance Indicators. Denver, CO: Education Commission of the States, 1994.

Ewell, P. T. "From the States Accountability with a Vengeance: New Mandates in Colorado," *Assessment Update* 12, 5 (September-October 2000): 14-15, 16.

Ewell, P. and D. P. Jones. *The Effect of State Policy on Undergraduate Education.* Boulder, CO: NCHEMS, 1993.

Ewell, P. T. and D. P. Jones. "Pointing the Way: Indicators As Policy Tools in Higher Education," in *Charting Higher Education Accountability: A Sourcebook On State-Level Performance Indicators,* edited by S. S. Ruppert. Denver, CO: Education Commission of the States, 1994.

Ewell, P. T. and D. P. Jones. *Making Quality Count In Undergraduate Education.* Denver, CO: Educational Commission of the State, 1995.

Executive Office of the Governor. Florida's Final Budget Report and Ten-Year Summary of Appropriations Data 1990-91 through 1999-2000. Volume 22. Tallahassee, FL: EOG October 15, 1999.

Florida Board of Regents. *State University Performance Based Budgeting.* Tallahassee, FL: FBR, May 8, 1996.

Florida Board of Regents. *Fact Book: 1999-2000.* Tallahassee, FL: FBR, May 2001.

Florida Community College System. *Briefing Paper on Performance Based Program Budgeting.* Tallahassee, FL: Division of Community Colleges, January 1996.

Florida Community College System. *The Fact Book: Report for the Florida Community College System.* Tallahassee, FL: Division of Community Colleges, February 2001a.

Florida Community College System. *2001-2002 Legislative Summary: Financial Affairs Briefing Package.* Tallahassee, FL: Division of Community Colleges, Bureau of Financial and Business Services, 2001b.

Florida Statutes. Available online at http://www.leg.state.fl.us.

Folger, J. and D. Jones. *Using Fiscal Policy to Achieve State Educational Goals.* Denver, CO: Education Commission of the States, 1993.

"Four-Year Public Institution Chief Academic Officers' Plan," submitted to the Council on Public Higher Education and to the Coordinating Board for Higher Education, January 1998.

Freeman, Michelle. *The Experience of Performance Budgeting on Higher Education at the Campus Level In the Past 20 Years,* unpublished doctoral dissertation: Knoxville, TN: University of Tennessee, 2000.

Freeman, T. M. "Performance Indicators and Assessment in the State University of New York System." In *Assessing Performance in an Age of Accountability: Case Studies. New Directions For Higher Education,* edited by G.H. Gaither, no. 91. San Francisco, CA: Jossey-Bass, Fall 1995.

Gaither, G. H. (ed.). *Assessing Performance in an Age of Accountability: Case Studies.* New Directions For Higher Education, 91, 1995. San Francisco, CA: Jossey-Bass, Fall 1995.

Gaither, G. H.; B. P. Nedwek; and J. E. Neal. *Measuring Up: The Promises and Pitfalls of Performance Indicators in Higher Education.* Report Five, ASHE-Eric Higher Education Reports. Washington, DC: The George Washington University, 1995.

Gaw, Steve, FFR Steering Committee member, personal correspondence to Robert Stein, September 27, 1995.

General Assembly, Senate Concurrent Resolution No. 93, Tuesday, March 5, 1996. 96 RS SCR 93/GA.

Gold, Steven D. *The Fiscal Crisis of the States: Lessons for the Future.* Washington, DC: Georgetown University Press, 1995.

Governor Patton to The Task Force on Postsecondary Education, March 26, 1997, with his Plan attached.

Graham, P.; R. Lyman; and M. Trow. *Accountability of Colleges and Universities: An Essay.* Unpublished, 1996.

Gray, M. J. *Enhancing The Quality And Use of Student Outcomes Data: The Final Report of the NPEC Working Group on Student Outcomes From a Data Perspective.* Washington, DC: NPEC, 1997.

Hall, Kimberley. *Tennessee Performance Funding and The University of Tennessee: A Case Study.* Unpublished doctoral dissertation. Knoxville, TN: University of Tennessee, 2000.

Halstead, K. Higher Education Report Card 1998: *Comparisons of State Public Higher Education Systems and National Trends.* Arlington, VA: Research Associates of Washington, 1998.

Hammer, M.; J. Champy. *Reengineering the Corporation: A Manifesto For Business Revolution.* New York, NY: HarperCollins, 1993.

HERC Report. *Report of the Governor's Higher Education Review Commission.* Frankfort, KY: CHE, vol. 1, 1993.

Hines, Edward R. *State Higher Education Appropriations 1992-93.* Denver, CO: State Higher Education Executive Officers, 1993.

Hines, Edward R. *State Higher Education Appropriations 1997-98.* Denver, CO: State Higher Education Executive Officers, 1998.

Hines, E. R. *State Appropriations.* Normal, IL: State Higher Education Executive Officers, 1994,1995, 1996, and 1997.

Holden, Governor Bob, *The Missouri Budget, Fiscal Year 2002*. Jefferson City, 2002.

Hollander, T. E. "Coordinating Boards Under Attack," *The Chronicle of Higher Education* 11, 33 (April 20, 1994): B-1.

Hutchings, P. and T. Marchese. "Watching Assessment Questions, Stories, Prospects." *Change Magazine* 22, 5 (Sept./Oct. 1990): 17-27.

James, William. *The Will to Believe*. New York, NY: Longmans, Green and Co., 1931.

Joint Committee on Accountability Reporting. *JCAR Conventions: A Need Answered: An Executive Summary of Recommended Accountability Reporting Formats*. Washington, DC: AASCU Publications, 1995.

Joint Legislative Committee. "Report of the Joint Legislative Committee To Study The Governance And Operation of Higher Education in South Carolina." Columbia, SC: Higher Education Study Committee, February 1, 1996.

Kiesler, Charles. Chancellor of the University of Missouri-Columbia, Correspondence to Commissioner of Higher Education Charles J. McClain, September 14, 1994.

Kingdon, John W. *Agendas, Alternatives, and Public Policies*. New York, NY: Harper Collins, 1995.

Kubler-Ross, E. *On Death and Dying*. New York, NY: Collier Books, reprint edition, 1997.

Langenberg, Donald N. "Team Scholarship Could Help Strengthen Scholarly Traditions," *The Chronicle of Higher Education* 39 (September 2, 1992): A-44.

Latimer, Dewitt. *A Case Study of the Twenty-Year History of Performance Funding at the University of Memphis*, Unpublished doctoral dissertation. Knoxville, TN: University of Tennessee, 2001.

Layzell, D. T. and J. K. Caruthers. "Performance Funding at the State Level: Trends and Prospects." Paper presented to the 1995 Annual Meeting of the Association for the Study of Higher Education. Orlando, FL: November 2, 1995, p. 71.

Layzell, D. and J. W. Lyddon. *Budgeting for Higher Education at the State Level: Enigma, Paradox, and Ritual*. Washington, DC: George Washington University, School of Education and Human Development, December 1990. (ERIC Document Reproduction Service No. ED 332 562).

Legislative Audit Council. *A Review of the Higher Education Performance Funding Process*. Columbia, Legislative Audit Council, 2001.

Lenth, Charles. "The Context and Policy Requisites of National Postsecondary Assessment," *Journal of General Education* 42, 1 (1993): 9-32.

Leonard, L. "Senate GOP'S Budget Would End College-Tuition Ceilings," *The Columbus Dispatch*, Thursday, May 17, 2001, News 05C.

Little Hoover Commission. *Budget Reform: Putting Performance First.* Sacramento, CA: Little Hoover Commission, 1995.

Lively, Kit. "Campus 'Accountability' Is Hot Again," *The Chronicle of Higher Education* 39 (September 23, 1992): A-25.

Lively, K. "Leaders of State Higher Education Agencies Face New Pressures," *The Chronicle of Higher Education* 11, 6 (September 29, 1992): A-30

Lorber, Jefferey. *Long-Term Effects of Performance Funding: A Case Study of 20 Years At Tennessee Technological University,* Unpublished doctoral dissertation. Knoxville, TN: University of Tennessee, 2001.

Massey, E. "Community College Accountability and Performance Funding Update." Paper presented to the Finance and Administration Committee of the Postsecondary Education Planning Commission, Orlando, FL, July 18, 1996.

MBEPC Report, Missouri Business and Education Partnership Commission, Approved January 14, 1991.

McClain, Charles J. "Economic Survival." Testimony before the Senate Committee on Education, in relation to Senate Bill 353, Missouri 1991.

McClain, Charles J. Commissioner of Higher Education correspondence to Presidents and Chancellors of Two-year Institutions, May 17, 1995.

McClain, Charles J. Commissioner of Higher Education correspondence to Chancellor Charles Kiesler, University of Missouri-Columbia, October 4, 1994.

McClain, C.J. and D.W. Krueger. "Using Outcomes Assessment: A Case Study in Institutional Change," In *Assessing Educational Outcomes. New Directions for Institutional Research*, edited by P.T. Ewell, no. 47. San Francisco, CA: Jossey-Bass, 1985, pp. 33-47.

McGuinness, A. C. *State Postsecondary Education Structures Handbook.* Denver, CO: Education Commission of the States, 1994.

McGuinness, A. C. "Linking State Policy for Higher Education to Financing: The Colorado Experience," *Draft National Center for Higher Education Management Systems.* Boulder, CO: March 27, 1995.

McGuinness, A. C. *State Postsecondary Education Structures Handbook.* Denver, CO: Education Commission of the States, 1997.

McKeown, Mary P. *State Funding Formulas for Public Four-Year Institutions.* Denver, CO: State Higher Education Executive Officers, 1996.

Meisinger, Richard J., Jr. *College and University Budgeting*, 2nd ed. Washington, DC: NACUBO, 1994.

Mercer, Joyce. "States' Practice of Grading Public Colleges' Performance Gets an F From Critics," *The Chronicle of Higher Education* 11 (September 1, 1993): A-39.

Minnesota Laws 1995, Chapter 212, Article1, Section 3 and 4. 1995 MN H.F. 1856 (SN) R1of20 P1 of 182 MN-Bills Term 1995. Minnesota House File No. 1856, Minnesota 79th Legislative Session, 1995.

Minnesota Laws 1994, Chapter 532, Article 3, Section 3 and 4. State Funding and State Goals: Linking Post-secondary System Appropriations to Outcomes with Coordinating Board Recommendation. Minnesota, January 20, 1994.

Minnesota Laws 1991, Chapter 365, Article 9, Section 9. State Funding and State Goals: Linking Post-secondary System Appropriations to Outcomes with Coordinating Board Recommendation. Minnesota, January 20, 1993.

Minnesota Planning. *At the Crossroads: Higher Education in Minnesota: A Report of the Commission on Post-Secondary Education.* St. Paul, MN: Minnesota Planning, 1992.

Minutes of Organizational Meeting of South Carolina Commission on Higher Education. South Carolina: Commission on Higher Education unpublished, July 3, 1996.

Missouri Constitution, art. 10, sec. 23.

Moore, K. M. and M. J. Amey. *Making Sense of the Dollars: The Costs and Uses of Faculty Compensation.* Washington, DC: George Washington University, School of Education and Human Development, February 1994. (ERIC Document Reproduction Service No. ED 368 255).

Morrison, M. *Quality Assurance in US Higher Education: A Case Study of Tennessee's Performance Funding Program with Learning Points for the Development of Teaching Quality Assessment in UK Higher Education.* Unpublished, 1995.

Mortenson, T. *State Tax Fund Appropriations for Higher Education, FY2000. Postsecondary Education Opportunity, Number 90.* Oskaloosa, IA: Center for the Study of Opportunity in Higher Education, December 1999.

Mortimer, Kenneth et al. *Flexibility in Academic Staffing.* Ohio: Association for the Study of Higher Education, January 1986. (ERIC Document Reproduction Service No. ED 284 523).

Musick, Mark. Personal conversation, May 9, 1995.

Musik, M. Conversation with President of the Southern Regional Education Board (SREB). Atlanta, GA, 1996.

The National Center for Public Policy and Higher Education. *A State-by-State Report Card on Higher Education: A Prospectus.* San Jose, CA: The National Center for Public Policy and Higher Education, 2000.

National Commission on Excellence in Education. *A Nation at Risk: The Imperative for Educational Reform.* Washington, DC: U.S. Department of Education, 1983.

Nettles, M. T.; J. J. Cole and S. Sharp. *Benchmarking Assessment: Assessment of Teaching and Learning.* Ann Arbor, MI: National Center for Postsecondary Improvement, May 1997.

Office of Program Policy Analysis and Government Accountability. *Justification Review of the State University System.* (Report No. 01-28). Tallahassee, FL: OPPAGA, May 2001.

Ohio Board of Regents. *Ohio's Instructional Subsidy Formula: A Review of Its History, an Analysis of Its Features, and Possible Ideas for Change.* Unpublished report. Columbus, OH: Ohio Board of Regents, 1992.

Ohio Board of Regents. Budget Review. Unpublished report. Columbus, OH: Ohio Board of Regents, 1996a. (*http://www.regents.state.oh.us/perfrpt/perf_rpt_links.html*).

Ohio Board of Regents. *Performance Funding for Public Higher Education Arrives in Ohio.* Unpublished report. Columbus, OH: Ohio Board of Regents, April 19, 1996b.

Ohio Board of Regents. *The Master Plan.* Columbus, OH: Ohio Board of Regents, 1996c.

Ohio Board of Regents. *Higher Education Funding Commission: Final Report and Recommendations.* Columbus OH: Ohio Board of Regents, November 15, 1996d.

Ohio Board of Regents. *Director's Summary.* Unpublished report. Columbus, OH: Ohio Board of Regents, November 1998.

Ohio Board of Regents. *Ensuring Student Access and Achieving Student Success.* Unpublished report. Columbus, OH: Ohio Board of Regents, 1999a.

Ohio Board of Regents. *Final Draft of Allocation of Success Challenge, At Risk Baccalaureate Degree Completion.* Unpublished report. Columbus, OH: Ohio Board of Regents, 1999b.

Ohio Board of Regents. *Final Draft of Allocation of Success Challenge, Timely Baccalaureate Degree Completion.* Unpublished report. Columbus, OH: Ohio Board of Regents, 1999c.

Ohio Board of Regents. Process for Scoring Success Challenge Unpublished report. Columbus, OH: Ohio Board of Regents, 2000a. (*http://www.regents.state.oh.us/hei/success/atrisk.html*).

Ohio Board of Regents. *The State-supported Ohio College and University Performance Report: Student Outcomes and Experiences.* Unpublished report. Columbus, OH: Ohio Board of Regents, 2000b.

Ohio Governor's Office. *Governor's Budget Request 2001-2003.* Unpublished report. Columbus, OH: Ohio Governor's Office, January 2001.

Osborne, D. and T. Gaebler. *Reinventing Government: How the Entrepreneurial Spirit Is Transforming the Public Sector.* New York, NY: Penguin Books, 1994.

Palmer, J. C.; E. R. Hines; M. Juanita; and J. M. Reed. "Fact File: State Appropriations for Higher Education, 2000-1," *The Chronicle of Higher Education* 47 no. 16 (December 15, 2000): A-35.

Performance Funding: Sector Committee Guidelines (*http://che400.state.sc.us/che/perform/secguide.htm*).

Performance Ratings for 1996-97, 1997-98, 1998-99, 1999-00 (*http://che400.state.sc.us*).

Perkins, G. "Notes on the Allocation of the 1997-98 Performance Based Program Budgeting Appropriation, Approved by the Board of Regents May 29, 1998." Unpublished manuscript, Board of Regents, Tallahassee, FL: Board of Regents, March 1999.

Postsecondary Education Planning Commission. *Outcomes Assessment in Postsecondary Education.* Tallahassee, FL: Department of Education, March 1992.

Postsecondary Education Planning Commission. *Accountability in Florida's Postsecondary Education System.* Tallahassee, FL: Department of Education, January 1994.

Postsecondary Education Planning Commission. *Proceedings of the Joint Meeting of the Board of Regents, State Board of Community Colleges, and Postsecondary Education Planning Commission.* Tallahassee, FL: PEPC, June 12, 1996.

Postsecondary Education Planning Commission. *Postsecondary Accountability Review.* Tallahassee, FL: Department of Education, October 1996.

Postsecondary Education Planning Commission. *The Development of an Enrollment Projection Model.* Tallahassee, FL: Department of Education, November 1997.

Postsecondary Education Planning Commission. *Workforce Development Funding Issues.* Tallahassee, Florida: Department of Education, December 2000.

Research Universities Sector Committee. Report on Performance Funding. South Carolina: Commission on Higher Education, unpublished, 1996.

Richardson, Richard C. Jr. "Effectiveness in Undergraduate Education: An Analysis of State Quality Indicators," in *Charting Higher Education Accountability: A Sourcebook On State-Level Performance Indicators*, edited by S. S. Ruppert. Denver, CO: Education Commission of the States, 1994.

Roaden, A. L. and Associates. *A Statement of Policy by the State Higher Education Executive Officers Program and Institutional Assessment.* Denver, CO: State Higher Education Executive Officers, 1987.

Ruppert, Sandra S. ed., *Charting Higher Education Accountability: A Source Book On State-Level Performance Indicators.* Denver, CO: State Higher Education Executive Officers, 1994.

Ruppert, Sandra S. *Focus on the Customer: A New Approach To State-Level Accountability Reporting And Processes for Higher Education.* Denver, CO: State Higher Education Executive Officers, 1998.

Russell, Margaret. *Performance Funding in Tennessee: A Twenty-Year Perspective*, Unpublished doctoral dissertation. Knoxville, TN: University of Tennessee, 2000.

Schmidt, P. "Rancor and Confusion Greet A Change in South Carolina's Budgeting System," *The Chronicle of Higher Education*, April 4 (1997): 26-27.

Schmidt, P. "Arkansas Colleges and Legislative Allies Curb Power of State Coordinating Board," *The Chronicle of Higher Education* 44, 8 (October 17, 1997): A -42.

Schmidt, Peter. "A State Transforms Colleges with 'Performance Funding,'" *The Chronicle of Higher Education* 45, 43 (July 2, 1999): A-26.

Seagren, Alan T. *The Department Chair: New Roles, Responsibilities and Challenges.* Washington, DC: George Washington University, School of Education and Human Development, October 1993. (ERIC Document Reproduction Service No. ED 363 265).

Serban, Andrea M. "Performance Funding for Public Higher Education: Views of Critical Stakeholders," In Burke, J. C. and A. M. Serban. *Current Status and Future Prospects of Performance Funding and Performance Budgeting for Public Higher Education: The Second Survey.* Albany, NY: Rockefeller Institute, 1997: 7-34.

Serban, A.M. and J. C. Burke. "Meeting The Performance Funding Challenge: A Nine-State Comparative Analysis," *Public Productivity & Management Review* 22, 2 (December 1998): 157-176.

Seymour, Daniel T. *On Q: Causing Quality in Higher Education.* Phoenix, AZ: American Council on Education, Oryx Press, 1993.

Shaw, Thomas. *An Evaluation of Tennessee's Performance Funding Policy at Walters State Community College*, Unpublished doctoral dissertation. Knoxville, TN: University of Tennessee, 2000.

South Carolina Commission on Higher Education. *Minding Our P's and Q's: Indicators of Productivity and Quality in South Carolina's Public Colleges and Universities.* Columbia, SC: South Carolina Commission on Higher Education, 1999.

South Carolina State Appropriation Bill H. 4775. South Carolina, 2000-01.

State of Colorado, House Bill 94-1110 in A. C. McGuinness, Jr. *Linking State Policy for Higher Education to Financing: The Colorado Experience.* Boulder, CO: 1995.

State of Colorado, HB 95-1196 in A. C. McGuinness, Jr. *Linking State Policy for Higher Education to Financing: The Colorado Experience.* Boulder, CO: 1995

State of Colorado, *Concerning Five Specific Policy Areas for Additional Funding in Higher Education,* HB 96-1088.

State of Colorado, Colorado Commission on Higher Education. Performance Indicators, HB 96-1219. CO: CCHE, 1997

State of Colorado, House Bill 97-1352

Steering Committee, Agenda For March 27, 1997, Meeting, Attachments.

Steering Committee, Minutes of Meetings. Performance Funding. South Carolina: CHE unpublished, 1997.

Steering Committee. "Performance Funding Plan, As Recommended by the Steering Committee To the Commission on Higher Education, To be voted on May 1, 1997 by the Commission on Higher Education." Columbia, SC: Commission on Higher Education, 1997.

Stein, R. B. "Performance Reporting/Funding Program: Missouri's Efforts to Integrate State and Campus Strategic Planning." In *Performance Indicators in Higher Education: What Works, What Doesn't, What Next?*, edited by G. H. Gaither. Proceedings from the preconference of the American Association of Higher Education symposium. Washington, DC: AAHE, 1996.

Stein, Robert B. "Missouri Coordinating Board for Higher Education: Funding for Results," Lessons Learned from FIPSE Projects IV, Fund for the Improvement of Postsecondary Education-U.S. Department of Education, (2000): 209-220

Stein, R. B. and A. L. Fajen. "Missouri's funding for results initiative," In *Assessing Performance in an Age of Accountability: Case Studies.* New Directions for Higher Education, edited by G. H. Gaither. San Francisco, CA: Jossey-Bass, 1995.

Study Group on the Conditions of Excellence in Higher Education. *Involvement in Learning: Realizing the Potential of American Higher Education. Final Report of the Study Group on the Conditions of Excellence in American Higher Education.* Washington, DC: National Institute of Education, 1984.

Taft, B. Letter to Roderick Chu, November 23, 1999.

Task Force Academics. "Final Report, Performance Funding." South Carolina: Commission on Higher Education, unpublished, September 18, 1996.

Terenzini, P. *Student Outcomes Information for Policy-Making: Final Report of the National Postsecondary Education Cooperative Working Group on Student Outcomes from a Policy Perspective.* Washington, DC: NPEC, 1997.

"Time for Results," *Report of National Governors' Association's Task Force on College Quality, NGA Chair's Initiatives 1985-2002.* Washington DC, 1991.

Trombley, W. "Performance-Based Budgeting: South Carolina's New Plan Mired in Detail and Confusion," *National CrossTalk* 6 (1996): 1.

Trombley, William. "Performance-based budgeting: South Carolina's new plan mired in detail and confusion," *National CrossTalk* 1 (Winter 1998): 1.

Trombley, William. "Academic Audits," The National Center for Public Policy and Higher Education, *National CrossTalk*, 7, 3 (Summer 1999).

Vandament, William E. *Managing Money in Higher Education.* San Francisco, CA: Jossey-Bass Publishing, 1989.

Wildavsky, Aaron. *Speaking Truth to Power: The Art and Craft of Policy Analysis.* New Brunswick, NJ: Transaction Publishers, 1993.

Williams, R. D. "Performance Funding," *OATYC Journal* 22, 1 (1996): 9-13.

Wingspread Group. *An American Imperative: Higher Expectation for Higher Education. An Open Letter to those Concerned about the American Future.* Racine, WI: Johnson Foundation, 1993.

Worthen, B. R.; J. R. Sanders; and J. L. Fitzpatrick. *Program Evaluation: Alternative Approaches and Practical Guidelines.* New York, NY: Longman, 1997.

Wright, D. and A. Spencer. "I've Looked at Performance Funding from Both Sides Now: The Development of a Performance-Based Program Budgeting System for Florida's Community Colleges." Paper presented at the 26th annual conference of the Southeastern Association for Community College Research, New Orleans, LA, August 1997: 3-6.

NOTES ON CONTRIBUTORS

E. GRADY BOGUE is Professor of Educational Administration and Policy Studies at the University of Tennessee. He served as chief academic officer for the Tennessee Higher Education Commission for six years. During that period, he directed the Performance Funding Project, the first state level performance funding initiative for higher education in the country and now in its twentieth year. Dr. Bogue has written seven books and over fifty articles on higher education subjects.

JOSEPH C. BURKE is Director of the Higher Education Program and Senior Fellow at the Rockefeller Institute of Government and SUNY Professor of Higher Education Policy and Management. He was President of the State University of New York at Plattsburgh for 12 years, followed by nine years as Provost and one as Interim Chancellor of the SUNY System. Dr. Burke has written extensively on assessment, accountability, and performance in higher education.

JUAN C. COPA is a Policy Analyst with the Florida Council for Education Policy Research and Improvement. He has worked for the Council (formerly the Florida Postsecondary Education Planning Commission) since 1999, providing assistance in quantitative research methods. In addition to his duties as a policy analyst, Juan is currently a Ph.D. candidate in Political Science at the Florida State University.

PATRICK DALLET is currently Deputy Executive Director of the newly authorized Florida Council for Education Policy Research and Improvement (K-20). Prior to that he served as Assistant Executive Director of the FL Postsecondary Education Planning Commission for over 16 years. Previous experience included policy analysis for the FL Commissioner of Education and the FL Senate Education Committee and teaching at both the K-12 and postsecondary levels.

TERRI LESSARD is the Senior Research Associate at the Higher Education Program at the Rockefeller Institute of Government. She is currently working on her doctoral dissertation in the Department of Educational Theory and Practice at the State University of New York at Albany, with a concentration in research and evaluation. Terri brings nine years of research and evaluation experience to her position, most of which is specific to education, ranging from pre-kindergarten to the graduate level.

GARY MODEN is Associate Professor and Program Coordinator for Higher Education in the Department of Counseling and Higher Education in the College of Education at Ohio University. He previously served as Associate Provost and liaison to the Ohio Board of Regents' institutional research during the development and implementation of performance funding. Prior to that position, Dr. Moden was Director of Institutional Research at Ohio University.

DR. ROBERT B. STEIN serves as an associate commissioner with the Missouri Coordinating Board for Higher Education. As chief academic officer for the state he works closely with institutional personnel in the design and implementation of public policy initiatives. Dr. Stein is involved in several national networks and is author of numerous publications on academic affairs issues including performance funding, dual credit programs, K-16 initiatives, and collaboration among colleges and universities.

MICHAEL WILLIFORD is Director of Institutional Research at Ohio University and and is an associate professor in the College of Education. He has written and consulted on institutional research, institutional effectiveness measures, and student outcomes assessment.

DAVID L. WRIGHT is a Policy Director for the newly authorized Council for Education Policy Research and Improvement, which advises the Florida Legislature and Board of Education on education matters. A doctoral candidate in Higher Education at Florida State University, David served as Institutional Research Director at Tallahassee Community College prior to joining the CEPRI staff.

INDEX

Commissioner of Higher Education, Missouri, 108, 109–10
Commission on Colleges, Southern Association of Colleges and Schools, 100
Commission on Higher Education (CHE), South Carolina, 195–215
  reorganization of, 198–200
Community College Program Fund (CCPF), Florida, 155
community colleges
  California, 35
  Illinois, 35
  Kentucky, 238
  Ohio, 175
  performance indicators and, 274, 279–80, 287–88
Community College System, Florida, 138, 154–56
  accountability reporting, 141
  appropriations, 139, 159–61
  dual-enrollment courses, 148
  dual performance budgeting/incentive funding program, 147–48
  funding amounts, 163
  funding distribution measures, 148–49
  funding impacts, 154–56, 154–58
  initiative funding, 140–41
  performance-based budgeting measures, 165
  performance budgeting, 143–49
  performance incentive funding, 144–47, 155
  performance measures, 165
  performance points, 164
  Workforce Development Act and, 153
comparative core indicators, 41–43
comparison with peers indicators, 71
completers measures, 148–49, 165
Conference of Presidents, Kentucky, 234
Connecticut, xiii, 32
cooperative academic degree programs, 237
Coordinated Plan for Missouri Higher Education, 126
Coordinating Board for Higher Education (CBHE), Missouri
  assessment recommendations, 109–10

Committee on Teaching and Learning, 117
Coordinated Plan for Missouri Higher Education, 126
Critical Choices Report, 113
  funding recommendations, 114, 116
  institutional accountability requirements, 112–13
  performance efficiency index, 125
  powers of, 108
cost-plus budgeting, 20
costs
  administrative, 70
  data collection and analysis, 277–78, 280
Council on Higher Education (CHE), Kentucky, 230, 234
Council on Postsecondary Education (CPE), Kentucky, 238
Cox, Gary, 234
CPE. See Council on Postsecondary Education (CPE), Kentucky
Critical Choices Report, Missouri, 113
critical disciplines indicators, 124, 130–31
Critical Success Factors, South Carolina, 199
curriculum, criticism of, 4
curriculum and planning indicators, 72
customers, of higher education, 11

data analysis costs, 277–78
data collection costs, 277–78, 280
decentralization
  accountability and, 271
  recommendations, 280
degree attainment measures, 178
degree/certificate productivity indicators, 124, 131
degree ratio indicators, 151
Department of Higher Education (DHE), Arkansas, 219–25, 224–25
diversity indicators
  faculty/staff, 69, 70
  individual mission, 274
  students, 70
diversity issues, 273–74